# Fixing Gender

# Oxford Studies In Gender And International Relations

Series editors: Rahul Rao, University of St Andrews, and
Laura Sjoberg, Royal Holloway University of London

*Windows of Opportunity: How Women Seize Peace Negotiations for Political Change*
Miriam J. Anderson

*Women as Foreign Policy Leaders: National Security and Gender Politics in Superpower America*
Sylvia Bashevkin

*Gendered Citizenship: Understanding Gendered Violence in Democratic India*
Natasha Behl

*Gender, Religion, Extremism: Finding Women in Anti-Radicalization*
Katherine E. Brown

*Enlisting Masculinity: The Construction of Gender in U.S. Military Recruiting Advertising during the All-Volunteer Force*
Melissa T. Brown

*The Politics of Gender Justice at the International Criminal Court: Legacies and Legitimacy*
Louise Chappell

*The Other #MeToos*
Iqra Shagufta Cheema

*Cosmopolitan Sex Workers: Women and Migration in a Global City*
Christine B. N. Chin

*Intelligent Compassion: Feminist Critical Methodology in the Women's International League for Peace and Freedom*
Catia Cecilia Confortini

*Hidden Wars: Gendered Political Violence in Asia's Civil Conflicts*
Sara E. Davies and Jacqui True

*Complicit Sisters: Gender and Women's Issues across North-South Divides*
Sara de Jong

*Gender and Private Security in Global Politics*
Maya Eichler

*This American Moment: A Feminist Christian Realist Intervention*
Caron E. Gentry

*Troubling Motherhood: Maternality in Global Politics*
Lucy B. Hall, Anna L. Weissman, and Laura J. Shepherd

*Breaking the Binaries in Security Studies: A Gendered Analysis of Women in Combat*
Ayelet Harel-Shalev and Shir Daphna-Tekoah

*Scandalous Economics: Gender and the Politics of Financial Crises*
Aida A. Hozić and Jacqui True

*Building Peace, Rebuilding Patriarchy: The Failure of Gender Interventions in Timor-Leste*
Melissa Johnston

*Rewriting the Victim: Dramatization as Research in Thailand's Anti-Trafficking Movement*
Erin M. Kamler

*Equal Opportunity Peacekeeping: Women, Peace, and Security in Post-Conflict States*
Sabrina Karim and Kyle Beardsley

*Gender, Sex, and the Postnational Defense: Militarism and Peacekeeping*
Annica Kronsell

*Good Victims: The Political as a Feminist Question*
Roxani Krystalli

*The Beauty Trade: Youth, Gender, and Fashion Globalization*
Angela B. V. McCracken

*Global Norms and Local Action: The Campaigns against Gender-Based Violence in Africa*
Peace A. Medie

*Rape Loot Pillage: The Political Economy of Sexual Violence in Armed Conflict*
Sara Meger

*Critical Perspectives on Cybersecurity: Feminist and Postcolonial Interventions*
Anwar Mhajne and Alexis Henshaw

*Support the Troops: Military Obligation, Gender, and the Making of Political Community*
Katharine M. Millar

*From Global to Grassroots: The European Union, Transnational Advocacy, and Combating Violence against Women*
Celeste Montoya

*Who Is Worthy of Protection? Gender-Based Asylum and US Immigration Politics*
Meghana Nayak

*Revisiting Gendered States: Feminist Imaginings of the State in International Relations*
Swati Parashar, J. Ann Tickner, and Jacqui True

*Out of Time: The Queer Politics of Postcoloniality*
Rahul Rao

*Gender, UN Peacebuilding, and the Politics of Space: Locating Legitimacy*
Laura J. Shepherd

*Narrating the Women, Peace and Security Agenda: Logics of Global Governance*
Laura J. Shepherd

*Capitalism's Sexual History*
Nicola J. Smith

*The Global Politics of Sexual and Reproductive Health*
Maria Tanyag

*A Feminist Voyage through International Relations*
J. Ann Tickner

*The Political Economy of Violence against Women*
Jacqui True

*Queer International Relations: Sovereignty, Sexuality and the Will to Knowledge*
Cynthia Weber

*Feminist Global Health Security*
Clare Wenham

*Bodies of Violence: Theorizing Embodied Subjects in International Relations*
Lauren B. Wilcox

# Fixing Gender

*The Paradoxical Politics of Training Peacekeepers*

AIKO HOLVIKIVI

# OXFORD
UNIVERSITY PRESS

Oxford University Press is a department of the University of Oxford. It furthers
the University's objective of excellence in research, scholarship, and education
by publishing worldwide. Oxford is a registered trade mark of Oxford University
Press in the UK and certain other countries.

Published in the United States of America by Oxford University Press
198 Madison Avenue, New York, NY 10016, United States of America.

© Oxford University Press 2024

All rights reserved. No part of this publication may be reproduced, stored in
a retrieval system, or transmitted, in any form or by any means, without the
prior permission in writing of Oxford University Press, or as expressly permitted
by law, by license, or under terms agreed with the appropriate reproduction
rights organization. Inquiries concerning reproduction outside the scope of the
above should be sent to the Rights Department, Oxford University Press, at the
address above.

You must not circulate this work in any other form
and you must impose this same condition on any acquirer.

**CIP data is on file at the Library of Congress**

ISBN 978–0–19–777404–5

DOI: 10.1093/oso/9780197774045.001.0001

The manufacturer's authorised representative in the EU for product safety is
Oxford University Press España S.A. of El Parque Empresarial San Fernando de Henares,
Avenida de Castilla, 2 – 28830 Madrid (www.oup.es/en orproduct.safety@oup.com).
OUP España S.A. also acts as importer into Spain of products made by the manufacturer.

*For äiti and isi, who helped me start this book,
for Jason, who supported me in writing it,
and for Ellis, who got me to finally finish it.*

# Contents

*Preface* xi
*Acknowledgements* xxi

1. Introduction: The Politics of Pedagogy 1
2. Fixing Gender: The Curriculum 30
3. Emotional Pedagogy: Knowing Wartime Rape 65
4. Resistance: Struggles for Meaning in The Classroom 91
5. Small Subversions: Feminist Pedagogical Moments 118
6. Conclusion: Practising Paradoxical Politics 154

*Notes* 171
*References* 173
*Index* 187

# Preface

Of late, it seems that whenever an instance of discrimination or violation in an institution is exposed, the response to the problem includes (and sometimes even centres on) providing gender training for all concerned. Whether the problem is with how corporate managers award promotions and raises; how police officers deal with complaints of domestic violence and sexual assault; how development professionals account for the lives and priorities of women in their project design and activities; or how peacekeepers interact with the local population in the area they are sent to; gender training is now reliably presented as the solution. The institutionalization of gender training prompts a number of different responses. Advocates of gender equality within organizations, often referred to as 'femocrats', tend to view the mandate to conduct training as an opportunity to get their foot in the door and to begin to effect institutional change. *Finally*, something is going to be *done* about the issue. What a victory for feminist concepts and theorizing, to be invited into the official practices of the institution! Others are sceptical. There is the cynic who belittles the importance of addressing gender discrimination, asking: Why are they (a police service, say) doing gender training? Don't they have bigger and more important issues to address? Then there is the radical critic (often a feminist academic or activist), who argues that the military and police are institutions shaped by misogyny, homophobia, and racism, and set up for the exercise of violence. They are murderous institutions. How could gender training in such a setting do anything besides provide a shiny veneer to rotten institutional politics?

I first became familiar with this debate from the former position. In 2011, as a fresh political science graduate, I started work at an international foundation based in western Europe, working on projects related to gender and security sector reform. In this role, I was often asked to provide gender training to security sector personnel, especially military and police services with a focus on the NATO region, eastern Europe, and West and Southern Africa. Equipped with the enthusiasm of a twenty-five-year-old who had landed her then dream job; the theoretical knowledge acquired in one graduate-level feminist theory class; and the patient mentorship of senior colleagues,

I initially embarked on this task with little critical reflection and a basic-at-best grounding in gender concepts and gender analysis. Figuring out how to design an engaging session and building the confidence to take charge of a room full of security professionals, most of whom were older than me, took up all of my energy and focus. It did not occur to me at that point that the exercise could be anything other than what it said on the tin: a step toward gender equality.

I spent five years in this role, and as time went by, I became more experienced and confident as a trainer, with approaches of my own and lots of opinions about how to best to do training. I had always enjoyed academic research and debate, and so I engaged in a number of workshops designed to bring us so-called practitioners into dialogue with feminist academics. Thanks to these events, I also became better educated in feminist analyses and was exposed to the critical feminist position. I will not lie, being confronted with this critique made me defensive, but it simultaneously provoked my curiosity about the political and epistemic effects of training. The more training sessions I facilitated, the more the questions posed by critical feminist academics haunted me. I wondered: Do we need to start every workshop with the sex/gender distinction? What effect do we think teaching these police officers about it will have? What about Judith Butler's (1986) contention that sex was always already gender? What exactly do we think gender is and does? What *does* a 'gender-responsive military' look like? Is that not an impossible paradox? How far can we push a feminist analysis before it causes an irreconcilable break with the logic of the military? Who am I to be telling these people about sexual violence? And: Is this really a responsible use of development assistance funds, to spend tens of thousands of *kroner* sending me to West Africa to position myself as an 'expert'[1]? In other words, my work in the field of gender training increasingly left me in an uncomfortable position, unsure as to whether what we were doing was, after all, good feminist politics.

I was not alone in feeling this contradictory pull. During my time working as a gender 'expert', I was mentored by and developed training practice together with a number of thoughtful colleagues who named their political commitments as feminist, pro-LGBT rights, anti-racist, and anti-colonial. My colleagues were by no means oblivious of, or even unsympathetic to, scholarly feminist critiques that highlight the complicities of global governance feminism with colonial structures, heteronormative thinking, and neoliberal agendas. Nonetheless, many of my colleagues—myself included—felt these academic critiques to be somehow too totalizing in their negative assessment. We felt that they often failed to account for the complexity and nuance that we saw in our daily practice. Yes, there were many unfortunate aspects to this kind of institutional engagement, but the general feeling among my colleagues was that it wasn't all bad. Surely, sometimes, to get meaningful change done in the real world, you sometimes had to get your hands (or your principles) a bit dirty? Not everyone can afford to maintain theoretical purity. I very much understood and felt this position, but it did not resolve the critical questions for me.

So while I initially came to the practice of gender training from a kind of default position of the optimistic femocrat, I came to write this book from a more complicated stance, torn between the democrat and the critical feminist. Eventually, I felt that there were limits to how I could grapple with this tension in my work as a practitioner, and so I decided to take the time to pursue these questions through academic research. I thus embarked on a PhD programme with the intention of settling for myself, once and for all, the question of whether gender training is good or bad feminist politics. If you continue reading, you will find that the trajectory of research since then disappoints this initial ambition. In this book, I argue that gender training is *both* good *and* bad feminist politics, and that this tension is in fact a paradox—something that resists resolution. More on this conclusion in later chapters. For the moment, the point is that the backstory of how I came to this research has some enduring implications for what follows in the book, and that bears pointing out from the outset.

First, this backstory meant that I knew that the research had to involve participant observation. As anyone who has ever taught anything is well aware, there is only ever a weak and contingent correlation between what is taught by the teacher and what the student learns. Interactive classrooms are unpredictable, exhilarating, and slightly chaotic settings. If we want to understand the effects of training, it is imperative that we contend with these messy dynamics.

I remember the moment this realization hit me. I was conducting a training workshop with a colleague. On day one, we facilitated an exercise on the sex-gender distinction. The activity involves sticking a post-it labelled 'Women' on one flipchart, and another labelled 'Men' on a second flipchart. The trainer then invites participants to contribute examples of activities or attributes traditionally associated with women (e.g. wearing make-up, being kind, looking after children, giving birth) or men (e.g. wearing trousers, being strong, earning money, growing a beard). Once the group has a number of items listed for both, the trainer removes the post-it notes and sticks each one to the other sheet: the list of women's attributes is now titled 'men' and vice versa. The trainer then asks the group whether it is *possible*, even if it is not common, for, say, a man to wear make-up. The trainer circles all things that are possible (growing a beard tends to be the subject of much humorous debate) and explains that these are examples of gender—things that we associate with men or women not because it is only possible for a man or woman to do them, but because of social construction. Just because women have traditionally been expected to care for children does not mean that men are somehow innately incapable of doing so. Those few that are not transferable (at least in this cis-normative schema, e.g. giving birth) are explained as biological sex and crossed out. The exercise went as planned. On day two of the workshop, we started the day by asking the participants what they had learned on the previous day. 'Sex versus gender!' someone volunteered. 'What did we learn about that?' I probed. 'That women can do more things than men can!' came the response. My colleague and I looked at one another in a moment of confusion, until we realized, first, that there had been an imbalance in the number of gender attributes we had discussed for women than for men, and that second, we would have to revisit the sex-gender distinction if we wanted to get the point across. What did *I* learn on day two of the workshop? That what training participants learn from an activity may be only tangentially linked to what the trainer had planned. Five years later, approaching the question as a researcher, I knew that it meant that understanding the politics of training requires observing training in practice.

In other words, my entanglement in the practice of gender training portends that, from its inception, two key aims of the book were to (1) provide an empirical account of the practices of gender training that accounted for complexity, and (2) to interpret or 'read' this complexity with a view to developing a conceptual grammar up to the task of contending with the messiness of this practice. The book is, in other words, committed to providing an on-the-ground account of feminist engagements with martial institutions that does not attempt to write out or smooth over tension and contradiction. It is this attention to the contradictions of the practice of training that has nuanced the line of inquiry that brought me to this project. My initial question of is-gender-training-good-yes-or-no has thus evolved into a more constitutive account: What are we/they doing when we/they are training on gender? What are the politics of this practice?

Second, my entanglement in the field of practice presented important ethical considerations for an academic research project. At the outset was the question of what to do with the knowledge that I already had before I started the research project. Clearly, I did not have informed consent to use anecdotes and quotes that had stuck with me from my time as a practitioner in my writing, which seemed to rule out the possibility of drawing on these experiences as 'research data'. Then again, it would be disingenuous to proceed as though these formative experiences did not shape where I looked, how I read, what questions I asked, and what lines of analysis I pursued and what, conversely, I did not. How could they do anything but? The lines were further blurred when I interviewed people I had worked with in my past professional life: If they recounted an anecdote from a training session that we had both been in, did that make it fair game? The question of what could and could not be included in the writing thus required ongoing contextual judgements rather than a blanket policy. Ultimately, I have assessed the admissibility of such examples based on whether any individual could be identified, and whether the inclusion of the account could result in harm to anyone. In the end, I have tried to ensure that in the few instances where I draw upon knowledge built outside of the formal research endeavour, I focus on the lesson rather than the story, blurring out the details to ensure full anonymity.

The ethical dilemmas, however, did not end there. Arranging interviews and participant observation of training sessions meant drawing on the network I had built up in my years at the international foundation. This was vital for the project, as security institutions are set up to be guarded against outsiders, and so obtaining access to them would otherwise have been very difficult. I used what more strictly socially scientific-minded inquiries describe as 'snowball sampling' where some of the research centred around my previous contacts, but these also led me to meet new research participants and sites of research. This was incredibly generative for tracing the workings of a transnational community of practice, but it also produced the awkward situation not only of writing about people I know personally (many of whom I am fond of) but also of formulating critical analyses of their work. These are busy people, so I don't presume all of them will read my analysis, but I know some will. I have written the book in that knowledge. Another ethical question then was how to represent my research participants in writing.

Of course, responsible representation should not only be a concern when one expects one might be personally confronted by those one writes about but the situation certainly does something to highlight to the author the responsibilities of representation. In the end, I have sought to address this question through how the analysis itself is conducted and written. Let me expand.

The analytical work in the book is inspired by post-structuralist methods, and I describe it as 'reading' training interventions. Aptly for illustrating my concerns, there is a double entendre to this term, in that 'reading' is commonly used in queer vernacular to describe criticism, or mocking another for comedic effect, as popularized to mainstream audiences by Jennie Livingston's 1990 cult documentary *Paris Is Burning* and subsequently the television show *RuPaul's Drag Race* (2009–present) (Butler 2014, 241; Halperin 2012, 204). I want to highlight here that it is not my intention to 'read' research participants in this sense of the term. I do not mean—to stick with the vernacular of queer culture—to be shady, although I do recognize that this may be an unintended consequence of my analysis, which is often critical in its tone.

To moderate this impression, I want to underscore that the primary objects of my analysis are discursive formations and knowledge practices. My intention is to interrogate what kinds of logics and politics any particular statement or action align with. Importantly, I understand these as exceeding any individual's subjectivity. I do not claim to make pronouncements on any person's subjectivity; pronouncements which I would regard as analytically and ethically suspect. Following from my understanding of categories such as gender, race, and sexuality as processes of subjectification rather than ontological pre-givens, I recognize that people may be and often are 'discontinuous, divided subjects caught in conflicting interests and identities' (Bhabha 1994, 42). In agreement with this epistemic stance, I follow Spivak's suggestion to cede that 'knowledge of the other subject is theoretically impossible', and to understand representations as relating 'to the divided subject in an indirect way' (Spivak 2010, 48, 33). As such, the writing in this book tries to resist fixing subject positions—whether that of the feminist, or the racist, or the homophobe—onto individuals, even when I interrogate what kinds of logics any practice or utterance aligns with. I believe that it is important, both analytically and politically, to resist the facile understanding that only a racist would say or do something racist. Classifying people in this way not only flattens and caricatures often complicated positions but also severely limits our ability to address pervasive structures of inequality. It disadvantages any attempts to investigate the complicities of those of us who might consider ourselves innocent when it comes to structures of power, and it is exactly these kinds of complicities that are so crucial to expose. Circling back to the question of how to represent research participants in writing, I have interpreted my political responsibility as one of not shying away from critiquing structures of oppression. I do not, however, understand this as carte blanche to analytically savage the research participants who generously and kindly lent their expertise and time to this project. In walking this ethical tightrope, I have sought to highlight that in critiquing systems of meaning making it is not my intention to criticize or to 'read' any individual.

In addition to the distinction between criticizing individuals and critiquing systems, I find it helpful to engage with the differentiation between criticism and critique that Saba Mahmood proposes. Criticism, according to Mahmood (2005, 36), is an oppositional exercise in which one looks for faults and failings with the intention of invalidating the opposing view. In the context of my research, this would mean engaging with gender training practices (and, pointedly, gender trainers) with a pre-determined mission to expose how they betray feminist political commitments. In contrast, Mahmood urges us to think about critique as an exercise in which one remains committed to understanding the perspectives and values of those one engages with, an exercise that 'leaves open the possibility that we might also be remade in the process of engaging another's worldview, that we might come to learn things that we did not already know before we undertook the engagement' (2005, 36–37). Though her work is situated in a distinct empirical field of inquiry (the politics of piety in the Islamic revival), Mahmood teaches all of us about the importance of thinking with the politics of practices that our political formation may have primed us to dismiss out of hand. This is a particularly valuable lesson, because it is not an easy course to maintain. In the process of conducting and writing this research, I know I for one have felt constant social and political guilt: either I have felt that I am being insufficiently critical of murderous institutions or that I am an ungrateful and treacherous recipient of my research participants' time and goodwill. With each crisis of guilt, however, I have circled back to my conviction that accounting for and grappling with the politics of gender training in a way that remains committed to seeing both the good and the bad is politically necessary for feminist strategizing.

One of the factors that kept alive the sense of guilt about being insufficiently critical is that this book was written based in an interdisciplinary department of gender studies and in conversation with many inspiring, radical, scholars. This location fostered an acute sense of political accountability, but it also importantly influenced my analysis. The approach of this book is intensely (perhaps wildly) interdisciplinary. I draw from work across a range of disciplines from critical cultural studies to international relations; and from diverse but also often overlapping theoretical perspectives, including feminism, post-structuralism, psychoanalysis, queer theory, and de- and postcolonial thought. I maintain that there is a certain commensurability to these perspectives, as all have importantly informed the development of both gender studies and pedagogical thought. While imposing a strict typology differentiating between traditions of scholarship is not my aim here, what is important is to name and acknowledge some important contextual differences. There are certainly political dangers to my theoretical framing strategy, as some understandable objections may be raised to taking analytical techniques devoted to understanding (and improving!) the conditions of liveability for marginalized subjects, and using these to study gender training conducted by typically relatively privileged gender experts in powerful (murderous) institutions. Though gender and feminist knowledge occupies a relatively marginal position in martial institutions, in recruiting the help of liberatory theories to think through the politics of gender training, I do not mean to imply that gender trainers occupy a comparable material or historical position to colonized and/or queer subjects seeking out ways of surviving and thriving in a world that is not invested in their living (though is often invested in their exploitation). I acknowledge the very different conditions of life and survival of those who seek, voluntarily and from a position of relative power and privilege, to practise feminist politics in military institutions from those subjects about and for whom postcolonial and queer theory was written. Reading dominant texts 'against the author's intention and ideology' is a well-established method of critique in postcolonial and queer theory (Bhabha 1994, xii). It must be admitted, however, that my evoking of their theoretical insights carries a concomitant risk of doing exactly the same to liberatory theories. This is by no means my intention.

My intellectual and political commitments include striving (though undoubtedly often also failing) to resist martiality, colonial thinking, and heteronormativity as logics of meaning making. I want to nonetheless underscore that there are contextual limits to how far and in what ways the insights of these theories can be applied to gender training interventions in peacekeeping enterprises. Rather than attempting a mechanistic application or transposition of these theories to the context I examine (a context which is not the primary originator of these theoretical insights), my approach is more accurately described as a *thinking through* and *reading with* the help of these theories. Such 'reading with' is not a question of inserting objects of analysis into a pre-given theoretical framework (substituting gender trainers for the subaltern, for example), but rather examining how exposure to these theoretical insights rearranges the landscape of what we are able to 'see', analytically speaking (Sedgwick 2003, 178). This theoretical framing can be described in Spivak's terms as analogy rather than transference of theory; as a 'productive catachresis' (2010, 49). This analogical mode of thought generates the conceptual vocabulary with which I examine gender training. I have found the lessons of these theorists instructive in thinking about what to make of contemporary contestations around gender, and for making strategic feminist decisions about when to engage and on what terms. I hope, dear reader, that you too find this a generative engagement.

# Acknowledgements

I imagine writing acknowledgements is a challenging business for any feminist committed to thinking seriously about the intersubjective nature of knowledge production and the relationships of interdependence that make our lives liveable. In a project that has taken nine years to bring to book form, but that in many ways started over a decade ago, I have accumulated a hefty pile of feminist debt (a term I borrow from Sumi Madhok)—one hardly knows where to start!

Perhaps most foundationally, the knowledge claims I put forward in this book are only possible because feminist thinkers before me have built the community, designed the concepts, crafted the language, and indeed created the very conditions of thinkability for these arguments can be made. The bibliography is a closely related genre to acknowledgements, and while that concludes the book, I would like to also start by reiterating this intellectual debt.

This specific research, however, would not have been possible without the generosity, labour, and care extended by particular individuals. The research participants described in the pages of this book generously lent their time and shared their expertise for this project. Protecting their collective anonymity means that I cannot name individuals here, but they know who they are. Thank you for taking time out of your busy schedules and for taking risks in allowing me to access your courses. I am very appreciative of how warmly I was hosted, which included covering some of my meals, accommodation, and transportation costs. That you were willing to do so is testament not only to your kindness but also to your dedication to developing gender work in a collaborative spirit.

The intellectual support, friendship, and good humour of Marsha Henry has been my constant companion from the early days of this research. I am fortunate to have worked with a scholar whose standards one is constantly inspired to try and meet. Working with you has been a masterclass in responsible research and feminist citation practices; and the many long conversations around peacekeeping and what really are the politics of engaging in these institutions (only to be disrupted by one of us having to run for a train) have been a lifeline.

Elisabeth Prügl, Ania Plomien, Sumi Madhok, Clare Hemmings, and Wendy Sigle: your engagement with this work, your mentorship, and your advice and guidance in taking the project forward have been invaluable over the years. Thank you.

I had the good fortune of meeting Aaron Belkin just at the moment when the central arguments of this book were beginning to crystallize. When I first heard him point out that transformation wasn't necessarily the point of engaging with military institutions, this shifted my thinking into a completely different mode of political thought. Our shared anxieties over the political credentials of the work we were engaged in provided rich ground for discussion and debate. Thank you for engaging so wholeheartedly and with such generous spirit with this work, and for pushing it forward in so many different ways.

Kate Millar, Audrey Reeves, and I met in 2008, and since then we have been the sisterhood of the feminist travelling book club (and, Kate, HLPs). I'm not sure I know who I would be or how I would think if I hadn't met you. Thank you for the companionship, friendship, and constant co-production of knowledge.

I didn't start this project with the ambition of being a feminist academic, but I finished it with a burning desire to be just that. This is due to the intellectual home in which this project grew, namely the LSE Department of Gender Studies. To the faculty, successive PhD cohorts, and MSc students I have known, read, and debated with—you are an inspiration, and you have profoundly shaped who I am as a scholar.

Many kind souls have read drafts of this work in different stages and for different purposes, and in doing so helped push the arguments and finessed their presentation. I extend my gratitude to: Kimberly Hutchings, Laura Shepherd, Rahel Kunz, Callum Watson, Hannah Wright, Atusko Ichijo, Hayo Krombach, Anne Sisson Runyan, Annika Bergman Rosamond, Swati Parashar, Lewis Turner, Georgina Holmes, Sabrina White, Hannah West, Roisin Read, Andrew Ross, Sarah Smith, Paul Kirby, Henri Myrttinen, Julia Welland, Cristina Masters, Philipp Schulz, Jelke Boesten, Emma Spruce, James Mayer, Billy Holzberg, Jenny Chanfreau, Aura Lehtonen, Priya Raghavan, and Meg Millar.

The Oxford Studies in Gender and International Relations series editors Laura Sjoberg and Rahul Rao, and Angela Chnapko and Alexcee

Bechthold at Oxford University Press have been a wonderful source of support throughout preparing the book for publication. Thank you for the energizing and motivating discussions, for providing such clear and unambiguous guidance, responding to my many queries so quickly, and for your support for the project! I am grateful to two anonymous reviewers for their generous engagement with the manuscript and suggestions for improving it. Thanks are also due to Nirenjena Joseph for managing the production of the manuscript.

My daughter Ellis was born while the book manuscript was out for review. Her arrival has brought me unimaginable joy, but also a newly heightened awareness of the amount of caring labour and housework it takes to sustain human life, let alone intellectual labour. In that spirit, I would like to extend my particular thanks to the people who helped so much with the often invisible but absolutely vital academic housework that every research project involves: Kate Steward, Zoe Gillard, Annie Robinson, Violet Fox, Henriettta Burr, and the dearly missed Hazel Johnstone MBE. As ever, thank you to the family and friends whose loving care made this work—and anything else I do—possible.

This work was supported by the Economic and Social Research Council [grant number ES/V006126/1]. The research also benefited from an LSE PhD Studentship and an LSE Centre for Women, Peace and Security fieldwork grant. I gratefully acknowledge the financial support that made this research possible.

# 1
# Introduction

## The Politics of Pedagogy

This is a book about the epistemic life of gender and the political work that this lively concept does. The term 'gender' has played an indispensable role in feminist theoretical innovation and political interventions. It is a concept that has travelled far and wide: it has been employed by diverse actors, ranging from grassroots feminist movements to the United Nations and other institutions of global governance. It is a malleable concept that has been made to do all manner of political work, from contesting patriarchal logics of sexual difference to providing a progressive veneer to the operations of powerful institutions. It is a lively concept, one that constitutes the object of ongoing contestation and debate. Anti-feminist forces generate moral panic around the language of gender in school curricula and government policies. At the same time, feminists note with concern that the widespread take-up of the term through frameworks such as gender mainstreaming risks collapsing it into *sexgender*, compromising the concept's radical potential by rendering it politically safe. The concept of 'gender' is, in other words, invested with myriad political desires and disavowals, demonstrating the continued urgency, for feminist theory, to track what meaning the term 'gender' is imbued with, how it is known, and what political work the concept can or should be made to do.

The concept of 'gender' has travelled far and wide because it is expected to do some heavy lifting when it comes to feminist political work. Gender, the theory goes, can help undo hierarchies of oppression by demonstrating the constructed rather than given nature of sexual difference. When addressed with attention to race, class, and sexuality, it can expose and contest systems of marginalization. At its most basic, the investment in 'gender' is that the analytics of the term alerts us to the fact that if the world is made rather than found, then it could be made differently, made less violently. That so many attach tangible consequence to the concept and its ability to help us imagine different worlds is evident in the fact that knowledge about gender has been described as the solution to a number of problems. Over the last few decades, its epistemic life has taken on a new incarnation, in the form of gender training for professionals of various stripes. This type of training sometimes addresses gender tout court, but other familiar examples include training on diversity and inclusion, on unconscious bias, or against sexual harassment and assault. Police officers, university students, government officials, international development workers, management consultants, and military personnel are some of the groups who have received gender training in recent years. Indeed, the popularity of gender training has rendered it, according to observers, 'one of the most widely used tools for supporting the implementation of gender mainstreaming strategies in public and private organizations worldwide' (Bustelo, Ferguson, and Forest 2016b, 1, 6). Knowledge about gender, in this paradigm, is the prerequisite to taking action to remedy inequalities and oppression.

The uptake of gender training as a strategy is so widespread that it is now established practice in what are arguably surprising spaces. This book examines the take-up of the term 'gender' in one of these unlikely contexts: the training of military and police peacekeepers. Martial institutions—like the military and the police—have long been described by feminist scholars as institutions of hegemonic masculinity, shaped by normative misogyny and homophobia. Nonetheless, these institutions now (somewhat) systematically provide gender training to the personnel they send on international peacekeeping missions established in conflict or post-conflict zones by international organizations like the United Nations. This juxtaposition between feminist knowledge and an institution of hegemonic masculinity provokes a number of questions: How can gender be made to work in and for martial institutions? Does or can such training mitigate some of the harms wrought by institutions of state violence? What happens, in other words, when gender is inserted into this context, and what are the implications for feminist strategizing? Feminists have long been divided about the potential and perils of engaging with institutions of state power, with some arguing that it is necessary to cultivate transformative politics, and others cautioning that such endeavours result in the co-optation of feminist knowledge to serve markedly different purposes than the ones they were intended for.[1] It is this introduction of an analytical category of feminist lineage—gender—into the institutions of war, and attendant debates about feminist strategizing, that set the stage for the normative contestation that this book examines.

In what follows, I trace how gender is rendered a knowable object in peacekeeper training, what the pedagogy of gender entails in these spaces, and how we might make feminist sense of the political and epistemic effects of such training. I examine policy mandates and training curricula and draw from extensive participant observation of gender training for military and police peacekeepers in Europe and Africa to provide a picture of how the meaning of gender is inflected at the site of training. I argue that gender training for uniformed peacekeepers constitutes a deeply ambivalent enterprise from the point of view of feminist political commitments. It involves the co-optation of feminist concepts to serve the purposes of martial politics at the same time as it contains within it the possibilities for disrupting racism, coloniality, misogyny, and homophobia (all key ingredients of martial politics) as logics of meaning making. In contending that co-optation, resistance, *and* subversion are all taking place, simultaneously, in gender training settings, the analysis in this book sets out to complicate the given terms of opposition in favour of sketching a picture of a deeply ambivalent enterprise. Rather than attempting to resolve the contradictions that inhere to this project, I suggest that the politics of gender training are best understood through the concept of paradox and seek to develop the conceptual grammar for a productive engagement with paradox. In so doing, I lay out a case for feminist analytical efforts to continue to track where the concept of 'gender' travels, and to contest the terms on which it is put to work.

## Training Peacekeepers on Gender

Over the last two decades, gender training has become a requirement for uniformed peacekeepers who are sent to (post-) conflict zones to provide security.[2] Framed as (part of) the response to gendered harms previously ignored in, or actively caused by peacekeeping missions, training represents an attempt to remedy or fix gendered problems in peacekeeping, alongside efforts to deploy more female peacekeepers and the establishment of gender advisory positions. Introduced against the backdrop of the adoption and evolution of the international Women, Peace and Security (WPS) agenda, states in different parts of the world increasingly agree that gender training is a necessary part of the preparation of peacekeepers for deployment and have developed training curricula and offered courses on gender and related topics. Some states limit such training to specific modules prior to deployment, but others also integrate gender topics and modules across basic training and professional military education, beyond peacekeeping missions. This practice is being developed across different areas of the world, rendering it a transnational phenomenon. Though precise numbers of how many have been trained remain elusive, since the year 2000, an increasing codification of policy commitments and training initiatives mean that tens, if not hundreds, of thousands of military and police peacekeepers are receiving gender training, rendering it a significant emergent practice (Holvikivi 2021). While certainly at present not all military and police personnel who deploy on peacekeeping missions receive such training, and many states in practice deprioritize its delivery, few states have argued—or even seem poised to argue—against the *principle* of training their troops on gender.

Such training was instituted as transnational practice in the context of several strands of advocacy and political discourse that drew attention to the linkages between gender and armed conflict. Gender training for peacekeepers was introduced against the backdrop of persistent reports of sexual exploitation and abuse committed by peacekeepers deployed to conflict zones (Bauer and Molinari 2017; Westendorf 2017; Henry 2013; Simić 2010). It was importantly propelled forward by the call to 'stop rape now', that is, demands to address wartime sexual violence articulated by advocacy groups and taken up by the United Nations (Kirby 2015; Eriksson Baaz and Stern 2013). Beyond the advocacy efforts of women's organizations and international NGOs working on issues of sexual violence, concern with gender and women's rights were also instrumentally deployed at the time by the US administration, with support from the group Feminist Majority, to portray the invasion of Afghanistan in 2001 as a mission to protect Afghan women from abuses at the hands of the Taliban; mobilizing feminist political concepts to justify an imperial military excursion (Shepherd 2006; Mahmood 2005; Young 2003). The recent history of the war in Afghanistan is one example of a broader constellation of truth claims that establish women's rights (or violations thereof) as, paradoxically, both a cause of and justification for war and military intervention (Abu-Lughod 2013; Cockburn 2010). This framing provides further rationale for providing gender training to military audiences: to persuade them that women's rights are inextricably linked to military missions and their objectives.[3] Against this backdrop, gender training efforts seek to provide peacekeepers with the knowledge and skills to address women's security concerns among the 'peace-kept' (Henry 2015, 374) population—especially to prevent and respond to conflict-related sexual violence. (Some) gender training also aims at preventing peacekeepers themselves from committing abuses against the local population, notably through acts of sexual exploitation and abuse.

These recent events are best understood as a series of moments in which the gendered dynamics of and harms caused by conflict and military intervention have become particularly visible and have occupied space in the media and in policy debates. It is important to note however, that this framing of gendered problems in conflict and intervention derives from a combination of media attention and policy responses to specific gendered harms, which is not the same as saying that any of these phenomena are new. Conflict and military intervention have long had gendered impacts on those affected, whether or not these impacts were recognized by politicians or military planners (Blanchard 2003). Conflict-related sexual violence has been documented across conflicts spanning a wide geographic and historical range (Goldstein 2003, 332; Enloe 2000, 108). Sexual harassment and assault have long been part of military institutions, to the extent that they may even be considered integral to their functioning, as a normalized and tolerated—if not accepted—part of military training (Wadham 2017, 243; Belkin 2012, 99).

Not only do these gendered issues have a longer history than the recent policy response might imply but also they are not exhaustive of the ways in which conflict, military intervention, and martial institutions are produced by and productive of gender and violence. That these three issue areas have been framed as *the* gendered aspects of conflict does not reflect some underlying truth as to where gender operates. Rather, the production of these phenomena as gendered simultaneously implicates the production of a series of omissions and silences around where gender is to be found. For example, domestic abuse committed by military or police personnel, particularly after deployments, rarely receives mention in policy discourses on the gendered aspects of conflict and security (Gray 2016; Whitworth 2008). The more subtle configurations of power that enlist women's gendered service to the military as cleaners, laundresses, sex workers, and supportive spouses likewise elude public attention in these discourses (Enloe 2000). The military is arguably adept in the production and mobilization of norms of masculinity and femininity in ways that foster acquiescence to, or even enthusiasm for, the exercise of collective violence (Belkin 2012, 24; Whitworth 2004, 104; Elshtain 1982). Close attention to the ways in which the military makes use of gender norms lends itself to the suggestion that, in fact, all military training can be thought of as 'gender training'. The development of specifically designated gender training in martial institutions demonstrates that certain phenomena are made to qualify as gender, whereas other gendered aspects of conflict and military intervention are rendered invisible. In other words, the emergent media and policy attention to gender in situations of armed conflict is best understood as a process of making and giving significance to gender as an analytic category and political problem, rather than assuming that it is simply a reflection of new problems, or all actually existing ones.

If it is the case that the gendered harms that gender training purports to respond to are not new or exhaustive of gender issues in peacekeeping, the corollary is also true: training does not somehow emerge as a natural or inevitable response to the harms identified. Gender training as a practice is not unique to peacekeeping enterprises: it is prevalent in other structures of global governance, notably in international development; in multinational and national structures such as the UN, the European Union, and their member states; the private sector; and civil society (Bustelo, Ferguson, and Forest 2016a; Kabeer 1991). Indeed, there are striking similarities between gender training in international development and peacekeeping. Training in both fields typically departs from the sex-gender distinction and analyses relations and processes that socially construct gender. While international development training then moves to examine the gendered division of labour and rethink the meaning of production (Kabeer 1991), a parallel is clear in that peacekeeper training often examines gendered security needs and prompts a rethinking of what counts as security. Both pedagogic moves are premised on centring people (men, women, boys, and girls, as peacekeeper training materials typically put it) in analyses, rather than abstractions such as 'the economy' or 'the conflict zone'. Accounts from trainers in both fields attest to the fact that such training often prompts forms of resistance that centre on cultural essentialism, and that evoke both trivialization of the matter at hand through humour or outright hostility (Kabeer 1991, 192; see also Lombardo and Mergaert 2016). Finally, both types of training often aim to 'shift the focus from what *is* to what *could be*' (Kabeer 1991, 194, emphasis in original). In sum, these similarities alert us to the fact that the development of gender training for peacekeepers is premised and builds upon the existence of training as a model in the broader field: it is one articulation of a broader trend.

Further, gender training in the field of international development is not simply portrayed as a rational solution to objective problems identified in development work. Rather, its practitioners describe gender training as a practice indebted to feminist activism and inspired by feminist consciousness-raising practices developed in the 1970s and 1980s (Ferguson 2019a, 114; Sexwale 1996, 53; on the notion of feminist debt, see also Madhok 2020). Some observers also draw parallels between the institutionalization of feminist politics in the academy and through training practices, describing gender training as 'a branch of Women's Studies' (Sexwale 1996, 54). Many gender trainers see training, not as a problem-solving tool—for example, as a fix to problems of sexual assault—but rather as a constellation of 'interventions aimed at changing the gender order' (Cornwall 2016, 75) and to 'combat patriarchy' (Sexwale 1996, 53) through 'an approach that aspires towards social justice by seeking to transform systems of power and privilege in ways that are participatory, reflexive, inclusive and non-hierarchical' (Ferguson 2019a, 116; see also Plantenga 2004). In other words, the development of gender training has roots in feminist activism, which invested the practice with transformative hopes.

## Feminist Contentions

While many trainers contend that gender training can and should effect feminist transformation, they also note with alarm the many ways in which this practice is amenable to co-optation by the politics of patriarchal institutions. Training practitioners in the field of development lament the ways in which the focus of gender training has shifted from political consciousness-raising to the framing of gender as a question of technical skills and checklists (Mukhopadhyay and Wong 2007, 114). Their accounts expose the many ways in which the transformative feminist politics of gender training become 'depoliticized' through 'technicist' solutions 'geared ... to reform rather than to transformation' (Sexwale 1996, 53). First, gender training practices often replicate inequitable global power structures. The field is dominated by Global North gender experts, who derive both material remuneration and epistemic authority from their position as trainers, often appropriating the knowledge produced by women of colour (Sexwale 1996). White trainers typically fail to account for their own location in structures of oppression and contribute to the erasure of local feminisms in the contexts where they work (Enderstein 2018; Kunz 2016; Rich 2003). Second, the training enterprise is imbued with the neoliberal governing rationalities of temporality, market efficiency, and individualism (Davids and van Eerdewijk 2016; W. Brown 2015). Institutional demands abound to deliver training in less time, and the messaging of the training itself privileges the language of market efficiency and individual transformation over commitments to social justice and analyses of structures of oppression (Enderstein 2018; Sexwale 1996). Finally, this inattentiveness to structural analyses and intersecting oppressions is often facilitated by lax standards of who is thought to possess the requisite expertise to deliver training. Gender trainers and gender experts typically have the title bestowed upon them by their employers without requiring prior studies or research, leading South African trainer Bunie Sexwale (1996, 60) to caution us to be suspicious of gender 'expertise' by offering an African proverb: 'be suspicious of a naked man who offers a shirt'. In short, trainers and scholars of this practice warn that the transformative potential of training is often thwarted by and comes to reinforce existing power structures in the form of 'nonfeminist or event antifeminist' gender training (Ferguson 2015, 386). Clearly, any unquestioning conviction that any gender training is better than none and uncritical celebration of the introduction of gender training into institutions of state power fails to take into account that training is a political process, and one that intervenes in particular institutional, cultural, and historical practices. Gender training is not simply the process of introducing new technical and politically neutral knowledge into an epistemic void. It is a political intervention in an institutional setting with its own set of knowledges and political investments. The politics of this practice are shaped through these pedagogical encounters.

The tension between feminist transformative projects and existent institutional politics is particularly stark in the case of gender training of peacekeepers. This practice has to contend within a structuring contradiction of peacekeeping itself—that of relying on soldiers to create conditions in which peace may be achieved. A. Betts Fetherston famously noted (1998, 167):

> There is no switch inside a blue helmet that automatically turns a soldier trained for war-fighting into an individual prepared to work non-violently and with cultural sensitivity in a highly militarized environment.

Problem-solving scholarship on peacekeeping has since examined the uses of training to socialize soldiers into 'cosmopolitan peacekeeping commitments' (Holohan 2019; Curran 2017, 12; Leeds 2001; Duffey 2000). At the same time, critical and feminist literature has insisted that we retain in view the ways in which peacekeeping itself is foundationally structured by contradiction. This is not simply a question of soldiers lacking specific technical skills or even that their attitudes are unsuited to peacekeeping. Rather, critical feminist scholarship points to a deeper contradiction, stemming from the 'ways that race, gender, and sexuality are privileged sites in the creation of a soldier' (Whitworth 2004, 104; see also Holmes 2019). The military is an institution that is dominated by men and that valorizes and rewards martial masculinity (Hearn 2012). Scholarship on military masculinities reveals the complex hierarchies of multiple masculinities at work, demonstrates the primacy of homosocial bonding in these environments, and exposes how femininity and marginalized masculinities are subordinated to the military ideal (Mäki-Rahkola and Myrttinen 2014; Belkin 2012; Higate 2003; Connell 2002; Barrett 1996). Notably, critical work on military masculinities consistently points to military training as a site at which these masculine ideals are inculcated (Duncanson and Woodward 2016, 5; Welland 2013; Cockburn 2010, 150).[4] An attentiveness to the reliance of peacekeeping on military personnel thus draws attention to the war-like nature and purpose of the martial institutions which now offer gender training.

Not only are the gendered and sexualized politics of martial institutions largely at odds with feminist transformative projects but also the peacekeeping endeavour itself cannot be construed as a reliably benevolent exercise of power on behalf of conflict-affected populations. Peacekeeping is imbricated with racialized and gendered structures of inequality, inflected through the specific frames of martial institutions and neoliberal governing rationalities. Peacekeeping operations are militarized environments, but they also contribute to the militarization of troop-contributing countries themselves. The practice provides national militaries with opportunities to acquire new and updated material, training and combat experience, diplomatic prestige, and even a raison d'être, justifying the maintenance of a military institution in countries not otherwise involved in conflict (Henry 2012, 19–20; Whitworth 2004, 183).

Peacekeeping re-inscribes a global colour line. Contemporary peacekeeping operations are largely reliant on the labour of Global South peacekeepers, whose voices are underrepresented in decision-making positions in the structures of global governance, but who constitute a cheap source of surplus labour, readily available for what Marsha Henry (2012) dubs 'peacexploitation'. The practice produces the imaginary of 'conflict prone Third World countries', portraying populations in the Global South as disorderly and chaotic, and opening up spaces for intervention by force (Pratt 2013; Razack 2004; Whitworth 2004, 38; Paris 2002). Against this backdrop, instances of violent and exploitative behaviour by peacekeepers can be understood 'as colonial or racial violence rather than simply violence typical of the hypermasculine world of militaries' (Razack 2004, 86).

If peacekeeping constitutes states in the Global South as a legitimate field of paternalistic intervention, it is also closely related to the exportation of modes of (neo)liberal governance (Richmond 2011; Zanotti 2008; Duffield 2001). Peacekeeping involves the deployment of force to end violence, while at the same time obfuscating the role of the neoliberal global economy and modern state system in producing that violence in the first place (Väyrynen 2004, 129). Not only is the imposition of a (neo)liberal global order enacted through the deployment of peace operations but also these logics permeate the ways in which peacekeeping operations are practised and the discourses that shape these practices. Neoliberal economic logics of peacekeeping facilitate violence against women, including through a political economy of peacekeeping and post-war reconstruction processes that render them vulnerable to exploitation and abuse (Duncanson 2018; True 2014).

We may thus reasonably expect that the risk of a feminist politics of gender training being co-opted by powerful institutions is particularly pronounced in peacekeeping contexts. Against these odds, however, some observers cultivate an optimism for the recuperability of feminist politics in engagements with the military, arguing 'against deterministic approaches toward the gender-military nexus that deny possibilities for change within military institutions' (Duncanson and Woodward 2016, 4). They insist that if feminist scholarship views gender as a social construction and hence changeable, surely this same analytical persuasion should apply to military institutions as well. Consequently, the argument goes, feminist analyses should be open to the notion that militaries could be gendered differently. Indeed, some writing in this tradition place their hopes in peacekeeping, as a different type of cosmopolitan-minded military activity, to catalyse change within national militaries (V. Brown 2020; Bergman Rosamond and Kronsell 2018; Duncanson 2013; Carreiras 2010). Further, some accounts characterize gender mainstreaming efforts as a way for feminists to get a foot in the door and work to reshape global security structures (Deiana and McDonagh

2018). However, such optimism is temperate as best. There is little evidence to suggest that a significant transformation is underway (Kronsell 2012, 146).

On the one hand, analyses of gender mainstreaming of peacekeeping have pointed to an implementation gap in commitments: marginalization of gender work through under-funding and under-staffing, non-implementation of training commitments, and a persistent failure to deploy more female peacekeepers (Bastick and Duncanson 2018; Pruitt 2016; Hendricks 2015; Higate 2004). Further, a number of critical accounts suggest that what change does take place is more likely to be assimilated into existing power structures rather than to meaningfully challenge them. Feminist analyses have drawn attention to the ways in which gender mainstreaming empties 'gender concerns of their critical content' and how gender, as a result, 'does the work of the status quo' (Whitworth 2004, 17, 140). While the presence of female soldiers is often considered a potential disruption to norms of hegemonic masculinity, critical feminist accounts have demonstrated the ways in which individual women are assimilated into norms of masculinity, and how traditional gender norms are thus re-asserted (Holmes 2019; Simić 2010; Sasson-Levy and Amram-Katz 2007). Further, gender mainstreaming often re-inscribes global inequalities, insofar as institutions of global governance assume that gender mainstreaming efforts of the Global North are superior to and take precedence over practices emanating from the Global South (Pruitt 2018). Gender, in mainstreaming discourse, becomes equated with 'other' women and their vulnerability; and discussions of men, masculinities, and power are thereby silenced (Kronsell 2012, 111; Higate and Henry 2009, 154; Whitworth 2004, 136). In other words, many critical accounts insist on seeing hegemonic discourses and institutions of governance as dexterous, capable of folding in calls for transformation while maintaining existing configurations of power.

In the face of such obstacles, it is reasonable to question whether a transformative feminist politics is even possible in the martial institutions of peacekeeping. The evidence for it does not look good. The corollary of this argument, however, need not be to write off the entire endeavour as singularly colonial or violent. Taking critiques of the transformative potential of gender training seriously does not automatically mean that the right feminist strategy is to abandon it altogether. Instead, taking these critiques seriously should serve as impetus for excavating the political work being done in the present. Sherene Razack, an ardent critic of peacekeeping practices, contends that retaining in view the often-violent politics of peacekeeping 'does not mean that we should stay at home when genocides are in progress ... We must go, but *how* we go is critical' (2004, 150, 164, emphasis in original). Indeed, critical accounts of peacekeeping practices typically locate possibilities for engagement not in the recuperation of transformative promise, but at the margins of hegemonic discourses. This amounts to a strategy of engaging and working with the ambivalent politics of training, rather than glossing over these contradictions. In this vein, Tarja Väyrynen advocates for '[a]llowing dissident ... voices to be heard' as a means of offering 'an element that celebrates uncertainty and multiplicity' and bringing 'in an alternative thinking on peace, war and gender' (2004, 140). Marjaana Jauhola (2010, 45) draws upon Judith Butler's theorizing in reading gender mainstreaming discourses against the grain, looking for disjunctures within hegemonic narratives, and providing alternative readings of 'subversion from within'. Read together, these accounts suggest political potential in critical engagement, not grounded in an expectation that gender mainstreaming will radically transform existing structures, but rather in an understanding that hegemonic discourses are marked by contradiction and instability.

Nonetheless, this literature has so far tended to assume the futility and co-opted nature of gender training without careful empirical engagement with this practice. My aim in this book is therefore to expand on a 'narrow awareness of the everyday' (Higate and Henry 2009, 8) through an interrogation of training as a mechanism through which 'people are educated to participate in the social, how they are interpellated into practices that leave the trails of violence in their wake' (Razack 2004, 57). Such an empirically grounded analysis is important, I argue, in order to investigate tensions and contradictions within the everyday practices of training. I attach importance to training not because I expect it to directly produce revolutionary action leading to structural transformation. Rather, I see training as a practice which shapes the epistemic rules that determine political possibilities: it involves a knowledge production process which shapes a 'grid of intelligibility' (Foucault 1998, 93) and 'makes possible particular identities, fixes categories of things and people, and makes various forms of conduct thinkable' (Prügl 2010, 4–5). Grounded in this epistemic stance, the overarching question that animates this book can be expressed as: *What political and epistemic work does gender training do in martial institutions involved in peacekeeping?*

## Pedagogy as Intersubjective Practice

What, then, does the political and epistemic work that gender training does look like in practice? Gender trainers themselves, and many researchers who study them, are remarkably open in their assessment of what feminist gender training should achieve. Rahel Kunz suggests that there is a need to move 'away from an understanding of feminist knowledge as expertise towards gender as a critical analytical category for *disruption and contestation*' (2016, 110, emphasis added). Rather than imparting knowledge, on a predictable track toward measurable training outcomes, such a gender trainer primarily disrupts established ways of knowing things. This understanding of training aligns with Naila Kabeer's explanation as to why her training does not offer 'blueprints for action': 'Empowering women must . . . begin with the individual consciousness and with the imaginative construction of alternative ways of being, living, and relating' (1991, 194). In Kabeer's account, knowledge is contextual and it is up to individuals to develop political consciousness and vision, as opposed to these being imposed by a blueprint for gender training. Yet other gender trainers describe their aims not as producing readily measurable learning outcomes, but rather as creating 'transformative encounters/moments' productive of 'transformative courage' (Ferguson 2019b, 91). Accordingly, what is needed to reclaim the feminist politics of gender training is the development of a practice of 'ethical encounters', and one that privileges quality of process over quality of outcomes (Ferguson 2019b, 16; Kunz 2016, 100; Prügl 2016, 26). In short, what all of these accounts of gender training have in common is their reluctance to assign a straightforward measure of success for gender training. There is no standardized test in which a point score over a certain threshold would indicate a successful training session.

Instead, these understandings of a specifically feminist politics of gender training point toward the importance of classroom encounters, and the skill of the trainer in creating moments that allow for the development of critical consciousness, subverting established knowledges, and producing transformative moments through ethical encounters. In other words, they call for a renewed attention to and deliberation over what constitutes feminist praxis in gender training. This requires specific pedagogical skills on the part of the trainer because exactly what will happen in each classroom or training session is unknowable in advance (Enderstein 2018, 49). Accordingly, what makes for a good gender trainer, argues Lucy Ferguson, is a question not only of subject matter knowledge but also of facilitation skills grounded in feminist pedagogical theory (2019b, 71, 85). This understanding of gender training contests institutional understandings of what knowledge about gender is, how it can or should be taught, and how it might be learned. In institutions of global governance, definitional and measurement biases favour assessing the success of gender training through standardized measures such as whether trainees can recite a formal definition of gender or list a number of actions peacekeepers can take to improve the gender-responsiveness of their practices. This stands in contrast to feminist gender trainers' quest for transformative moments and consciousness-raising. In navigating this double-edged potential, some scholars of gender training call for a closer alignment of practices of gender training with feminist pedagogical theorizing in order to ensure that training serves transformative purposes (Ferguson 2019b, 71; Enderstein 2018, 52). This understanding of pedagogy locates knowledge not in the text of the curriculum, but rather in the related processes of teaching and learning, where no automatic correspondence can be assumed between what is taught and what is learned. It identifies, in other words, the site of pedagogy in the *encounters* between subjects and knowledges (Britzman 1998, 19). I ground my conceptualization of pedagogy in these theories, not because I assume that gender trainers in martial settings hold feminist pedagogical visions or practise feminist pedagogy (most do not), but because these theories provide conceptual tools with which to gauge what is happening in this training, and with which to arbitrate what its political effect may be.

Because training is an intersubjective process, the political work that it does is determined by pedagogical practices. In other words, how curricula are devised and delivered, and how they are made meaningful in the classroom, are significant in shaping what the politics of the training are. These insights give rise to more specific, practical questions about the training process itself: How is gender made a knowable object? Who is authorized to know it? How is it learned? What processes of translation and contestation are involved in this learning? Guided by these questions, this book seeks to track the meanings that gender acquires in training contexts. It is centrally concerned with knowledge as process—how knowledge about gender is produced, and how training participants come to know gender.

It is worth highlighting that these are epistemic questions, constitutive in nature. This is not a causal investigation, and provides no direct answers to the positivist question 'Does gender training work?' Responding to such a question would presume that we already know what gender is and what it would mean to successfully train it; it assumes that we already know to what end such training should work. Here I make no such assumption. My inquiry is focused precisely on what meaning(s) gender acquires in the process of training, and what kinds of politics these meaning(s) open up or foreclose. This is a project that is interested in how discursive constructions of knowledge condition the limits of possibility for being and acting in the world. There is, in other words, an important epistemic difference between the question of 'Does it work?' and 'What work does it do?', and this book is primarily interested in the latter. The constitutive nature of my guiding questions does not, of course, suggest that this is a politically disinterested inquiry. To the contrary, the question of what epistemic and political work gender training does implies a normative question that is also a deeply practical one: Is gender training good or bad feminist politics? What should those of us who name our political commitments as feminist do with it?

## Studying Gender Training

This insistence on the importance of understanding pedagogy as an intersubjective practice has, of course, methodological implications. On the one hand, the focus of this book on the constitutive epistemology of gender training and its political potential means that rather than attempting to measure any causal impact of training on trainees' subsequent behaviours or performance, this book focuses on what happens in training itself. Formalized training curricula, such as the UN's Core Pre-Deployment Training Manual, provide some insight into the truth claims that gender training makes, but these are never fully predictive of the pedagogical encounters training produces. In practice gender trainers exercise a considerable amount of freedom in how they conduct training—sometimes to the extent of fully freewheeling. The text of a curriculum only communicates the desires of those providing the training, obscuring from view how these texts are taken up by those who are giving or receiving the training, and how the meaning of these texts is subsequently inflected at the scene of pedagogy. This recognition means that in order to assess the politics of gender training, we need to consider the intersubjective encounters that take place in the classroom, rather than simply examining training materials. It requires, in other words, a research method that allows analytical access to training sites;

to 'the micrological texture of power' that Spivak suggests is so important to understanding how subject formations operate (2010, 33).

Accordingly, the ways in which this book sets about exploring these questions is through what can be described as a multi-sited ethnography. The analysis in this book draws from a research archive that comprises participant observation of training courses; interviews with trainers and training participants; and examination of training materials and related policy documents.[5] What this means in practice is that I examined what kinds of commitments related to gender training are included in the relevant policies, and critically examined existing training curricula, manuals, and handbooks. I also conducted twenty-three semi-structured interviews with gender trainers and gender training designers. But the core of the book's analysis draws from time spent hanging out in gender training courses. Though I had worked in this field before researching it, for this book, I spent a total of eight weeks with the specific purpose of conducting participant observation on seven different training courses.

Five out of the seven courses were specialized gender courses, devoted to gender in their entirety, and aimed at gender advisers, gender trainers, and general military or police audiences. In addition to these specialized courses, I observed national pre-deployment training and a gender lecture provided as part of professional military education in a national setting. With the exception of one course for police officers in West Africa, the courses were primarily aimed at the military, although training audiences and facilitation teams also included a handful of police officers, civilian experts, and civil society representatives. Such specialized courses involve primarily middle-ranking officers—rather than enlisted soldiers or police officers from the lower ranks—meaning that the audiences were on average older and more educated than in a typical pre-deployment training attended by all ranks and functional specializations. Additionally, as many course participants told me, women are more likely than men to apply to or be selected for specialized gender courses, meaning that the courses were remarkably gender-balanced. In contrast to the overall low numbers of women in police and military institutions, women counted for roughly half of all participants in the gender courses I observed.

These courses took place in East Africa, the Nordic region, West Africa, the Western Balkans, and western Europe. Peacekeeper gender training remains a relatively small professional circle, and so in order to protect the anonymity of the research participants, I do not specify national or institutional location further. These training course sites should be understood more as nodal points in a transnational network of gender training than as discrete national (or, as it were, regional) case studies. Attention to the transnational aspect of peacekeeper gender training is not simply a question of examining different local articulations of a globally mandated policy. Rather, gender training involves a transnational community of practice. A loosely bounded community of gender trainers are involved in the design and delivery of training across multiple institutional and geographic sites, designing courses and debating best practice in meetings held at the UN in New York, NATO in Brussels, and the Nordic Centre for Gender in Military Operations in Sweden. They then travel to regional and national peacekeeping training centres to conduct training as international experts, and many do the same when deployed on peacekeeping missions. This circulation of people is associated with a circulation of knowledges: one often comes across the same trainers and training activities, examples, and presentation slides across a range of locations in ways that a process of policy diffusion and global standardized curricula simply cannot account for. There are continuities to the practice of training, in other words, that are not the direct result of the diffusion of a top-down policy mandate, but that are forged through the horizontal travelling of knowledges. It is this transnational community of practice on gender training that constitutes the object of inquiry for this study. My examination of gender training as a transnational practice thus tracks a story that unfolds across multiple institutional and geographic locations.

Much of this research was conducted through relations of 'critical friendship' with gender trainers, and from the vantage point of an 'empathetic collaborator' (Chappell and Mackay 2021; Holvikivi 2019; Prügl 2016). By this I mean that the research was conducted in the context of ongoing personal and professional relationships that exceeded the temporally and spatially bounded encounters that the terms 'participant observation' and 'interview' imply. These relations of proximity produced a dialogic relationship with research participants, which meant allowing the research questions and direction to be shaped by the conversations I had with research participants in the spirit of ethnographic inquiry. The participatory dimension of the research varied, from relatively passive observation to highly participatory engagement. In a number of cases, my permission to observe courses was granted in exchange for my agreement to support the course facilitation team, including by delivering training sessions, facilitating small group work, and collecting anonymous participant feedback. This active participation provided a way to practise reciprocity with the individuals who gave their time and insight for this research, and who lent their professional capital to vouch for my presence in their courses; a practice commonly used in feminist research to attempt to ameliorate the unequal benefits of research encounters (Huisman 2008, 374; Jacoby 2006, 166; Wolf 1996, 24). The practice of reciprocity did, however, have specific impacts on the research process.

On the one hand, being part of the facilitation team meant that I was invited to team meetings and gained valuable insight into how the trainers envisioned the course and their goals, and reflected on the pedagogical process throughout. It gave me access to course materials, such as anonymous feedback forms from participants. On the other hand, participating in the course delivery meant that I was perceived by the training participants as an instructor, which doubtless shaped on what terms participants were willing to discuss the course content with me. My role as an instructor in some ways increased the positional power that I held in the research encounter, and could have proven problematic in that no feminist approach to methodology advocates *increasing* the power of the researcher (Jacoby 2006, 154; Cook and Fonow 1986, 22). However, in practice, training participants seemed keenly aware of the fact that I exercised no institutional power over them in military and police hierarchies, and negotiated my ambiguous status on the course through humour, dubbing me, among other monikers, their pet civilian and course mascot, and on one course deciding to give me an honorary officer rank (of captain, which made me the lowest-ranked person present!). While this behaviour suggests that the participants read me as mostly harmless, norms of politeness nonetheless circumscribed how critical of the course delivery they were likely to be with me.

It is also worth noting the ways in which this research archive was produced through interactions inflected by gender, race, and class. That the researcher's positionality impacts the fieldwork process and subsequent knowledge claims is well established in the feminist methodological literature (Henry 2003; Wolf 1996; Harding 1993; Fonow and Cook 1991). The ways in which research participants read my positionality doubtless shaped the types of conversations they would have with me or in front of me. In agreement with the feminist literature on positionality, I contend that this is not a problem that can be overcome, but rather advocate for accounting for the ways in which positionality affects what knowledges are available to the researcher.

As the fact that I obtained the moniker 'pet civilian' attests to, and as is discussed in the feminist critical military studies literature, military culture can be suspicious of civilian presence (Gray 2016, 77; Cohn 2006, 98). Nonetheless, being consistently read as a young cis woman moderates this suspicion somewhat, and I encountered the phenomenon that Carol Cohn describes, of benefiting from the fact that naïveté about the military and national security is most likely to be forgiven in a young woman (2006, 96). Indeed, many of my interlocutors were notably willing (often eager) to take time to explain military culture to me.

Femininity shaped my experience in other ways as well. When speaking with a male NGO trainer I call Malcolm, we swapped stories of informal coffee-time encounters with training participants on a course we were both involved in. As we compared notes, we identified important differences in what stories we had heard. I had had military culture patiently explained to me, and learned a great deal about the lives of training participants—stories of lost spouses; traumatic experiences of witnessing violence in peacekeeping missions; reflections on the gendered division of labour in their homes; and worries over children's health and schooling. That such stories were readily shared with me suggested that my interlocutors were reading feminine qualities of nurturing and caring onto me. Malcolm, in turn, had been told that deployment on peacekeeping missions was a great opportunity, because it meant you could have a girlfriend in the mission area in addition to your wife at home. This was despite the fact that Malcolm had delivered a training session on the UN policy of zero tolerance for sexual exploitation and abuse, *and* had outed himself as a gay man! At the same time, Malcolm said that he felt judged by the trainees for his status as a civilian man against a backdrop of cultural norms that associate soldiering with masculinity. How our gendered subject positions were interpreted by the training participants had clearly shaped what kinds of stories we were made privy to.

My attention was drawn to the dynamics of gender and class when a western European military gender adviser I call Katie, in a session on dealing with resistance, noted that sometimes a male commander will feel that he must be respectful of women, and that a female gender adviser might circumvent possible resistance because of this politesse. Her remark prompted me to reflect on whom I was conversing with as trainees. In specialized gender training courses, most participants were officers—a role that is often linked to a particular class positioning—and as such were likely to have been professionally socialized to regard themselves as 'an officer and a gentleman'.

Further, as a researcher from a well-known and well-regarded university, military officers probably estimated that I shared their class positioning (see also Gray 2016, 77). Such concerns likely dissuaded them from sharing overtly negative comments or crude jokes about gender training with a female trainer and feminist researcher.

Racialization was another factor impacting positionality and hence what I, as the researcher, was able to hear. I often pass as white, and given my institutional location and education in the Global North, I came to the research encounter equipped with, as Suruchi Thapar-Björkert and Marsha Henry put it, the 'colonizer's language/tools/knowledge' (2004, 370). An entry in my field notes from a multinational course in East Africa reads:

> The challenge of doing fieldwork in an international environment: national/linguistic/racial grouping of participants. At dinner, I noticed how I keep finding myself among the European/Anglo/white participants—not the African and South Asian participants. Must make more of an effort to speak to people equally.

In other words, I noticed that participants, trainers, and myself tended to drift into national/linguistic/racial groupings during a multinational course. While I tried to ensure I spent equal amounts of time conversing with all participants, I was not always able to transcend my association with whiteness. In particular, although I wanted to formulate a postcolonial critique of some of the racial dynamics of the training, I noticed that Black African participants were particularly cautious in criticizing Eurocentrism to me. My association with the colonizer circumscribed what trainees would say in front of me and undoubtedly also what I was able to understand. In sum, the research archive that informs this book is, as all knowledge is, inflected by dynamics of gender, race, and class.

I read the material of this research archive through an interpretive lens informed by discourse analytical techniques: this book seeks to understand what the internal logic of training interventions are, what epistemic traditions they draw from, what assumptions they rely on, what accepted truths they cite, whom they invite us to be, and what makes them work as true. In order to get at these questions, I examine three features of discursive formations: subject positioning, authoritative knowledges, and instability and contradiction.

First, part of the epistemic and political work that gender training does is that of interpellation, shaping how we can be and act in the world by recruiting us to particular subject positions. This means it is important for us to analytically 'see' what subject positions training discourse makes available, how the relationships between different subject positions are set up, and what kinds of understandings of the self this discourse encourages. The 'officer and gentleman' who is courteous about gender training in polite company, demonstrates a widely available subject position that shapes how one might behave. I am interested, in other words, in the 'question of the epistemological position to which we are recruited' (Butler 2016, xii). This question also implies an interest in how the process of interpellation works. It is therefore not only a question of which subject positions are available but also a question of how one comes to invest in that subject position. Following Ahmed, I suggest: 'The narrative invites the reader to adopt the "you" through working on emotions' (2014, 1). Appeals to emotions shape our desire to take up a particular subject position. In other words, my reading of the knowledge formations of gender training examines not only how different subject positions are constructed but also how, in terms of an emotional pedagogy, trainees are invited to occupy different subject positions.

Second, related to the epistemic and political work that training does are questions of how gender is rendered a knowable object, and what processes of translation, negotiation, and resistance are implied in this process. These questions suggest an attentiveness to where training discourses gain their authority, and what earlier knowledge/investments they presuppose. Discursive utterances gain their power through reference to already accepted truth claims. Our previous example only works because institutional military discourses and broader cultural narratives have convinced the subject that being a military officer is an honourable vocation and that being a gentleman is what one should aspire to. Citation of existing power is what makes for authoritative speech; its 'constitutive historicity' is established because an action '*accumulates the force of authority through the repetition or citation of a prior, authoritative set of practices*' (Butler 1993, 19, emphasis in original). Following from this understanding of discourse as citational, I examine what makes certain knowledge claims work as true by examining what accepted truths they cite, and to what effect.

Third and finally, I contend that discourses are often ambivalent, encompassing contradictory claims (Bhabha 1994, 95). Because discourses are iterative in structure, repetitions pose 'a structural risk'; they are a 'site where a politically consequential break is possible' (Butler 2016, 24). Accordingly, the third aspect of my close reading strategy involves looking for tensions, inconsistencies, instabilities, and slips within the training discourse. These are plentiful because, as noted earlier, peacekeeping itself is structured by contradiction: are peacekeepers war-fighters or peace-makers? It is moments of doubt such as this one that foster critical practice by provoking new questions and unsettling given truths, such as: peacekeeping is a benevolent exercise, sexual violence is a problem there but not here, or men and women are equal in the military. Exposing the ambivalence underlying these claims presents windows for imagining how the world might be organized differently, which is why tracing them and working the contradiction is central to this book's analytical mission.

What is common to all of these interpretive strategies is that they engage in an analytical practice of tracing the limits of a discourse. They are founded on a conviction that knowledge could be constructed differently, and so 'read against the grain' of the text (Bhabha 1994, 36). The impulse to look beyond the text, to see what it is foreclosing, makes this a disobedient practice. What enables the practice is a body of critical scholarship which provides forms of 'counter-knowledges' that make it possible to think about how these understandings could be constructed differently (Bhabha 1994, 33). Accordingly, in this task, I engage in a practice of *reading with*, drawing on critical feminist, queer, and postcolonial insights as critical material in order to see what the training discourse is 'doing'. This analysis lends itself to my reading of the political potential and limitations of these interventions, with the empirical material serving as a catalyst to generate a conceptual vocabulary with which to consider the implications of the practice of gender training for feminist strategizing.

## Paradoxical Politics

Overall, this book demonstrates that gender training produces multiple and often contradictory political effects. From the point of view of normative commitments to feminist politics, training is a deeply ambivalent practice. On the one hand, gender is deployed in training as a concept that sustains binary, heteronormative thinking, and that reproduces colonial logics of difference. In this sense, my findings are wholly sympathetic to, and build on, critical feminist scholarship that points to how gender becomes depoliticized when it is deployed in gender mainstreaming efforts (Whitworth 2004, 140; see also Carson 2016). The concept of 'gender' often loses its critical edge in training, and is emptied of its potential to serve intersectional, queer, and postcolonial feminist projects. Not only is this political potential lost but also the concept itself becomes a tool that abides by martial logics and proposes the use of force as an appropriate solution to the problems identified. This analysis echoes the findings of feminist scholarship in critical military studies and beyond, pointing to the ways in which feminist concepts are already or are made amenable to imperial politics; that '[t]he project of gender integration will always be subject to forces intent on removing any commitment to the political goals of feminism' (Otto and Heathcote 2014, 8; see also Pratt 2013; Young 2003). In this sense, my findings lend themselves to the argument that, from the point of view of feminist politics, gender training for peacekeepers is a co-opted practice.

It is worth acknowledging at this juncture that '*feminism* [is] not a uniform referent even for those of us who regularly [deploy] it to name the politics of our intellectual investments' (Wiegman 2016, 86, emphasis in original). I describe the political work that gender training does to be at odds with feminist politics when gender is made to support the use of martial force, to justify imperial incursions, to bolster cis- and heteronormativity, and to re-inscribe racial hierarchies. However, as has been well documented, there *are* articulations of feminism which are not inherently or necessarily opposed to such politics. Not all feminists oppose militarism, and many have brushed aside concerns over militarism when lobbying for women's right to serve (Kennedy-Pipe 2017; Sasson-Levy and Amram-Katz 2007). Feminist analyses and politics have importantly contributed to the (re)production of racialized hierarchies and helped justify imperial incursions abroad and discriminatory policies at home by portraying non-Western populations as backward and in need of white saviours (Farris 2017; Mohanty 1988). Some strands of contemporary feminist politics insist on biological dimorphism to exclude trans* subjects from feminist politics, while forms of liberal feminism emphasize individual betterment, echoing the mantras of neoliberal projects (Phipps 2020; Hines 2019). Notably, these types of political commitments do not give rise to an understanding of the politics of peacekeeper gender training as ambivalent. The assessment of co-optation, then, is a self-consciously political one. It stakes a claim to feminism not just as an empty signifier but also as a particular kind of feminist commitment.

Even with this insistence on a feminism that opposes colonial violence and attends to multiple systems of oppression, an ambivalence persists within gender training practice. This book identifies a contradictory dynamic, whereby some gender training, at times, serves to destabilize these very same structuring logics of heteronormativity and coloniality. As explored particularly in Chapter 5, gender training demonstrably opens the door to moments of feminist pedagogical practice, denaturalizing colonial and heteronormative constructions of gender and disturbing the logics of martiality. My conceptualization of feminist pedagogical practice is importantly indebted to broader work, beyond the security sector, on gender training as a transformative feminist strategy (Ferguson 2019b; Mukhopadhyay 2014). However, my findings depart somewhat from this body of scholarship, in that I do not suggest that these subversive feminist practices, in the context of peacekeeper training, will necessarily produce cumulative causal effects that lead to structural transformation in the long run (they do not necessarily amount to a slow drip of change). I hesitate to make such claims both because my methodology does not lend itself to an assessment of cumulative transformative change and more importantly because I suggest that the nature of these subversions does not put forward a coherent demand for an alternative, transformed future. They constitute what Gayatri Chakravorty Spivak calls a 'practical politics of the open end'; a form of everyday political labour that sustains resistant politics, rather than a solution for doing away with structural violence (Spivak and Harasym 1990, 105). I thus depart from some of the feminist literature on gender training in that I call these moments 'small subversions' rather than transformative moments in an effort to capture their resistant—rather than future-producing—orientation.

The findings of this book, then, point to contradictory political effects of gender training for peacekeepers as simultaneously 'good' and 'bad' feminist politics. These findings leave us with the question of how to think about such ambivalent dynamics beyond the eminently reasonable but analytically and politically unsatisfying conclusion of 'it is both'. The titular suggestion of this book is that this dynamic is most usefully thought of as a paradox: a proposition that is both true and false at the same time. A paradox is inherently irresolvable (Scott 1996). Thinking of training as a paradoxical practice within a feminist tradition of thought therefore necessitates the development of conceptual thinking that engages with the question of how to sit with a tension, how to work with a paradox in a way that is not politically paralysed, but productive (W. Brown 2000). In this task, I take up Dianne Otto's suggestion that feminist analyses of such engagements abandon what she calls, following Clare Hemmings (2011), 'progress narratives' in which feminist politics can always be recuperated to secure a better future, in favour of an attention to the 'politics of the present'. This attention to the present, Otto argues, demands that whether or not we are invested in the long-term transformative potential of interventions like gender training, we are nonetheless obligated to develop ways of engagement that are more resistive and less amenable to institutional capture in the present (Otto 2014, 158).

If, following Otto's suggestion, we put aside for a moment the demand that gender training produce a different, transformed future, and attend to its paradoxical nature in the present, this allows us to consider the value of small acts of subversion that destabilize hegemonic narratives, at the same time as we remain vigilant of the dangerous co-optations that are taking place. If we take the stance that the future is by definition unknowable, and disinvest from long-term transformation as *the* criterion for an activity being politically worthwhile, can we think of a feminist investment in gender training that is 'optimistically cruel', as Robyn Wiegman (2016, 91) reworks Lauren Berlant's (2011) famous 'cruel optimism'? Berlant's cruel optimism is a relation in which 'something you desire is actually an obstacle to your flourishing' (2011, 1). In contrast, Wiegman (2016, 91, emphasis added) suggests that feminism's attachment to an object (in her case, the academy), can be optimistically cruel:

> our ongoing attachment to an object ... is only possible because *we know it will not deliver what we most want from it*. In this context the cruelty of our optimism—to be attached to an object that 'impedes the aim' that brought us to it—is a potent form of inoculation against the threat of institutional complicity.

Wiegman's thinking about feminism in relation to academia as optimistically cruel, finds, I believe, a parallel in thinking about feminism's relation to gender training. Thinking with Wiegman's conceptualization means accepting that gender training 'will not deliver what we most want from it', that is, it will not undo intersectional structures of oppression (2016, 91). Rather than producing apathy and resignation, being optimistically cruel means that any value we attach to the practice is not contingent on its producing long-term transformation. Importantly, it liberates us from considering anything falling short of long-term transformation as failure.

Instead it provides the basis for acknowledging and developing forms of political engagement that are less amenable to institutional capture.

Drawing on these ideas, this book develops a conceptual vocabulary aimed at fostering feminist political strategizing in an ambivalent historical present. Rather than celebrating gender training as an unambiguous normative good (which clearly it is not), or consigning it to a scrap heap of lost and misguided feminist causes (which involves discounting and discarding a huge amount of feminist political work), I argue that there is scope within this practice to develop feminist strategies of resistance. Despite all the issues with gender training—and there are many—how we know gender continues to matter. It matters because it has implications for how it could be known otherwise; how such knowledges could be used to create new ways of being and acting in the world. Engaging in knowledge production and world building projects in diverse epistemic communities is particularly important in the current political climate, in which a hostility to feminist thinking appears resurgent. I argue therefore for developing forms of critical engagement that resist the amenability of the concept of 'gender' to serve the purposes of imperial politics. Rather than retreat to a position in which any compromise is unacceptable and any risk too risky, we need debate and to invest effort into thinking about what feminist pedagogies might look like and how they might be practised. There is political value in exploiting the margins of hegemonic discourses to introduce strategies of disruption and subversion. To do so, we need to keep following the concept of 'gender' around on its travels and to take part in the contestations over the political meanings of the term, while at the same time recognizing that such approaches are always messy, imprecise, and corruptible.

## Organization of The Book

The point of departure for this book is a certain agnosticism about the exact meaning and content of 'gender'. What gender is and does in training are constitutive questions for this inquiry, rather than pre-established facts. The concept of 'gender' can be defined in a variety of ways and can thus be made to do all manner of epistemic and political work. Critical, queer (and) postcolonial feminist scholarship has demonstrated how gender can be and has been defined in ways that produce deeply marginalizing effects by closing off or silencing 'other' ways of being. Accordingly, the empirical analysis begins with an overview of what gender training is. Chapter 2 examines the scope and content of gender training for peacekeepers and considers what work gender is made to do against the insights of critical feminist literature, which demonstrate what is closed off or silenced by defining gender in a particular way. This reading practice aims to bring sustained attention to bear on the political effects of producing gender knowledge. Through an investigation into how training curricula are produced, this chapter describes how gender becomes fixed as a knowable object, and how the political economy of knowledge production involved in this fixing privileges certain actors and forms of knowledge. More specifically, it sheds light on how the curriculum design process privileges expertise in the Global North, while marginalizing other knowers and forms of knowledge. It demonstrates how training curricula omit consideration of race and non-normative sexuality to produce a narrow understanding of gender. It also discusses the ways by which the military setting shapes the epistemic rules governing who is a credible knower, and the demands placed on what gender knowledge should do in and for the institution. Throughout this discussion, I remain attentive to the potential for contention around what counts as gender in training, reading against the grain to suggest how gender could be and sometimes is conceptualized differently in training. This analytical tension exposes that the racialized and sexualized subjects exiled from the episteme nonetheless continue to haunt its foundations, keeping alive contradiction and ambivalence at the heart of gender knowledge.

However, and as discussed above, gender knowledge is produced through social interaction: We must understand pedagogy as an intersubjective practice, in which there is no automatic correspondence between how training designers imagine the practice and goals of gender training, what is set in the curriculum, what happens in the classroom, and what training participants learn as a result of these encounters. Chapter 3 thus moves from an examination of texts, of training curricula, to an examination of classroom dynamics in order to interrogate knowledge production processes at work in training. This chapter suggests that knowledge can be thought of as produced through affective processes to highlight the ways in which training fosters specific types of epistemic and political investments. This mode of analysis speaks to the question of how gender is learned in a training setting. Substantively, through an attentiveness to how conflict-related sexual violence is treated as a training topic, Chapter 3 sketches out the ways in which training fosters investments in martial logics and the use of force as well as the ways in which training participants' emotional investments may also alert them to the limitations and shortcomings of martial action.

Sitting with the interest in how training participants come to accept, modify, or reject knowledge presented to them in the training setting, Chapter 4 focuses specifically on resistance to feminist politics and analyses in gender training. This type of resistance follows, I suggest, patterns or scripts that can be performed by both trainers and training audiences. This chapter charts different scripts through which trainers and trainees alike seek to undermine the radical potential of gender knowledge, suggesting that resistance involves ways of undermining the training through humour, distancing gender from feminist politics, and projecting the issue of gender onto racialized others. Throughout this analysis, I highlight that resistance is a dynamic and often politically ambivalent process, examining how struggles over meaning are staged in the training context in ways that defy a simple resolution to political contestations.

The analysis in Chapters 2 through 4 demonstrate primarily the ways in which gender is rendered a knowable object through an epistemic lens that privileges martial and neocolonial logics. This finding—that martial institutions militarize gender knowledge and make it serve their own purposes—will likely come as little surprise to critical feminist observers schooled in intersectional analyses. However, this discussion is punctuated throughout with an attentiveness to moments of instability for or rupture from the hegemonic discourses of martial institutions. In Chapter 5, I shift modes of analysis to pay more systematic attention to these moments, which I describe as subversive. This chapter offers a reparative reading of some training practices as engaging in feminist pedagogical practice. I do not go so far as to call these practices transformative; they do not necessarily provide an alternative future for martial institutions. Rather, I characterize them as 'small subversions'; moments of delinking, disruption, and instability against hegemonic discourses. I argue that we can think of feminist pedagogical moments as effecting a Spivakian notion of a 'practical politics of the open end': not a politically decisive solution, but a practice that keeps alive resistance to hegemonic logics and ways of thinking and acting differently.

In the concluding chapter, I take stock of the ambivalence that characterizes the story this book lays out: that gender training works to depoliticize the concept of gender, rendering it safe and ready to serve the interests of martial institutions; and at the same time, that it has the potential to subvert the hegemonic logics of these institutions. Setting up this contradiction as paradox, I ask, finally, what does the nature of this paradox mean for feminist politics? Are we to abandon gender training as a lost political project? Perhaps not. I suggest that a transformed future is not the only standard that renders feminist political projects viable and desirable. Instead, I argue for a disinvestment from liberal progress narratives, and a concomitant embrace of a politics of subversion and ambivalence. Such a shift in modes of political thought allows for an engagement with the present that is—following Wiegman—'optimistically cruel' (2016, 91). Building on this argument for a recognition of the political worth of subversive gender training practices, I conclude by reflecting on the implications of this argument for feminist political strategizing and for engagement with practitioners and policymakers.

# 2
# Fixing Gender
## The Curriculum

'Gender' is a term that—despite its potential for contention—is frequently deployed in the structures and policies of global governance of peace and security. The UN, its Security Council, and troop- and police-contributing countries mandate gender mainstreaming, establish gender policies, conduct gender analyses, deploy gender advisers, and, of course, mandate and deliver gender training. Policymakers, gender trainers, and a number of scholars agree that training is required for gender mainstreaming and that the key to successful training is for peacekeepers to learn what gender is. What is remarkable about this seemingly straightforward claim is that it presumes the pre-existence of gender as an object of knowledge. It gives gender a stable and reliable ontology, assuming that we already know what gender is and does—that we agree on that definition—and can easily impart this information.

The reason I draw attention to this assumption will be familiar to many working in the field of gender and feminist theory. To state that 'gender' has been a hugely productive concept for feminist activism and scholarship would be an understatement. At the same time, its broad analytical purchase has meant that the concept has been imbued with different meaning depending on who has used it, when, and for what purpose. These different conceptualizations of gender have done different types of political work. The take-up of the term by feminists in the 1970s to insist that gender is socially constructed opened up avenues for arguing that if gender is constructed, it could be constructed differently. It allowed feminists to contest the idea that biology is destiny, breathing new life into Simone de Beauvoir's famous maxim 'one is not born, but rather becomes, a woman' (de Beauvoir 1997, 295; see also Strathern 2016; Friedman 1996, 78). The troubling of the sexual binary in turn lent itself to queer and feminist arguments that aimed to denaturalize heterosexuality and that developed a vocabulary for contesting the pathologization of trans* and intersex subjects (Butler 2007a, 2004; de

Lauretis 1989). At the same time, Black feminists in the United States and the United Kingdom brought critical attention to bear on the ways in which gender has been racially coded as white in feminist politics and scholarship, erasing from view the intersectional oppression experienced by Black women (Cho, Crenshaw, and McCall 2013; Collins 1989; Carby 1982). Post- and decolonial feminists have exposed how gender operates, historically and in the historical present, to construct colonial difference (Lugones 2007; Mohanty 1988). And of course, at the heart of feminist deployments of gender is a paradox, whereby feminists use 'woman'—a category of sexual difference—as a basis from which to formulate political demands, while at the same time (often) seeking to do away with sexual difference (Scott 1996).

While this brief reference to some ways in which gender has been theorized and problematized is necessarily selective, it reveals the importance of asking a foundational question when approaching the practice of gender training: What exactly *is* gender, this knowledge object that is at the core of the training? Or perhaps more accurately: What or whose version of gender is being operationalized? My point here is not to establish an essential truth to gender or a correct definition that one could use as a yardstick against which to assess gender training initiatives. Even a brief overview of feminist theorizing on gender casts suspicion on any definitive pronouncements of what gender is and does. Rather, my point is that the process by which gender is imbued with meaning is itself a selective epistemic act, and one which has political effects. Judith Butler (2007b, xxii) alerts us to the fact that:

> The question... of what qualifies as 'gender' is itself already a question that attests to a pervasively normative operation of power, a fugitive operation of 'what will be the case' under the rubric of 'what is the case'.

Any attempt to fix meaning to the concept of 'gender' is, in other words, underwritten by an operation of power; a power that operates through its own invisibilization, posing as natural or as common-sense. Accordingly, the point of departure for this book's analysis of gender training is an interrogation of what meaning gender acquires in this practice: How is gender constructed in gender training and to what effect? I am interested, in other words, in the process by which gender acquires a certain 'thingness'; how it is rendered an object to be known (Sedgwick 2003, 6).

The process by which gender takes form in the pedagogical project of peacekeeper training starts with the design of training courses and curricula. In this chapter, I examine the training curriculum as a site at which knowledge about gender is produced and made to work as true. The notion of 'fixing' gender has at least two meanings here. The writing of a curriculum on gender exemplifies an effort to fix an understanding of what gender is and does; it is a process that renders gender knowable. This fixing is also a process of remedy: what is included in curricula is what is seen as necessary to fix problems associated with gender. This process implicates a number of actors, working in and through constellations of power, who are able to claim the authority to know and teach gender, constituting a political economy of knowledge production. The questions that guide this inquiry can be expressed as follows: Who is authorized to know gender? How is gender rendered a knowable object? Who can teach it? By drawing attention to the process of fixing meaning to the term 'gender', my aim is to expose how this process produces the social facticity of the term itself. As Teresa de Lauretis (1989, 2) argues, gender works as a technology (here too) that determines the horizons of the possible. This approach insists on seeing the meaning of gender, what it means to teach it, and what the outcomes of gender training are, as open-ended, ongoing processes rather than given facts. It could be described as an anti-ontological conceptualization of gender and a bottom-up, empirically informed understanding of what gender means in any given context. It follows that this is not a quest to identify moments of misrepresentation or miscognition of an underlying truth of gender in training curricula. Rather, I seek to trace how gender as a concept is produced, what knowledge about gender circulates, and with what effects, while remaining attentive to how it might be produced otherwise.

## A political Economy of Knowledge Production

In principle, all peacekeeper gender training is guided by official curricula set by powerful institutions. These curricula determine what counts as gender, delimit the scope of training, and prescribe solutions to problems they identify as having to do with gender. Because curricula are incarnations of epistemic authority—they establish what the problem is and what should be done about it—they are a site at which many different actors vie for influence. As with any knowledge-production process, critical feminist sensibilities point to the importance of asking who is in a position to authorize knowledge, who is recognized as a knowing subject, and what kinds of knowledge are licensed as a result. These considerations are of crucial epistemic importance: they determine whose experiences and concerns inform the conduct of peacekeeping operations. These questions also have material consequences because those recognized as knowing subjects, as experts on gender, gain professional advantage and monetary remuneration for their work.

## Whose Curriculum?

The United Nations is the primary international organization that mandates peacekeeping missions, placing it in a position of authority to prescribe or recommend gender training. It establishes this mandate through the Security Council's Women, Peace and Security Agenda, which calls for gender training of peacekeepers (see e.g. UN Security Council Resolution 1325 [2000] para. 6 and Resolution 2106 [2013] para. 8). The UN Department of Peace Operations provides all troop- and police-contributing countries with a standard training package intended for delivery prior to deployment on a peacekeeping operation, called the Core Pre-Deployment Training Materials.[1] These materials include lessons on a number of topics that have an explicit gender focus: women, peace, and security; conflict-related sexual violence; and sexual exploitation and abuse. The curriculum is designed to be delivered through national training programmes as well as by regional peacekeeping training centres. Once deployed, peacekeepers receive further in-mission training to contextualize broader gender topics to the area of operations. This process, centred on an official UN curriculum which is delivered to all staff, regardless of job function, national origin, or where they are deploying, is notable for its top-down conceptualization of gender knowledge. It suggests that what should be known about gender can first be established in general terms and subsequently applied to local mission contexts. The epistemic effect of such a process is to privilege an understanding of 'gender' as a universally applicable and transnationally consistent term. In this sense, peacekeeper gender training follows similar patterns to the development of gender expertise across a range of fields of global governance, where observers point to a 'geographic hierarchisation' of gender knowledge (Kunz, Prügl, and Thompson 2019, 34). In this knowledge-production process, experts located at the headquarters of international organizations such as the UN are in a position to identify and name problems and set the terms of discussion. Their knowledge and vantage point is thus privileged over that of socioculturally specific epistemic communities.

Of course, the UN is not the only organization that oversees peace operations, nor is it the only institution that has a stake in the design of training curricula. Troop- and police-contributing countries also send personnel to African Union, NATO, and European Union missions, each of which set their own training mandates and requirements. Owing to the complex division of labour between institutions of global governance and troop- and police-contributing countries, many national institutions that offer training or courses on gender prepare their personnel to deploy to different organizations' missions. Indeed, in the gender training courses I observed, course participants almost without exception were deploying to or have deployed on diverse types of missions: some were or will be involved in UN peacekeeping, some in NATO-led operations, some in European Union missions, and yet others in African Union missions. Many of the courses run by national and regional peacekeeping training centres are certified by multiple organizations, and their training practices respond to multiple institutional requirements simultaneously. Further, many of the instructors involved in the design and delivery of training have worked for a number of different organizations, and speak across institutional boundaries. Some come from a military or police background, others count civilians who are employed by UN, NATO, or the European Union, or by national ministries of defence. In practice, then, training courses often meld together different training requirements set by a number of institutions, and address both military and police peacekeepers.

This diversity of missions reveals the complexity of the institutional environment in which training is carried out. The intertwining of institutional mandates in the delivery of training produces dual effects. On the one hand, it means that the curriculum design process is characterized by interinstitutional contestations over what the scope and purpose of gender training should be, and which institution owns which approach. Institutions mark out their approach as distinctive by, for example, developing a form of branded terminology: whereas UN training materials refer to 'conflict-related sexual violence (CRSV)', NATO speaks of 'conflict-related sexual and gender-based violence (CRSGBV)'. Each organization thus signals how they consider the nuances of the issues at stake and what their member nations promote.

On the other hand, the involvement of a diversity of institutional actors to some degree harmonizes knowledges, because it produces a community of practice around gender training. These institutional crossovers can often be traced in the career paths of individuals within this knowledge community, with several senior gender experts changing posts during the course of their careers between institutions like the UN and NATO.[2] This circulation of individuals across different institutional sites also entails a horizontal circulation of knowledges. It contributes to the creation of a shared language and terms of contestation around the question of gender. Importantly, it means that peacekeeper gender training is not (only) a transnational phenomenon insofar as it entails localized articulations of a globally mandated training requirement. Rather, gender training involves a transnational community of practice of gender experts and trainers.

## Whose Knowledge?

While the mandate for gender training derives from political authorities' policy guidance, such as Security Council resolutions or regional and national action plans on women, peace, and security,[3] the official source of knowledge for this training is something called 'operational demands'. Reports from ongoing military and peacekeeping operations are used to identify training requirements, which are then translated into learning topics and introduced to the training curriculum as learning outcomes.[4] These training needs are often enumerated on the basis of who needs to know and what, given their rank and functional specialization. In military gender training, these are usually disaggregated as the tactical, operational, and strategic levels. In this neat feedback loop, what makes it into gender training curricula is determined by problems identified by military actors on the ground. However, in reality, a greater diversity of actors contribute to the production of knowledge about gender.

Many organizations that do not have a governmental mandate to send troops abroad and therefore to train them nonetheless partake in contestations that shape the field. Primarily international non-governmental organizations, these include the likes of the International Peace Institute in the United States and the Geneva Centre for Security Sector Governance in Switzerland. These organizations lack the institutional authority to mandate training requirements, but nonetheless develop training materials on gender, including for police and military personnel.[5] Their training materials are regarded as valued resources by many individuals working in the UN and NATO contexts and inform the design of training by these institutions. Further, representatives of these organizations actively partake in shaping gender training practices: they advocate for certain approaches by publishing policy papers; they attend stakeholder meetings such as the NATO Committee on Gender Perspectives annual meeting; and they send trainers to assist in the delivery of gender courses. Their presence in official proceedings and in training courses is welcomed as a source of expertise by some, and regarded with suspicion given their outsider status by others. Overall, the participation of non-governmental actors in the process demonstrates Rahel Kunz's observation that knowledges about gender in the field of global governance 'circulate in many different ways and directions, defying the simplistic, linear top-down version of the transfer scenario' (2016, 111). The range of actors who partake in the negotiation of what merits inclusion in gender training curricula is not therefore limited to peacekeepers on the ground, as the problem-solving 'operational demands' scenario would suggest, but also includes gender experts from non-governmental organizations who have the ability to access institutional debates and curriculum design processes.

The key to understanding what types of actors are involved lies precisely in identifying who is able to *access* institutional curriculum design processes. Two key organizations that develop gender training for peacekeepers are the UN and NATO, whose curricula are designed in New York (UN); Brussels (NATO Headquarters); Norfolk, Virginia (NATO Allied Command Transformation); and Stockholm (Nordic Centre for Gender in Military Operations, NATO Department Head for Gender Education and Training). While the geographic location of these centres is not the sole determinant for which outside actors are involved, location does hint at the types of organizations and individuals who are able to provide input on the process. Indeed, those who are involved in the curriculum design process hail almost exclusively from the Global North/minority world. This of course does not mean that Global South peacekeepers are somehow uninvolved in gender training. The majority of the world's peacekeepers come from the Global South nations, which also design and deliver gender training (Holmes 2019; Henry 2012). However, experts from the majority world rarely provide input on the training curricula of these dominant international organizations.[6]

An illustration of this division of labour between those who do gender work on the ground and those who are positioned as knowing gender for the purposes of designing training is succinctly illustrated by a 2021 article on female peacekeepers in *The Economist*. The central question this article grapples with is why more women should be deployed as peacekeepers, and why so few are. The article lists the countries that deploy the most peacekeepers, including women, all of which are located in the Global South/majority world. The piece also makes specific mention of the innovative deployment of all-female peacekeeping units by India and Bangladesh. The article's analysis, however, is driven by interviews with eleven experts on gender and peacekeeping, all of whom work in North American and European institutions. These experts draw from their knowledge of the Global South: military officers and educators based in the United Kingdom, the United States, and Canada explain gendered dynamics of conflict in the Democratic Republic of Congo, Nigeria, and Mali ('Female Soldiers Are Changing How Armed Forces Work' 2021). This one article thus neatly captures the geographic division of labour that characterizes the political economy of knowledge production around gender and peacekeeping, which locates knowing subjects in the minority world and objects of knowledge in the majority world.

The design of peacekeeper gender training curricula thus concentrates expertise in the Global North. However, this does not mean that the gender knowledge that makes it into these curricula is exclusively from or of the Global North. Transnational gender expertise is an economy of knowledge production that often involves the appropriation of knowledge from the South to the North. Gender knowledge in peacekeeping, like that in international development, is marked by patterns of intellectual dispossession enabled by professional codes which are remarkably lax in their standards of citation. It is common to come across the same examples and activities in different training settings, even when these are not part of the officially prescribed curriculum. Indeed, training practices circulate, and one may see the same training activity used in courses in the Western Balkans, in East Africa, and in the Nordic countries. Naila Kabeer generously describes this recycling of training materials in the realm of international development as reflective of 'the true "hunter-gatherer" manner of trainers', where trainers forage for knowledge and examples in different locations (1991, 186). A problem arises when the trainers who use these activities rarely mention, or are even aware of, the provenance of the materials and activities they use. That such practice amounts to knowledge extraction is pointed out by South African gender and development expert and trainer Bunie M. Matlanyane Sexwale, who observes that the recycling of materials often involves the appropriation of knowledge from women in the Global South. The benefits of this knowledge, materialized as 'expert' status and the monetary remuneration that accompanies it, are reaped by those working in the North, leaving the labour of women in the South unpaid for and leading Sexwale (1996, 59) to ask: 'Are Western institutions regressing to slavery or have I just simply been blind, naïve and too trusting of humanity!?' Gender training is thus characterized by a political economy of knowledge production that concentrates not only epistemic authority but also the material remuneration that comes with it in the minority world.

Peacekeeper gender training draws its authority from the Women, Peace and Security agenda, and derives from it the mandate to improve the lot of conflict-affected women. Although the design of this training is dominated by experts located in the Global North, the training itself establishes the figure that sam cook (2016) describes as the 'woman-in-conflict'—imagined as a woman in the Global South—as a figure of central concern to international peace and security. The curriculum design process then produces a disjuncture between concern for the figure of the *Woman*-in-conflict and taking seriously the experiences of actual *women* in conflict, to borrow Chandra Talpade Mohanty's famous distinction between the universalized third world Woman (singular, upper-case) and women (plural, lower-case) as 'real material subjects of their collective histories' (1988, 62–63). If gender experts and trainers from the Global South are a rare presence in curriculum design processes, conflict-affected women are completely absent. Training materials often mention the need to consult women among the local population, but this is the task of the lowly soldier on patrol, and the Woman-in-conflict is positioned as the soldier's informant. She is not consulted on the content and priorities of training curricula at the design phase. The Woman-in-conflict therefore informs the development of training curricula as a figure whose range of possible needs and priorities is already known; she does not partake in the curriculum design process as a subject considered to be in possession of the type of knowledge that must inform training initiatives. The conflict-affected Woman thus emerges in the curriculum design process as an object of knowledge rather than a knowing subject; as the one who is spoken for rather than the one who speaks; as Gayatri Spivak's 'gendered subaltern', as 'the one most consistently exiled from episteme' (Spivak and Harasym 1990, 102–103).

This exile from the episteme is not limited to the embodied subjects who partake in designing training curricula, the exile also works on an epistemic level, in defining what knowledge is deemed relevant. The policy framework within which training operates, as well as the mission requirements that determine training needs, frame gender training as always-already a response to the operational demands of the peacekeeping mission. This entails, for example, that there is limited space to address concerns that are deemed to be internal to the peacekeeping endeavour. Problems such as sexual assault of colleagues or of the peace-kept population only factor in when they are deemed to have 'operational effects', affecting either the extent to which the peacekeepers are setting a 'good example' to the local forces in the peacekeeping area, or undermining relationships with the host community. The range of possible concerns or priorities that women in conflict have about the gendered dimensions of peacekeeping is circumscribed by what is deemed relevant by and to the peacekeeping mission. Combined with the dominance of gender knowledge from the Global North, which advances an understanding of gender as a universal knowable, the knowledge paradigms of gender training involve conflict-affected women (in whose name, we must remember, these interventions are carried out) only in terms of what Nikita Dhawan (2012) describes as 'hegemonic listening', where the scope of what can be heard and understood is already set. The political economy of knowledge that informs curriculum design thus privileges the authority of military experience articulated as operational demands and Eurocentric gender expertise and works to marginalize 'other' perspectives on gender and peacekeeping.

## What Gender is and Does

Even with the exclusion of so many actors and ways of knowing from the curriculum design process, what exactly gender is and does is not always a point of agreement. Although a broad consensus exists that peacekeepers should be trained on gender, what exactly this should involve is a subject of negotiation and compromise. The first point to negotiate is the role and import of the concept of 'gender' to the training. Many academic observers and training designers alike attach high importance to the concept. Lisa

Carson, in her examination of gender training for Australian peacekeepers, posits: 'In order for the goals of gender training to be achieved, *peacekeepers need, first and foremost, to understand what "gender" means*' (2016, 277, emphasis added; see also Mackay 2005, 269). This much is agreed, and although the ways in which different training curricula define gender vary somewhat in their wording, their definitions largely align. The UN pre-deployment training package, as an illustrative example, states that whereas sex is 'biologically defined; usually determined at birth; [and] universal', gender 'is socially constructed; differs across cultures and time; [and] results in different roles, responsibilities, opportunities, needs and constraints for women, men, girls and boys' (DPKO & DFS 2017, 5). Of course, 'gender' could be and has been defined in different ways, and there are critiques that can be levelled against this particular definition of 'gender'. But before moving to consider critiques and contestations around the definition, I want to draw attention to the significance of insisting on a definition of 'gender' in this training in the first place.

It may seem an obvious fact that gender training needs to provide a definition of 'gender'. But, as Sara Ahmed reminds us: 'The obvious is that which tends to be unthought and thus needs to be thought' (2012, 19). Heeding this call, I want to pause for a moment to reflect on what work the concept of 'gender' is doing in the training curricula. Indeed, examining the other topics covered in gender training with a curiosity about what the definition of 'gender' is needed for casts some doubt on the *necessity* of defining 'gender' for the purposes of training. The main learning outcomes for peacekeeper gender training are to understand that conflict has a differential impact on men and women; that women's particular roles and responsibilities often lead them to be overlooked as actors in providing security and building peace; and that the peacekeepers' mandate includes protecting women from gender-specific harms. It then seeks to equip peacekeepers with skills in ensuring that women's differing experiences are taken into account; to devise ways of consulting and involving women in peacekeeping activities; and to take measures to prevent and respond to gender-based violence. It is not, I contend, clear how nuanced an understanding of gender is needed to grasp these learning items. That women and men often have gender-specific roles, responsibilities, vulnerabilities, and needs can be explained through a framework that relies on essentialist understandings of men and women; essentialist understandings, I might add, that peacekeepers are already well versed in. These learning outcomes do not, in and of themselves, *require* delving

FIXING GENDER: THE CURRICULUM   41

into the complexities of social construction. It is not therefore self-evident why an understanding of gender is required to achieve these learning goals.

Of course, if the course is called gender training, it would be impossible not to include a definition of 'gender'. This is already something training participants often demand more clarity on. However, many trainers insist on defining 'gender' even when the course name does not include the term. Note, for example, that the relevant modules in the UN training materials from which I take the illustrative definition of 'gender' above are not called 'gender' but rather these modules are named 'Women, Peace and Security', 'Conflict-Related Sexual Violence', and 'Sexual Exploitation and Abuse'. The United Kingdom subsumes military gender expertise under the broader rubric of 'human security', and related job roles are called Human Security Advisers and training Human Security Training. Often, 'gender' is left out of course titles precisely because the term is understood to be a politically volatile one. Particularly in a context of intensifying anti-gender politics, where opposition to the term is used to mobilize conservative political forces, the term is hidden within the curriculum. In other words, if the content of the course does not straightforwardly necessitate a definitional discussion of gender, neither does the title of the course.

Instead, I suggest that academics' and gender experts' insistence on introducing a definition of 'gender' in training stems from a political goal: if gender is understood as socially constructed, it could be constructed differently. The persistence in teaching definitions of 'gender' in training might, then, have less to do with technical, measurable learning outcomes of the training, and more to do with the political potential of understanding the world as constantly in-the-making, as changeable. Indeed, a western European gender trainer I call Mila was insistent that the definition of 'gender' should *do* something, rather than simply respond to training participants' demand for clarity and an easily fixed definition. Mila critiqued a training manual she had been working with to me in these terms: 'It's very much this: we'll tell you what gender is, and once you can define it and write it, that means you've learned it. But beyond that, no. Nothing to do with behavioural change'. In contrast, Mila was invested in the concept of 'gender' producing some kind of change within the training participants and how they conduct themselves. The persistence of framing training in terms of gender can therefore be explained not through any actual rational-cognitive demands dictated by a training curriculum that focuses on operational demands of peacekeeping missions, but rather through its indebtedness to the feminist roots of gender training as praxis and the politicizing potential of the concept of 'gender' itself. This recognition serves as a reminder to interrogate the political potential (or the foreclosing of it) of contentions around what gender is and does.

## Troubled Definitions

Precisely because the concept of 'gender' carries destabilizing potential for hegemonic norms, how exactly the definition of 'gender' is formulated and applied has been the subject of both academic critique and practitioner contentions. These debates centre on how gender is defined and what is omitted from this definition. Feminist analyses of gender training have lamented the ways in which the definition of 'gender' offered in training appears to have been emptied of feminist political goals. Carson's (2016) study of Australian peacekeeper gender training puts forward a critique of how gender is defined in it, arguing that the definition provided reduces gender to equivalent difference between men and women, obscuring questions of power and patriarchy. She juxtaposes the depoliticized definition of 'gender' used in training with the understanding of gender put forth by feminist activists who lobbied the UN to use the term in the first place; an understanding that was grounded in feminist analyses of patriarchal power. Carson's charge that the way 'gender' is defined in peacekeeping training has lost the originary meaning of the term is an accurate and necessary critique. At the same time, it bears echoes of what Clare Hemmings (2011) characterizes as a narrative of feminist loss, wherein the loss of past feminist commitments mark a betrayal in the present (see also Wiegman 2014). It is worth bearing in mind, as Hemmings insists we should, that a focus on such a narrative of feminist loss constrains our analysis by fixing a particular standard against which to measure how gender is understood. Such a narrative limits the analytical horizons of where we might look in order to locate exclusions. In this instance, it points to the necessity of building on the established critiques of gender training as depoliticizing the concept of 'gender' to further examine how 'race', coloniality, and heterosexism figure in this understanding of gender.

First, not only are power and patriarchy missing from how gender is conceptualized in training curricula but also race is primarily notable for its absence. I mentioned earlier that gender training curricula are underpinned by an assumption of the universal knowability of gender. This universalism is supported by a non-recognition of the ways of in which gendered power relations are always already racialized. 'Race' as a term is not articulated in training curricula in relation to gender, and a broad non-recognition of colonial histories mirrors what Ann Stoler (2011) describes as 'colonial aphasia', whereby colonizing powers foster a culture of ignorance around how they have dominated and dispossessed racialized others in the past, and how they continue to do so in the present. Although race and coloniality are not explicitly articulated in training curricula, I argue that their operative logics nonetheless inform the construction of gender at work. Gender training curricula focus on what María Lugones (2007, 190) describes as 'the light side' of coloniality, where gender is organized around biological dimorphism, heterosexualism, and patriarchy. This understanding of gender fails to take into account that these are Eurocentric, not universal organizing principles of gender. Further, it neglects that in European societies, a 'differential construction of gender along racial lines' persists (Lugones 2007, 206). It is not just women, but specifically white women who are understood to embody the attributes of normatively desirable femininity, such as chastity, innocence, and weakness. In contrast, women of colour have routinely been constructed through the tropes of sexual voracity and physical and emotional toughness, in a logic which both produces and justifies violence directed at them. Under the logics of colonial thought, not only are women of colour thus racialized but also their gender is constructed differently. They are located not on the 'light side' but the 'dark side' of coloniality. In contrast to the light side of coloniality, its dark side has involved the reduction of the colonized to inferior beings, and produced violences such as 'forced sex with white colonisers' (Lugones 2007, 206). Eurocentric understandings of gender, grounded in the light side of the modern/colonial gender system, therefore produce blind spots that fail to understand experiences of violence that are simultaneously gendered and racialized. This single-axis framework for understanding gender is facilitated by the fact that, as Lugones reminds us, '[t]hough everyone in capitalist Eurocentred modernity is both raced and gendered, not everyone is dominated or victimized in terms of their race or gender' (2007, 192). Gender training thus privileges the experiences of those dominated or victimized in terms of gender but not of race.

This inability to see and/or unwillingness to name 'the colonial difference' (Lugones 2010, 743) continues to inform how subject positions are produced in gender training. In privileging the 'light side' of coloniality, training establishes a Eurocentric understanding of gender as *the* yardstick against which to measure progressiveness. The use of this yardstick produces an understanding of relations of oppression and violence as gendered but not racialized, and differences between them as questions of scale, not substance. It facilitates an understanding of sexual exploitation and abuse committed by peacekeepers as the case of a few 'bad apples' in an otherwise good barrel, rather than as the systematic operations of the dark side of coloniality (Razack 2004, 6). In contrast, training underscores the incomparable scale of sexual violence committed by warring parties, typically presented through 'killer facts'[7]—shocking numbers of how many women have been raped—to underscore the gravity of the problem. It focuses attention on violences that are understood as both more serious and more prevalent, and which are invariably associated with black and brown bodies. It is in this move that race, while still unarticulated, becomes hypervisible. Training creates an understanding of conflict and violence as stemming from an inferiority of peace-kept populations, who come 'to be mythically conceived not as dominated through conquest, nor as inferior in terms of wealth or political power, but as an anterior stage in the history of the species, in this unidirectional path' (Lugones 2007, 192). In other words, a training curriculum which forwards an understanding of gender that fails to account for its imbrications with race erases colonial difference, thereby leaving unchallenged a discursive production of peacekeeping nations as inherently superior.

If the understanding of gender put forth in training obscures the ways in which gender is racialized, it also naturalizes understandings of biological dimorphism and heterosexualism. This understanding of gender is nonetheless haunted by sexual subjects who do not map onto, per Butler, the matrix of binary gender identification determining heterosexual desire (2009, 135). Training curricula rarely address or even acknowledge modes of being beyond compulsory heterosexuality, and many trainers I spoke with asserted that they specifically did not want to address the topic. This disavowal was not framed in overtly homophobic or transphobic terms but rather, inclusion of sexual orientation and gender identity was described as 'adding too much complexity', and as something, as explained by a western European military trainer I call Robert, that 'muddies the waters about what it is that we're trying to do, because it becomes such a wide subject'. Robert did not go so far as to assert a personal disavowal of non-confirming practices and identities, but instead framed them as inconvenient, as disruptive.

Trainers often project feelings of homophobia onto their training audiences, and pander to this assumption rather than risking their own position by addressing sexuality.[8] For example, a Nordic military trainer I call Max explained to me that his training incorporated discussion around what peacekeepers should do in different scenarios. These scenarios drew on Max's own experience of deployment on peacekeeping operations. One example he related to me was when he was out on patrol, and his unit came across local police officers who were beating two men, whom they accused of homosexuality (a crime in this context). Max explained that in this scene, the peacekeepers needed to consider how to prevent human rights abuses (i.e. protect the two men being assaulted) while at the same time maintaining good relations with local security forces (as the mission mandate was to support the local police). Max felt this example provided useful training material to prepare peacekeepers to grapple with dilemmas they were likely to encounter on deployment. However, when Max showed me the slide he had prepared for discussion, the scenario featured children being beaten by police, not (presumptively) gay men. When I asked what prompted him to change this description, Max responded that the example of children presented 'a clearer human rights violation'; one that 'aroused more feelings'. In other words, he presumed that his audience would be more troubled by violence against children than they would be by violence against gay men. This substitution is particularly striking, given the ways in which discourses around protection of children—symbolic of reproductive heterosexuality—are so often mobilized in service of homophobic politics (Edelman 2004). By framing the discussion around children, Max side-stepped the ways in which discussion of sexuality might destabilize the gender binary and re-centred heteronormativity in gender training.

In other contexts, this work of projection also does racializing work. For example, I attended a gender training in a West African context, where a team of West African police trainers were joined by a group of European trainers from donor countries. The training audience were exclusively West African police officers. Although sexuality was not explicitly mentioned in the training curriculum, one of the European trainers, whom I call Ralf, mentioned homosexuality several times during the course, but consistently coupled this with the caveat: 'Sorry to keep pushing the issue, I know that this is sensitive'. He persisted in this framing, despite the lack of any objections over the two-week course. The moment when one of the participants retorted: 'Don't worry, we are quite comfortable!' suggested that perhaps what was at play in framing the issue of homosexuality as 'sensitive' was more to do with a European self-understanding of progressive superiority over cultures deemed 'traditional' than any actual hostile reaction to homosexuality from the training audience. Ralf thus enacted a well-rehearsed script of sexual politics that asserts cultural superiority (see e.g. Rao 2020; Puar 2007): he projected the homophobia inherent in the erasure of queerness from gender onto the West African training audience.

Ralf, however, was exceptional in that he volunteered questions of sexuality to the discussion as a trainer. In contrast, most trainers are well-versed in reasons *not* to discuss non-conforming sexual subjects because training audiences persistently ask questions about sexual orientation and identity which they are unprepared to answer. Sexual orientation and identity are not included in training curricula, and so many trainers lack the vocabulary or knowledge to respond to these questions. Explaining that these questions are not gender proper, or that they are 'too complicated' or 'too sensitive' thus offers a way to circumvent such questions. In a Nordic course I observed, a trainer, when facilitating a session on gender concepts, was unable to answer questions students asked him about where trans* subjects fit in relation to sex/gender, or whether discrimination based on sexual orientation is also a gendered harm. I was seated at the back of the classroom, in observation mode, but the trainer asked me whether I could respond to these questions in his stead. He later asked myself and another trainer on the course to give a session on sexual orientation and gender identity, and carved out an hour from the course programme for us to do so. This was a rather unique occurrence—it seems unlikely that most gender training courses have a feminist researcher at hand to respond to questions about sexuality. What this example highlights is that although the design of training erases queer subjectivities from its conceptualization of gender, actual training practice reveals that these subjects persistently trouble the foundations of the binary gender order put forth. The act of fixing gender as binary and heterosexual is thus only ever contingent. The silence around sexuality is one that is actively produced and continuously reasserted by trainers, it is not an oversight.

On the surface, a critical attentiveness to 'race' and sexuality exposes that how gender is defined and operationalized in peacekeeping is marked by a series of omissions. In addition to the omission of power and patriarchy, gender training omits discussion of race and sexuality. But this is not a simple case of lack of attention or erasure. Racialized logics and colonial thinking inform how gender is understood. Training is consistently haunted by questions of sexuality. These hauntings are produced by a double move that, on the one hand, defines gender through whiteness and heterosexism, and on the other, refuses to name either. The definition of gender is thus best understood not through omission or lack, but rather as structured through contradiction. That there is an ambivalence at the site of constitution of the definition of gender is of course not an anomaly—postcolonial scholars like Homi Bhabha (1994) have long drawn attention to the fact that contradiction is a key characteristic of imperial discourses, and observers of contemporary militarism like Aaron Belkin (2012) have pointed to militaries as a site at which these contradictions are smoothed over and rendered unremarkable. It is precisely by directing our attention to the contradiction that we may locate moments of instability and destabilize their logics of domination.

## The (Wo)Man Question

Even though they are working with a binary understanding of gender that omits sexuality and race from discussion, those who oversee the development of gender training curricula still differ on how best to depict the roles and needs of women and men. Academic critiques have argued that a focus on gender as synonymous with women obscures the relationality of gender, eliding from view systems of oppression, and both male violence and male vulnerability (see e.g. Whitworth 2004, 125). Further, a focus on women is often coupled with children, constituting both through infantilization and vulnerability, as the conflated category Cynthia Enloe (2014, 1) refers to in compound form: 'womenandchildren'. On the one hand, such dynamics are reinforced by ongoing training practices. For example, the UN has associated gender with women by pursuing a number of initiatives to increase the number of women deployed on peacekeeping, including a dedicated female officers' training course on gender.[9] Its Department of Peace Operations has at times collapsed job functions into the position of a 'gender and child protection advisor', evoking the image of 'womenandchildren'. Training materials on gender habitually focus on women and their vulnerabilities. On the other hand, these debates are squarely on the radar of many policymakers and gender trainers. Those working within and outside of the UN have cautioned that efforts to raise the number of female peacekeepers perpetuate an essentialized understanding of women as kinder, gentler peacekeepers (Baruah 2017). Similarly, the establishment of training on gender and child protection was critiqued by some UN peacekeepers I spoke with, precisely on the grounds that it reinforces the association between women, femininity, and vulnerability.

In this ongoing contention of how the woman question is framed, those supporting initiatives to include more women, and to subsume child protection in the remit of gender advisers defend their choices on pragmatic grounds. The fact remains that in many of the places peacekeeping operations take place, local women are better able to speak to female peacekeepers than their male counterparts. Providing specialized training, by the UN, to women military officers increases the chances that these women will be chosen for deployment on peacekeeping mission by their home country. One military officer lamented that if the gender adviser does not take on child protection issues, there is a tangible risk that the peacekeeping operation will not have anyone with a mandate for child protection.

In addition to these practical considerations, there are also political reasons to be suspicious of an automatic, categorical insistence on framing gender in any universally applicable way. There can be a streak of coloniality to the move to disavow any reference to particular skills or qualities women have *as women*, because this move can amount to the transnational projection of the concerns of white feminism. Take for example the worry that referring to women and mothers in association with one another reproduces ideas of women's traditional gender role as nurturing and passive. This is a culturally located anxiety. In *The Invention of Women* (1997), Oyèrónkẹ́ Oyěwùmí famously argued that Western gender categories were imposed on Yorùbá society, where social categories were relational rather than based on 'bio-logical' gender. In contrast to Western understandings of motherhood as linked to women's political disempowerment, Oyěwùmí (2016, 2011) proposes the notion of 'matripotency' to account for the social power and recognition Yorùbá mothers traditionally derived from carrying children. Motherhood, in her analysis, emerges as a mode of ascending social hierarchy and a position of power.

Nor is this analysis of Yorùbá society an isolated exception. In other West African societies, recent events have demonstrated the political power that can attach to motherhood, understood as a category of social seniority. Several accounts document an appeal to motherhood to claim authority in Liberian politics, starting with former President Ellen Johnson Sirleaf's (2009, 209) description of political leader and chair of Council of the State in 1996 Ruth Sando Perry as 'a widow and grandmother who declared herself "hard as steel" and determined to force the warlords into line'. Perry's claim to authority was bolstered by the fact that she was a grandmother who was seen as capable of 'scolding' the warlords into disarming, referring to the relational and social power associated with motherhood (Johnson-Sirleaf 2009, 210; see also Moran 2012). It is not my intention here to make definitive or generalized pronouncements of the operations of the category of motherhood across West African societies regardless of time and place. Such an endeavour would grossly exceed the kinds of knowledge claims I am qualified to make, and would doubtless gloss over important contextual determinants. My point here is to highlight that *any* universalizing approach to dealing with gender, women, and motherhood, is bound to (re-)produce an oppressive mode of political advocacy. In this sense, objections to initiatives to empower women as women, or to associate them with motherhood, stemming from a white feminist aversion to any claims smacking of essentialism, may in fact contribute to undermining claims to female authority in non-Western contexts. Accordingly, I suggest, following Spivak (in Spivak and Grosz 1990, 12), that in the debates surrounding how women are understood in gender training, it may be less important to insist on the theoretical purity of an anti-essentialist stance, and more important to recognize that some practical gender work may trouble commonly held theoretical commitments of feminism.

The discursive move sometimes put forth in gender training to counteract the equation of gender with women and essentializing arguments about them is to insist that gender is about, in a commonly used phrase, men, women, boys, and girls. This move to include men on the one hand draws on broader initiatives, such as UN Women's 'He for She' campaign, to cast men as 'gender champions' and allies for change (Duriesmith 2020). An alternative subject position available to men in this discourse is that of the also-potential-victim, in that training on conflict-related sexual violence increasingly recognizes that men may also be victims. While there can be no doubt that men and boys are also victims of sexual violence, that women can commit violent acts, and that men can work toward gender equality, this discursive framing pre-emptively omits discussion of male complicity in gender violence and perpetuation of inequalities (Kirby 2013; Sjoberg 2016). That this shallow analysis lends itself to doing away with questions of male violence is evident in the way some trainers emphasize women's violence and men's victimization in a purported attempt to deconstruct traditional gender norms. Occasionally, the focus shifts from an attempt to highlight the diversity of roles and experiences among women and among men and leads instead to attempts to reverse power relations and the victim–perpetrator positioning. This move lends itself to some wild arguments with weak substantiation, such as the claim made by a presenter in the West African course I observed, who argued that women commit rape more often than men do. It is clear in this instance that the demand to include men in the conceptualization of gender does not necessarily add complexity to the definition. Rather, it can be used as a vehicle to align the message of the training with deeply misogynistic 'men's rights' agendas that seek to negate or inverse gendered relations of power and violence. While at the outset of this section I suggested that feminist trainers and academics invest in the term 'gender' because of its radical transformative potential, these contentions demonstrate that others invest in the term because it allows them to direct discursive attention away from masculinized violence and the oppression of feminized subjects. In other words, the prioritization of gender as an analytical category carries ambivalent political potential—gender is used to *both* politicize *and* depoliticize the discourse of training.

## Doing Gender

The question of what gender 'does' is also a matter of ongoing contestation, evident in debates over what it is that should be taught and known about gender, beyond conceptual definitions. The policy framework which mandates gender training for peacekeepers devotes a great deal of attention to the issue of sexual violence. Given the transnational nature of peacekeeping enterprises and similar moves within the broader Women, Peace and Security agenda, training deals with questions of sexual violence through a distinction between internal and external gender issues. This distinction separates out sexual harassment within the organization, recruitment and deployment of female peacekeepers, and sexual exploitation and abuse as internal gender issues; and conflict-related sexual violence, liaison with and protection of the local population, and an analysis of the gendered effects of the mission as external gender issues. Because of the transnational nature of curriculum design, those issues deemed internal to the troop- or police-contributing country are usually sidelined in such training, as they are considered the responsibility of the individual nation, not the multinational mission.

Nonetheless, the linkages between internal and external questions of gender do not lend themselves to such a neat separation, and continue to be the subject of debate. Some training materials do note that internal and external gender dynamics are related, and training participants are often quick to point out the linkages between violence committed by the peacekeepers and that committed by local actors. Nonetheless, a dominant feature of training is the endeavour to keep internal and external questions separate. A UN report (Anderson 2012, 15) offers up the following quote from a senior military officer:

> We initially thought 'gender issues' were only about the behavior of troops... not realizing the operational interest, the added value to the effectiveness of the mission of integrating gender perspectives.
> —Brigadier General Jean-Philippe Ganascia, Former Force Commander of EUFOR/CHAD

The report then goes on to lament the fact that 'discussions of peacekeepers and sexual violence have disproportionately portrayed them as perpetrators rather than protectors' and that 'this has had the effect of distancing personnel from host populations, thereby limiting situational awareness of women's needs and risks' (Anderson 2012, 15). The report thus advocates for a focus on sexual violence outside of the mission rather than within the ranks, allowing peacekeepers to know themselves as protectors from violence rather than its perpetrators. It suggests that addressing internal gender questions—the behaviour of the troops—detracts from gender as an operational question, and calls for a reassertion of this distinction. While none of these discussions suggest that topics such as sexual exploitation and abuse and sexual harassment should not be part of peacekeepers' training, these topics are delegated to nations rather than 'gender training' thus conceived.

However, the extent to and terms on which these topics are covered in national training remains dubious. Robert showed me a gender training module he had designed for pre-deployment training in his western European country. As a slide on sexual exploitation and abuse came up, Robert quickly skipped over it, noting that 'this is nothing new for them... the types of things we're talking about, one could really dumb this down to being a decent human being, ultimately embedded in our Army leadership code'. Lasse, a Nordic soldier I spoke with during his pre-deployment training, scoffed at the mention of sexual exploitation and abuse in training on similar terms: 'For us this is a given, and sometimes in training you wonder, do they think we are complete morons?' Lasse juxtaposed his self-described commitment to gender equality with soldiers from other countries he had met in missions: 'Sometimes I wondered at how low a level some coming from African countries were. They had to be told that you can't just pick up a woman off the side of the road and rape her'. In making these statements, Robert and Lasse were both drawing on a widely available racialized script that frames European soldiers as already gender aware and not prone to committing abuse, and which thereby inscribes morality on white bodies (Razack 2003). In this discursive move, the purportedly internal gender issue of sexual exploitation and abuse is re-externalized, and constructed as the problem of the 'not-us' African soldier 'over there' along the familiar racial-sexual civilizational hierarchy that characterizes much of the work in the field of gender and conflict (Pratt 2013). In other words, the assertion of an internal/external distinction in training curricula appears to do the work of situating 'gender' as an external question, in a move which protects in particular Global North peacekeepers' sense of self: for *us* this is a given; *they* had to be told.

While sexual violence is a predominant theme in peacekeeper gender training, training curricula also aim to provide peacekeepers with broader skills for gender mainstreaming. Robert explained what he had learned on a Nordic training-of-trainers course:

> That's when you start to realise what [gender advisors] and gender focal points do, which is something again, it's not focused on the violence-exploitation side, but more on gender considerations in the military more widely. And so . . . if we're planning stability operations whereby we're trying to facilitate elections . . . and we gather information that suggests that 70% of the population is literate, we will go great, we will put out a leaflet campaign to tell people to vote. But if we don't sex-disaggregate the data, we won't find out that it's 100% men and 40% women, or what have you.

With this example, Robert explained how training attempts to alert peacekeepers to the persistence of gendered inequalities across a range of dimensions. In this example, Robert is explaining that peacekeepers who devise communication strategies with the peace-kept population need to take into account gendered differences in literacy rates. The training does also impress upon peacekeepers that they need to consult local women as well as men on the security issues they are facing, and to take into account gendered differences in security needs and priorities in their planning.

In promoting women's participation, students are encouraged to think about gendered constraints on mobility and time—for example when and where women might be able to attend a consultative meeting, given the particular security risks they face and caring responsibilities they have. All of these considerations feature concerns that are external to the mission. Even though local women may be more comfortable speaking to a female peacekeeper, gender training curricula notably do not provide space for discussion of what might account for the low numbers of women deployed as peacekeepers. Questions of discriminatory practices within military and police institutions do not form part of the training, often to the frustration and disappointment of women on these courses. That peacekeepers are encouraged to think of gender as an external question that does not imply a need for any profound change on their own part is sometimes unwittingly demonstrated by their own performance. On a western European training course I observed, students were given a scenario to contemplate in small group discussions on the topic of women's participation. Each group was then asked to nominate a representative to report back to the whole course on their discussions. Each and every group rapporteur was a man, despite the fact that women amounted for half of participants. This produced a rather ironic dynamic for a training session on women's participation. The question, for these students, was clearly what they needed to do to enable peacekept women to participate in their activities, not anything to do with their own ways of working. As with the question of sexual violence, here again training enforces a distinction between internal and external, where what gender 'does' is a question to do with racialized others, not a question that requires introspection. Gender training thus stays within the comfort zone of male peacekeepers, positioning them as subjects who provide solutions, rather than as part of the problem of gender.

## Facing The Uniforms

In fixing an understanding of what gender is and does, training curricula produce a theory of gender. As Spivak reminds us: 'no practice takes place without presupposing itself as an example of some more or less powerful theory' (in Spivak and Grosz 1990, 2). If we consider gender training as a way of theorizing of gender and read training curricula against the vast bodies of knowledge produced in gender studies, it is not exactly difficult to identify points of critique. However, in reading the theorization of gender in training curricula, we must also account for the fact that these are pedagogical texts. The purpose of a curriculum is not to advance scholarly thinking on gender, but to identify what about it can and should be known by training audiences who have little prior exposure to these questions. Gender theories typically question societal truths and read widely accepted norms against the grain. It would be unreasonable to expect peacekeepers who have may have been schooled their entire lives in liberal (or, as it were, illiberal) politics and positivist thought to be able to fully internalize, in a week-long training course (or less), the insights that it has taken feminist scholarship cumulative lifetimes to arrive at. Training is best understood as a strategic endeavour. Training curricula cannot simply be judged against the state of knowledge in the field of gender studies. Rather, they must be read as intervening in existing epistemic communities with their own assumptions and values. Curricula are designed bearing in mind the interaction of the students with the material that is presented. They represent pedagogical interventions designed to support understanding of the topic, and to prompt students to think about the world in a different way.

## The Sceptical Audience and The Happy Gender Trainer

Those involved in curriculum design often highlight that the peacekeepers to be trained are mainly men, and that they are at least sceptical of, if not hostile to, the idea of gender training. This much is evident from the accounts of two then senior gender advisors at the UN. Angela Mackay (2005, 267), who was instrumental in designing some of the foundational UN training materials for peacekeepers, describes the challenge she faced:

> here we would be developing training material intended for soldiers, task oriented, 90 percent male, who had most likely not given the subject too much attention in the past, and who were likely to be defensive. Yet, it was important to grab their attention, without alienation—in a maximum time frame of one day.

What is clear from Mackay's description of the challenge is that gender training curricula are designed with certain assumptions about the audiences they are intended for. In a similar vein, Nadine Puechguirbal, also reflecting on her experience as a UN gender adviser and trainer, reports that many of the students 'have never before heard the word "gender", or hold distorted and/or extremely negative views about what it means' (2003, 117; see also Higate and Henry, 2009). These reflections by those involved in curriculum design provide insight into what type of audience the training materials cater to: uniformed men, with scant knowledge of, and little interest in, the topic. As such, the design of training interventions must be understood as a strategic move which intends to persuade a hostile audience of the benefits of increasing their own gender awareness.

Accordingly, the strategies that these curriculum designers propose for training are, first of all, designed not to alienate the audience. As Puechguirbal puts it: 'it is important to use a "gender-friendly" approach, so as not to antagonize or "lose" the audience by being overly aggressive or confrontational' (2003, 118). Ahmed notes that this strategy of using language that is palatable to those in power is a strategy commonly used also by diversity workers in universities (2012, 64). Following this line of reasoning, in the training that I observed, I noted that trainers tend to avoid the kinds of 'red flags' thought to antagonize participants. Words like 'feminism' or 'patriarchy' are seldom heard in peacekeeper training. For some military participants, attempts to introduce gender-neutral language into the institution is another sore point. Some trainers go along with this, resulting in discussions that sound absurd to a feminist outsider like myself, such as talk about gender balance in 'manning' (staffing) or the number of female 'seamen' (sailors) in the navy. Further, some gender trainers in western Europe insisted that the term 'gender' should never be paired with the term issues: speaking of 'gender issues' was banned. The word 'issue', they explained, was negative and implied a problem. Gender, they argued, should be seen as a positive thing, an operational tool, a useful perspective.

On the one hand, this inclination to avoid confrontation with training audiences serves to protect the trainer from hostility. This is not just a question of personal emotional distress, but also serves a strategic purpose in the political economy of gender training. The foregrounding of a positive orientation toward the topic is doubtless fuelled by the ways in which training is evaluated. Evaluation is typically centred on methods such as collecting feedback questionnaires from students. Such questionnaires arguably measure less what the trainees learned, and more whether or not they liked the training and/or the trainer. Despite their dubious ability to measure learning, these evaluation scores serve as currency to demonstrate to donors that the training was successful and to secure mandates and funding for future training initiatives.

This concern with avoiding conflict is also framed in terms of a pedagogical imperative to foster a positive affective disposition toward the topic. In her account of designing training modules, Mackay stresses the importance of ending the last module 'on a *positive and proactive note*... for participants to leave the training with the recognition that they had not only a personal responsibility as well as power to act, to be a force for not only doing harm, but hopefully doing good' (2005, 269, emphasis added). The suggestion here is that a positive affective orientation toward the topic is thought to be more conducive to acting, in contrast to disengagement prompted by hostility or apathy produced by guilt. The ways in which this positive affect are maintained are linked to the hesitation to deal with questions of masculinity I introduced earlier. By introducing men and boys into the scope of the training by presenting them as also-potential-victims and as 'gender champions', the training assuages any sense of shared male responsibility for violence: it allows male students to know themselves as potential victims rather than potential perpetrators. The desire, on the part of curriculum designers, to cultivate a positive affect toward gender also dovetails with the focus on topics that are deemed external to the peacekeeping endeavour—topics that do not trouble the trainees' sense of self. This insistence on positive affect produces an unwillingness to confront what Deborah Britzman (1998, 2) characterizes as 'difficult knowledge', impeding the ability of training to address complicity in structures of inequality and violence and work through a range of reactions to and relations to the training material.

Not only does a strategy designed to keep sceptical or hostile military men on board rule out addressing important questions of complicity, it also risks pandering to the most extreme views. I argue that designing and delivering the training in a manner that is going to keep even the most hostile attitudes on board and not agitate them is likely to concede too much. It is important to interrupt the assumption that gender training audiences are uniformly hostile, and to bear in mind the possibility that some trainees may disagree (possibly privately, as suggested by Belkin 2012, 101) with overt expressions of patriarchal attitudes. It is worth cautioning that any attempt at making strategic allowances for hostile training audiences needs to also allow for a silent minority who are invested in gender equality, and for whom it may be empowering to see a trainer contest rather than concede to misogynist logics;

to use the situational power that anyone authorized to speak as a trainer and as an expert wields to disrupt dominant logics of meaning making.

In addition to maintaining a positive orientation toward the topic, trainers engage in a form of discursive bandwagoning where they present the endeavour of gender training as supporting goals that the martial institution already deems legitimate and important. I mentioned above that gender training is framed as a way of responding to operational demands, arguably the first priority for these institutions. In a similar move, which is sometimes strategic and sometimes stems from genuine conviction, trainers often underscore the importance of the training as a way of applying a 'gender perspective' in order to increase 'operational effectiveness', which scholars of diversity initiatives and international development are likely to recognize as a variant of the 'business case' for equality work. In this realm too, trainers feel that in order for their message to be heard, they need to speak the language of the organization, to cite already accepted truths (Whitworth 2004, 120; see also Butler, 1993, 19). This discursive move frames the topic (gender) as important, because it is linked to something that the students are already assumed to value highly (mission effectiveness). Training then goes on to demonstrate this value to the mission by providing concrete examples. As Mackay puts it: 'the focus had to be practical and of immediate relevance to the "soldier on the ground"' (2005, 268). She argues (2005, 270):

> Theory can be fascinating, experiences and anecdotes telling, but throughout the training it had to be possible to answer the 'So what?' question if a peacekeeper asked it. If the material could not be demonstrated to be relevant, then attention would fade, and we would have failed.

This reflection emphasizes the assumptions at work about the peacekeeper subjectivity—that they will only consider relevant what is deemed relevant for their professional identities. It portrays trainees as single-mindedly professional and rules out the possibility that this is not their primary identity or concern.

However, and in contrast, my observations of training suggest that such a singular professional identification is not consistent among training audiences. In some of the training courses I observed, students were asked at the outset to share their expectations of the course. What was notable was that many did not, in fact, frame their expectations in professional terms. They voiced instead a desire to learn something that they could take back to their home communities, to their family, to their church. Marketing the utility of gender training on such terms is unlikely to secure the formal approval of the military organization to conduct gender training, but these observations do suggest that military training audiences do not always engage with gender training through a single-minded task orientation. Rather, it reveals that military subjectivities, too, are fragmented and discontinuous (Bhabha 1994, 42). In appealing to students only in terms of their warrior or police subjectivities, gender training may be undermining its own potential as it rules out the possibility of the peacekeeper subject who wishes to transform gender relations in his (to repeat the assumed masculine subjectivity) personal life.

This expectation of a hostile audience is reproduced in specialized courses aimed at gender trainers and gender advisers. These courses often include sessions such as 'countering resistance', examining the terms on which colleagues and superiors are likely to dismiss the need for gender work. On the one hand, trainers I spoke with expressed a desire to prepare those they were training to face resistance. Malcolm, for example, explained that in his training he would sometimes ask participants to consider resistant statements:

> I have . . . been in a situation where people go to the gender training and think it's great, and then you realise you almost throw them under the bus because they haven't talked about this before, and they're not always completely aware that they're going to face resistance. So, I think once you've got people on board, it's important to arm them with resistance statements.

Malcolm, in other words, anticipated that his training participants, no longer hostile to the idea of gender themselves, would have to contend with the resistance of their colleagues and future trainees. Bearing this in mind, he sought to prepare students for resistance by prompting them to think in advance how they would respond. His attempts to prepare training participants for a hostile environment bears echoes of strategies outlined in feminist pedagogy: 'Students need skills for surviving and thriving as a feminist in a patriarchal society when the support of a women's studies program is gone' (Schniedewind 1987, 25).

Not only does some specialized gender training attempt to equip students with skills to deal with hostile audiences but also these courses are involved in building a community of support for those who work on gender.

During the end-of-course graduation ceremony in the Nordic training-of-trainers course I observed, the course director congratulated participants on completing the course, and welcomed them into 'the gender family'. She went on to describe various community fora, such as Facebook pages that the participants could use to keep in touch, and talked about an alumni network for those who had completed a gender course. This work of community-building also took less structured forms. During the course I observed in East Africa, one participant told me that she loved going on gender courses, because they were different. She explained: 'You always meet people who are passionate. And they are friendly. When I arrived, two people came to give me hugs. I've never been on another military course where I'm hugged, especially by the course director!' In other words, because gender trainers feel that they are under attack from the broader establishment, they work to support one another, providing gender trainers and advisors with skills and emotional support.

## Epistemic Authority

'I wouldn't call myself a subject matter expert, but I speak infantry'. This was how Max began his presentation during the gender training-of-trainers course I observed in the Nordic region. In making this assertion, Max spoke to a common concern among the gender training community, identified by Puechguirbal (2003, 126):

> Another critical challenge is to involve more men as gender trainers, especially military or ex-military, because they are sometimes better able than women to convince male trainees of the issue's importance.

These statements provide a wealth of information about how epistemic authority is embodied in the training endeavour. Martial knowledge is understood to be particularly valuable in the military context—hence why Max speaking infantry lends his training credence and makes up for what is lacking in subject matter (gender) expertise. Epistemic authority has a long tradition of being figured as masculine, but underlying Puechguirbal's call for involving more men as trainers is also the prevalent notion that when women speak about gender, they are perceived as pursuing a 'personal agenda' (K.A.M. Wright 2016, 351; see also Hurley 2018b). The gender trainer must not only provide a happy affect, it also helps if they are male and military to convey epistemic authority.

I want to note that there is a something of a facile assumption at work here: that male students would prefer to speak about gender with male instructors. This seems at odds with Mackay's assertion that having women constitute at least a third of the students in the classroom leads to 'an entirely different dynamic and provides a richer learning experience for everyone' (2005, 273). Indeed, it seems equally plausible that the presence of a male trainer might encourage male students to perform masculinity with more bravado than they would with a female trainer. Nonetheless, the desire for men to deliver gender training remains largely unchallenged by those who design curricula.

The importance attached to the trainers' masculinity is also observable in practice in efforts to disavow traits associated with femininity and queerness. For a man to work as a gender trainer was perceived by some of my interlocutors as risking their masculinity. I was told that in one Nordic training centre, none of the male trainers wanted to take responsibility for the gender training session. The man who did so in the end, said that he could deliver gender training because he was married and had several children. The implication in this statement is that being a gender trainer renders one's masculine image vulnerable; but that heterosexual marriage and reproduction inoculated him from being perceived as queer or feminized (as likewise observed by Hurley 2018a, 83). Under the conditions of normative masculinity, women working as trainers also have something to gain from distancing themselves from qualities associated with femininity. A UN gender adviser I call Fiona explained the terms on which she advocates for gender training: 'This is Security Council, this is not an option. We're not doing it because it's nice to do, we're doing it because it has to be done'. I read in Fiona's rejection of niceness an impulse to push back against the notion of women as caring and nurturing; and in her evocation of the Security Council mandate a desire for gender training to achieve normative alignment with a form of militarized masculinity. The more one is able to distance oneself from queerness and femininity, the more credible one seems to become.

Importantly, epistemic authority is embodied as not only male, but also military. Privileging the uniformed trainer constitutes not only an appeal to likeness, but also speaks to the ways in which epistemic authority is constructed in military communities. Joanna Tidy (2016) highlights the importance of 'ground truth' in claims to authoritative knowledge within military organizations. Ground truth is based on the belief that in order to speak authoritatively on a topic, the speaker must have first-hand experience: he or she must have experienced it 'on the ground'. This form of epistemic authority was enthusiastically validated by some of the gender training participants I spoke with, who expressed appreciation at hearing from instructors who had already been deployed as military gender advisers. As a military officer on the gender advisers' course held in East Africa put it to me: 'You learn more from experience than you learn from the book. Because the reality on the ground is different than what you read in the book'. This valuation of ground truth is inversely observable in the framing of theory in relation to the training. Mackay recalls (2005, 268):

> The theory was the main challenge. How could national troop trainers understand and learn themselves to be able to deliver? At the same time, the theoretical underpinnings had to be relatively invisible if the trainers were not to be scared off.

This inclination among curriculum developers was likewise borne out in my observations. Whether they found theory scary is debatable, but trainees did often critique sessions that included discussion of theory as 'too philosophical' or 'too academic', suggesting that it was less real, or that it held no relevance to them.

That being said, the epistemic authority of 'ground truth' is not always framed by training participants in exclusively military terms. For example, in feedback forms on a military course on conflict-related sexual violence, participants requested a more holistic approach, incorporating more civilian perspectives and more consideration of victims' perspectives (Axmacher 2013, 23–24). What this request suggests is that 'ground truth' is not necessarily a military prerogative. Rather, in the trainees' appreciation, participants to and victims of the conflict may also possess it. It is at this juncture that those exiled from the episteme in the design of curricula re-appear, if not as knowers themselves, then at least as valued informants. Mackay cites an example of the inclusion of community representatives (clergy, nuns, teachers, mayors, civil society associations, etc.) as a fruitful training practice (2005, 275). In a similar manner, on one course I observed, participants suggested that visiting a local women's organization would have been a useful activity for the course participants. In other words, it appears that the forms of epistemic authority that are considered valid in military training can be expanded to non-military subjects. While this broadens the scope of who is authorized to know gender, it does still position the local population more as 'native informants' rather than as knowers who have the authority to shape the training itself.

What is notable in the embodiment of epistemic authority as masculine and military, is the fact that much of the curriculum design, described in the first section of this chapter, involves primarily women and many civilians. A split is thus discernible between who is thought to have the requisite expertise to design curricula, and who is perceived as embodying epistemic authority. Indeed, expertise on gender seems to be a secondary consideration for who is an appropriate trainer. Max's admission that he might lack subject matter expertise was echoed by many male military gender trainers I spoke with. Robert, for example, noted that his training amounted to a job performed by 'enthusiastic amateurs'. Nonetheless, many civilian women who hold more extensive expertise on gender eagerly affirm that training is best delivered by a man in uniform. This tendency to re-centre masculinity in gender work is observable beyond the realm of training: consider for instance the fact that the NATO Committee on Gender Perspectives is the only NATO Committee to stipulate a gender quota—meaning that in practice NATO has all-male committees but explicitly disallows all-women committees (as pointed out by K. Wright, Hurley, and Gil Ruiz 2019, 77). Civilian women ceding epistemic authority to military men nonetheless happens from a position of relative power, as it is the designer of the curriculum who makes this determination in the first place. In the process, however, they concede not only their own epistemic authority but also the authority of others who do not fit this mould. Because of the hegemony of Global North gender experts in the design of gender training, these experts may be poorly qualified to evaluate forms of expertise that are expressed in different terms.

How figuring epistemic authority through the body of the white male military instructor works to silence other forms of expertise was brought to my attention during the multinational gender advisers' course I attended. One training session was delivered by a civilian gender expert from East Africa. Her presentation style differed from that of the Global North trainers who ran most of the sessions. After her presentation, a Nordic military officer I call William approached me and remarked that I had just gotten an example for my research of how *not* to do gender training. William's slight smirk and conspiratorial tone implied that he assumed I would share his conclusion that the session we had just witnessed was a pedagogical disaster. Nonetheless, when I reviewed the participants' feedback for that day, I found that many (I suspect that these included the African officers on the course, but cannot verify this as the feedback was anonymous) were elated with this particular presentation. Some feedback was very critical, but other students praised the East African instructor for her skill in presenting and her ability to involve participants. What I concluded from this episode was that the presenter was able to communicate in culturally specific forms that spoke to some (but clearly not all) of the participants; that she embodied a specific form of female authority that (again, some of) the participants responded to very positively. William was clearly not qualified to evaluate her training skills. Nonetheless, it is the Williams of this world who dominate training design and—by proxy—evaluation practices. That is to say, because experts from the Global North dominate training design, they are also in danger of constructing the ideal of a good trainer in their own image. Epistemic authority is thus produced as normatively male, military, and white.

## Conclusion

Gender trainers and curriculum designers, like many other practitioners and researchers who work on gender, often speak as though it is evident that we all share a common understanding of what exactly gender means. But when we begin to examine how gender is defined in training curricula and the contestations surrounding this definition, it becomes clear that what exactly gender is and does is far from self-evident. While gender training is presented as a rational solution to an objectively identifiable problem, I have sought in this chapter to offer a mode of analysis that runs counter to this proposition: a mode of analysis grounded in the supposition that the meaning of gender is produced rather than given. This mode of analysis allows us to see that the conditions under which knowledge about gender is produced are imbricated with power; the ways in which it is made to work as true uphold systems of marginalization and oppression; and how the forms of epistemic authority it draws from grants bodies marked in certain ways epistemic authority. In short, knowledge about gender is always produced from a particular epistemic location which sets the parameters of what can be said and heard and by whom. This epistemic location of course has deeply political effects. It entails that gender in peacekeeper gender training is produced by and reproduces epistemic structures which configure authority as white, male, and military; which obscure from view structures of oppression; and which marginalize the knowledge of racialized and non-conforming sexual subjects. In the process, the production of knowledge about gender also reproduces the contradictions inherent to all imperial discourses, as those exiled from the episteme continue to haunt its foundations.

An attentiveness to these contradictions in the curriculum design process does not yet provide an account of how the pedagogical processes of gender training play out. This requires an intersubjective account of knowledge production. While the discussion in this chapter has focused on the text of the curriculum—i.e. what curriculum designers *plan* should be taught and how—I have already begun to juxtapose these plans with accounts of how trainers and students interact with each other and the learning material. Not only do trainers have a considerable amount of flexibility in how they deliver training—sometimes to the extent of fully freewheeling—what students learn as a result may only be weakly linked to the content of the curriculum and the intentions of the trainer. I have drawn attention to classroom practices to demonstrate how the ambivalences of gender knowledge continue to haunt the pedagogical site of training. These dynamics hint at my broader argument of the need to extend the analytic gaze to the classroom. They demonstrate that examining what the curriculum prescribes is not sufficient to produce an account of what is *learned* in gender training. The next chapter takes up this task, devoting sustained attention to the dynamics of knowledge production through classroom interactions.

# 3
# Emotional Pedagogy

## Knowing Wartime Rape

That the figures of the sceptical military audience and the happy gender trainer, introduced in Chapter 2, feature in the minds of those who design gender training curricula suggests that there is something at work in gender training beyond the transfer of objective knowledge and technical skills. It suggests that learning is a process that is about more than just being presented with new information. In her exploration of pedagogy, Eve Sedgwick (2003, 167, emphasis in original) recounts the story of Elizabeth Palmer Peabody, a nineteenth-century educator in the United States, colliding with a tree:

> When Elizabeth Palmer Peabody one day walked right smack into a tree, she was naturally asked whether she had not seen it in her path. 'I saw it', she became famous for replying, 'but I did not *realize* it'.

Being presented with technical knowledge is the equivalent of seeing a tree. This is not the same as *realizing* what the significance of the tree being in one's path is, let alone changing one's course to avoid collision. The difference between seeing and realizing is the difference between being given information and learning. Returning to the sceptical audience and the happy trainer then, the invocation of these figures by those who design gender training amounts to a recognition that the attitude and emotional disposition of students matters for what they see and what they learn.

Gender training aims to effect shifts in how peacekeepers think and feel about their work. As scholars of peacekeeping have highlighted, the demands of peacekeeping work differ in important ways from the warfighting soldiers are trained in (Whitworth 2004; Fetherston and Nordstrom 1995). Peacekeeping requires skills in protecting and supporting civilian populations; cross-cultural communication; and non-violent conflict resolution. Add to this that gender training asks those trained in institutions of hegemonic masculinity to take seriously aspirations to gender equality in their work, and it becomes apparent that gender training involves reorienting peacekeepers' relationships with knowledge: rethinking whether their task is defined by warfighting or peacekeeping; who they are meant to protect and from what; and who may be valuable partners or informants in this mission. In other words, it asks training participants to *unlearn*—as critical educators refer to the process—how martial institutions have taught them to think and to relate to others, and to open themselves up to new forms of knowledge (Mehta 2019).

These processes of unlearning are contentious, emotionally charged affairs. They lay bare the ways in which knowledge is affective as well as cognitive, or rather, that the two are not easily separable. Indeed, feminist educators have critiqued the extent to which early forays into critical education for social justice were grounded in rationalist thought and animated by the assumption that if rational individuals were shown evidence of oppression, they would be convinced to work against it. In contrast to such cognitivist understandings, and in continuity with critiques of liberal epistemologies that insist on a binary separation of reason/emotion, mind/body, and public/private, feminist pedagogical approaches have drawn attention to the affective dimensions of learning, describing learning itself as a 'psychic event' (Britzman 1998, 3). Emotions matter in gender training, and not only because managing the emotional charge of the gender training classroom can help shield a gender trainer from dismissive comments and hostile questioning. They matter because of their deep implication in what knowledge is recognized and accepted as true. Megan Boler describes emotions as 'inscribed habits of inattention' which 'define how and what one chooses to see, and conversely, not to see' (1999, 172, 177). Emotions are implicated in encounters with knowledge because they underwrite investments in certain epistemic stances and subject positions over others. They shape how each of us makes sense of the messy world in which we find ourselves, and what we can accept as true.

Precisely because emotions shape what can be known, the pedagogical project of gender training has a vested interest in managing emotional expressions in the classroom. Emotions are never fully private affairs: from the language we have at our disposal to name what we feel, to what constitutes an appropriate emotional expression at any given site, emotional registers are intersubjectively produced. Further, emotions have social effects. As Sara Ahmed (2014) has shown, emotional orientations produce a sense of community, delineating boundaries between inside and outside, between us and them. Emotions are thus political: they enable certain forms of being and acting in the world. When managed through pedagogy, they can constitute either a site of social control or a site of political resistance (Boler 1999, 108). All of which suggests that the emotional landscape of gender training has important implications for its political effects. Accordingly, this chapter continues my exploration of gender training by shifting attention from how gender is taught to how it is learned. Focusing on the emotional pedagogy of gender training, the inquiry of this chapter is structured around questions of: What kinds of feelings does gender training evoke? How do these emotions shape how peacekeepers understand themselves and their task? How do those providing gender training manage and shape emotional expression? What can and cannot be seen as a result? To get at these questions, I examine classroom practices around one topic of gender training that enjoys particular pre-eminence in curricula: conflict-related sexual violence (CRSV).

Conflict-related sexual violence occupies a central space in international policymaking on gender and security and this intense but narrow focus is reproduced through gender training courses for peacekeepers, in which it constitutes a staple training topic. Although this novel attention to gendered violence in peacekeeping at the policy level is not a wholly unwelcome development—it is after all a step toward recognizing how experiences of security and harm are deeply gendered—it also simultaneously reinforces other processes of exclusion and hierarchical ordering. Feminist observers have levelled many excellent, incisive critiques of the 'policy hype' surrounding the topic (Hilhorst and Douma 2018). Though a brief summary of these analyses cannot do justice to their nuance and complexity, a few of their key contentions are worth outlining, because these importantly inform my reading of training in the topic. First: a singular, at times voyeuristic, focus on the phenomenon exceptionalizes wartime rape in ways that contribute to the banalization of other forms of conflict-related violence, including other forms of gender-based violence. Second: the focus on sexual violence, in policy and some research, has facilitated a colonial gaze productive of racialized understandings of sexual violence, its perpetrators, its victims, and protectors from it. Such understandings of wartime rape as something committed by 'barbaric' or 'wrongly gendered' racialized others has been widely critiqued for the ways in which they sustain a hierarchical approach to global governance, and facilitate a denial of more widespread and pervasive forms of gender inequality and sexual violence (Eriksson Baaz and Stern 2013, 26,

30; see also Mertens 2019; Motlafi 2018). In other words, this focus on sexual violence in peacekeeping policy and training is susceptible to the familiar ways in which Western feminist agendas sustain colonial imaginaries and support interventionist politics (Pratt 2013). In what follows, I take up these, and many other poignant critiques and combine them with an analysis of the emotional charge of peacekeeper training on sexual violence. This exploration allows me to get at the micrological texture of power, to examine the pedagogical processes through which peacekeepers come to feel and think about this violence and their own relation to it.

## Stoic/Emotional

In November 2016, I observed a pre-deployment training course for military peacekeepers in a Nordic country. During this course, I spoke at length with one of the training participants, whom I call Lasse. Lasse was an army reservist. He was about to deploy to a peace operation; the latest in a series of deployments he had undertaken to different mission areas. I asked Lasse for his opinion on the gender lecture, which formed one part of the overall course. His response was unenthusiastic, noting that it was 'OK', but that it had not really offered any new information. I probed further, asking Lasse, given his experience in previous missions, what he thought the gender lecture should contain. His response caught me by surprise:

LASSE: One could advise on response mechanisms—like what organizations can help. Otherwise there's nothing you can do when encountering victims, apart from offering condolences.
AIKO: That sounds like a difficult situation.
LASSE: Yeah . . . The training should tell what one might see in the area of operations. Like what it feels like to see a raped person, or a mutilated person, or a murdered person, or a dead person. Those kinds of things aren't everyday stuff for us. They should say that it might feel bad, and that's normal. At the point when it doesn't feel bad, that's when you need to start worrying.

My sense of surprise at this comment stemmed from the fact that the military environment in which we were in is frequently characterized—both in the literature as well as by military personnel themselves—as an environment of hegemonic military masculinity where talking about your feelings is off-limits (Goldstein 2003, 267–269). Against this backdrop, I experienced Lasse's introduction of feelings into the conversation as a rupture in dominant discourses. This sense of rupture appeared to be shared: as Lasse finished saying this, one of his course mates walked by, and Lasse invited him to join the conversation with the quip: 'Hey, come join us! Come talk to Aiko about your feelings!' The chuckles that followed suggested a sense of surprised amusement at the turn the conversation had taken: 'Come talk to Aiko about your feelings'.

This conversation with Lasse stood in contradiction with an understanding of soldiering masculinity as structured through an oppositional positioning of toughness and emotionality, where stoicism characterizes military masculinity and emotionality is disavowed. While official military discourses typically construct soldiering masculinity as stoic and unemotional, this conversation suggested that there is something about gender training that incites discourse about emotion, or even that *requires* expressions of emotion from peacekeepers. Indeed, and as I will unpack in this chapter, gender training consistently produces a vexed relationship between stoicism and emotionality. This contradiction prompted my curiosity: What kinds of feelings circulate in the training setting? How to account for the way in which these feelings trouble prevailing notions of unemotional military masculinity? What pedagogic work do emotions do? Emotion therefore informs my inquiry at two levels. Discourse about feelings constitutes the object of study, but emotion can, as Clare Hemmings (2012, 148) reminds us, also serve as a methodological tool, as what animates my curiosity is the sense of 'affective dissonance' that my conversation with Lasse provoked.

## Stoicism and Military Masculinity

Military masculinity is typically characterized as structured through a series of binary oppositions, such as masculine/feminine, aggressive/passive, heterosexual/homosexual, and strong/vulnerable, where attainment of properly masculine status is achieved by embodying the former and rejecting the latter (Belkin 2012, 38). Although the focus of the literature, and of my analysis, is on military personnel, police officers can similarly enact forms of military masculinity (see e.g. Bevan and MacKenzie 2012). Importantly, these binary oppositions often include a stoic endurance of hardship, as juxtaposed to an emotionality characteristic of femininity traditionally understood. These structuring binaries of military masculinity are inflected in particular ways in the peacekeeping endeavour and the Nordic context Lasse was speaking from. The peacekeeping mandate these soldiers undertake is structured around an appeal to masculinity as protective of women and feminized civilian populations. Flowing from this protective mandate, nascent forms of military peacekeeping masculinity valorize restraint over an eagerness for combat (Duncanson 2013, 92). Further, the Nordic countries have cultivated an image of the Nordic soldier as particularly apt in peacekeeping, as possessing the traits of being professional, neutral, and calm. This figuration of the Nordic peacekeeper is evident in both official imagery produced by Nordic governments, and in Nordic peacekeepers' self-representations (Mäki-Rahkola and Myrttinen 2014; Haaland 2012; Kronsell 2012; Penttinen 2012).

In many ways, gender training for peacekeepers reproduces the structuring binaries of military masculinity. Training materials on CRSV reveal that training relies on gendered binaries. Training scenarios depict victims of sexual violence as female, and peacekeepers as male, thereby upholding the opposition between masculine/warrior/protector and feminine/civilian/victim. These materials consistently locate sexual violence as a problem of conflict-affected areas, sustaining a binary opposition between us/protectors and them/perpetrators. Importantly for my purposes here, these training curricula also maintain a problem-solving orientation toward the topic, implicitly reproducing the stoic/emotional binary by circumventing discussions of feelings and privileging rational action. Gender training practices have been critiqued for presenting subject matter in a technical, problem-solving manner, divorced from political considerations, and training curricula on sexual violence are no different.

Such training typically begins with an interactive lecture on the nature and incidence of CRSV, sometimes incorporating video clips. Many training materials then present peacekeepers with short scenarios, which they work in groups to devise responses to. By way of illustrative example, a scenario in a training guide produced by United States Africa Command (USAFRICOM 2014, 26) reads:

> A squad-sized patrol is driving along a trail in an uninhabited area approximately three kilometers from the nearest village. They see a partially-clad woman crawling towards the trail and stop to render assistance. She

appears to be in a state of shock, but is able to say that she was getting water for her family and was abducted by four armed men and gang-raped. The men wore different mixtures of military-type uniforms and spoke in a language she did not recognize. The rape occurred about 500 meters away from their current location, and she believes the rapists are probably still in that vicinity.

This scenario is typical in both the level of detail it provides and its descriptive tone. It is concrete and unambiguous, and demands immediate action. Together with the scenario, trainees are given contextual facts regarding the operating environment, rules of engagement, and command structure, and must devise an appropriate response to the situation at hand. These exercises reduce the scenario to a problem to be solved, and any references to emotion—such as the woman appearing to be in a state of shock—are promptly circumvented. In this case, the problem posed by emotion is resolved, because the woman is nonetheless able to describe what happened to her. Further, concern for the victim is underplayed by an emphasis on describing the identifying characteristics and location of the perpetrators. In all of this, emotion is marked by an absent-presence. It is this type of training design that Lasse alluded to when he pointed out the silences that persist around sexual violence: it does not encourage or require talking about what it feels like to meet a rape victim, nor is it focused on what the patrolling soldiers might do to support the victim.

Although training curricula thus reproduce an understanding of military masculinity as stoic rather than emotional, it is worth bearing in mind, as Aaron Belkin (2012, 33) urges us to do, that the structuring binaries of military masculinity are not as stable or clear-cut as they might appear. Indeed, feminist theorizations of emotion already trouble this binary juxtaposition between stoic and emotional. They suggest that rather than understanding stoicism, toughness, or hardness as an absence of emotion, these types of expressions can in fact be understood as *a specific type of emotional orientation* toward others (Ahmed 2014, 4). Studies of Nordic peacekeepers demonstrate how such stoic emotional expressions are socially produced. Teemu Tallberg (2007) examines the workings of homosociality among a group of Finnish male peacekeepers, and describes how banter, gossip, and the consumption of alcohol are produced as socially accepted ways for men to deal with the stresses of deployment, presumably in lieu of discussing one's emotions. A discourse that does not express emotion is therefore, somewhat paradoxically, an affective discourse and an emotional investment in stoicism. Megan Boler's extensive examination of the role of emotion in education similarly traces the ways in which pedagogy has functioned as a site of the social regulation of expressions of emotion. She rightly contends that a demand to disavow emotion is best understood, not as unemotional, but rather a specific, politically informed coding of emotion: 'Simply stating that one does not express emotion in the classroom when in the role of authority is a culturally coded form of denial about what counts as "emotion"' (1999, 148). Accordingly, what is at stake in defining military masculinity as stoic is properly understood not as a lack of emotion per se, but rather as a form of defining emotion through negation. These discourses do not evacuate emotion, so much as they produce what are and are not acceptable emotions to express.

Indeed, military educators and trainers routinely implement pedagogical strategies to manage the emotional investments and orientations of military personnel, even though these strategies are not typically understood as dealing with emotion. During a gender training-of-trainers course that I observed in the Nordic region, participants were asked to consider training design from the point of view of the different domains of learning outlined in Bloom's taxonomy (see e.g. Martin and Briggs 1986). The instructor noted that many different kinds of training involve cognitive, affective, and psycho-motor skills, providing as an example how recruits are taught to clean their weapons. This training requires, the instructor explained, a *cognitive* understanding of how the weapon works, the requisite *psycho-motor* skills to carry out the cleaning, and, importantly, the belief, or *affective* investment, in the importance of cleaning a weapon regularly. In other words, military trainers and educators are aware of the fact that pedagogic projects aim to manage the affective lives of trainees. What is at stake in stoic military masculinity is therefore not a blanket refusal of emotion, but the operation of a discourse that manages and regulates emotion, setting the rules of what can and cannot be expressed.

## An Incitement to Discourse

Not only does the stoic/emotional binary not hold conceptually but also an empirical examination of training practices suggests a further contradiction. Namely, some training on conflict-related violence in practice encourages, or even requires, trainees to talk about their feelings. In courses that I observed, feelings often became 'something to say', resembling a Foucauldian confessional practice (1998, 32). One of the ways in which trainers encourage participants to talk about feelings is through the use of video clips in training. This training practice is often suggested by gender training curricula, and was advocated by the gender trainers I spoke with. The rationale for it was described by trainers as two-fold: video provides variation in the mode of delivery and therefore pre-empts boredom, but it also provides a sense of how things 'really are on the ground', thus evoking a claim to authenticity through another form of ground truth. As Puechguirbal explains, the use of video in training is thought to enable 'trainees to see other "realities"' (2003, 117). Though trainers themselves explained their desire to incorporate video into training in these terms, my observations of training suggest that the use of video also serves as a technique to incite participants to talk about their feelings.

For example, during the gender training-of-trainers course I observed in a Nordic country in March 2017, the class watched a documentary titled *The Greatest Silence* (2007) on wartime rape in the Democratic Republic of Congo (DRC). In this film, producer and director Lisa F. Jackson—a white woman from the United States—travels in the DRC, interviewing victims and self-professed perpetrators of sexual violence. The victim testimonies are highly emotive: the detailed descriptions of violent acts and close-up shots of tear-stained faces invite the viewer into personal stories, to witness suffering and partake in grief, in the familiar 'representational economy' described by critical literature on CRSV (Mertens 2019, 669). The film-maker herself tries to draw linkages between sexual violence across different contexts. She inserts herself in what Robin May Schott calls 'the circle of harm', beginning each interview by telling her own story of having been gang raped thirty years earlier in the United States (2015, 137). In this sense, the documentary appeals to a common sense of humanity while exposing harm, trauma, and suffering wrought by sexual violence. The film is action-oriented in its message: it begs the audience to take action to prevent sexual violence from occurring.

This documentary forms a part of the regular curriculum for the gender training-of-trainers course I observed. The course director, whom I call Vera, mentioned to me that in a previous iteration of the course, the film had been screened in the evening, with no debriefing after the viewing. Vera found this arrangement unsatisfactory, because the documentary is, as she described it, horrible and upsetting, and students need to be able to debrief after watching the film. In other words, Vera described the film as productive of emotion, and regarded this emotion as something that needs to be addressed. She was of course accurate in this assessment—the upset produced by the film was palpable in the classroom, and was voiced by participants in subsequent conversations as well as in their course feedback. Following the screening of the documentary, the atmosphere in the classroom was sombre. Many students mentioned that they found the film difficult to watch, and their shock circulated through utterances such as 'How can this happen?' These reactions were reflected in the course evaluation questionnaire, where trainees mentioned that the documentary 'touched me deeply', 'really influenced me', and was an 'eye opener'. In other words, these reflections on the documentary demonstrate a sense of having been touched by the film. The emotions that the film evoked were described by students as 'sad', 'terrible', 'scary', and 'powerful'. The viewing of *The Greatest Silence* catered precisely toward the emotional shortcomings of training that Lasse identified. While Lasse himself was not involved in this course, one of the students in their feedback form pointed to the ways in which the course responded to the training need Lasse had discussed with me months earlier: 'This [film] can be used also for the soldiers that are [sent] out to [the] mission area to prepare them [for] what they can encounter and prepare them to meet these difficult questions'. In other words, the viewing of the film was seen as productive of a discussion of emotions.

Nonetheless, I want to suggest that this discourse around emotion is not necessarily automatically produced by the film, or even the topic of wartime rape in and of itself. Rather, the way in which the film was presented amounted to an 'incitement to discourse' about emotion (Foucault 1998, 17). The class was warned prior to viewing that the film was emotionally distressing, a few shed tears while watching, and many spoke of their emotions after. Vera introduced the film to the class and, in voicing her concern about the upsetting nature of the film, could be read (as I suspect Lasse read me in our encounter) as embodying the kind of feminine nurturance and empathy that invited students to name their feelings. All of these factors coalesced to centre the witness to the violence, embodied here as the Global North peacekeeper, and their feelings on the topic. Talking about emotion thus became the norm in the classroom. In this context, it would have felt inappropriate not to display concern or to make light of the topic in this setting—akin to laughing at a funeral. In this way, the training invited or even compelled students to discuss emotional reactions to the film: it would have been difficult to report not being touched by the film.

The feelings of upset were coupled with efforts to understand what we had seen: How to make sense of these overwhelming feelings? What purpose do they serve in the training course? One student summarized in her learning diary: 'The document[ary] we saw in the morning was very awakening and brought up lots of emotions and thoughts. It was horribl[e] to watch it but still it was good to learn about these things'. In other words, there was an awareness that this film, and the feelings it evoked were important, they served a purpose, they were part of a learning process. This feeling was echoed by many students, who mentioned that the movie was 'very important', and provided a 'powerful message and motivator'. The students were reporting that the movie had *touched* them, in the sense that it produced emotion; and that it had *moved* them, in that it motivated them to act upon their knowledge of wartime rape.

## Tough Guys and Martial Frames

Training on sexual violence produces, then, a contradictory demand of peacekeepers. Predominantly military personnel, they are expected to embody an unemotional form of masculinity. At the same time, the training produces an incitement to talk about feelings and to violate its constitutive stoicism. In many ways, this confusing demand speaks to the foundational contradiction of peacekeeping, which asks soldiers trained in war-fighting to take on peacemaking and humanitarian tasks (Fetherston and Nordstrom 1995). The peacekeeping endeavour asks them to occupy two contradictory subject positions: that of the emotional humanitarian and that of the tough soldier. Research by Laura Miller and Charles Moskos (1995) suggests that in response to this contradictory demand, peacekeepers opt for one of two strategies: to act as a warrior or to act as a humanitarian. However, gender trainers are not oblivious to this contradiction, nor are they content with leaving peacekeepers with this binary choice. Either strategy on its own is unsatisfactory from the perspective of martial institutions equipping peacekeepers to prevent and respond to CRSV. In response, the training attempts to smooth over this contradiction by employing a particular form of emotional pedagogy.

## Towardness and Awayness

To return to the viewing of *The Greatest Silence* during the gender training-of-trainers course, though being touched and moved by this documentary were common features of the emotional scripts that circulated, it seemed that there were two different directions in which students were moved. These emotional reactions can be understood as establishing orientations toward others, producing or undoing boundaries and subject positions. Ahmed explains: 'Emotions are relational: they involve (re)actions or relations of "towardness" or "awayness" in relation to such subjects' (2014, 8). The students' reactions of horror, pity, guilt, and disgust seemed to combine in different ways to move them either toward or away from the subjects represented in the documentary.

On the one hand, trainees described their reactions in terms that placed themselves within the world of the documentary. Comments such as: 'What I learned was a reminder that the world is not [a] very nice place to live, especially for female persons', combined with the admission that it 'made me ashamed to be a man' suggest that the viewer is somehow complicit, through his manhood, in the acts of violence depicted in the documentary.[1] Such feelings prompted classroom conversations that were grounded in attempts to situate the peacekeeper self within the world of the documentary, and to explore how the presence of peacekeepers impacted on the dynamics of sexual violence. Consequently, students raised questions of sexual exploitation and abuse perpetrated by peacekeepers against the peace-kept population. Participants noted that peacekeeper violence fell on a continuum of harms experienced by the local population, and that at the very least, their responsibility was to make sure that peacekeepers did not add to these harms. Further, such feelings prompted some students to consider the needs and wishes of the victims of wartime rape, leading them to question whether the UN should really be paying to send tens of thousands of troops to conflict areas to conduct military patrols, and whether that money would not be better spent in providing medical and psychosocial support to victims instead (uncannily echoing arguments put forward by some critical feminist scholars, see, for example, Whitworth 2004, 186). In other words, an emotional script that locates the peacekeeper self within the world of the documentary appeared to lend itself to situating one's own role and responsibility vis-à-vis the violences depicted in the documentary, in an impulse that prompts a movement *toward* the subjects of the documentary.

In contrast, other students' reactions involved an effort to maintain a distance to the subjects of the documentary, ranging from a move to keep one's own subjectivity outside Schott's (2015, 137) 'circle of harm', to forceful expressions of disgust. This kind of distancing began with how Vera, the course convenor, introduced the film. Her framing of the film as upsetting implied that the phenomenon of wartime rape would come as new and shocking to the trainees, belying an assumption that the corporeal experience of sexual violence was a reality previously unknown to them. The trainees were positioned in Vera's framing as outsiders to the violence, rather than as subjects already having experienced or perpetrated it. Accordingly, some students reported in their learning logs that what they learned from the film was: 'Different cultures behave differently', and that 'war, as we take it in western countries, is something different in other places'. These types of comments demonstrate the ways in which wartime rape comes to be known as a problem that is essentially foreign, attributable to 'different cultures' and 'other places', thus allowing viewers to feel a sense of moral superiority. It facilitates an understanding of sexual violence as inhering to peace-kept societies, suggesting that peace-kept populations are morally lacking and potentially unsaveable. Such dehumanizing and racialized discourses, as documented in a number of studies, lend themselves to apathetic attitudes toward peacekeeping tasks (Jennings 2019, 35; Henry 2015, 385). In perhaps the most brutal articulation of this logic, one student responded to the film in their course feedback form: 'Proves my motto, that is Crap Obeys Gravity [sic] and the smell of it spreads around the continent'. The movement *away* from the subjects of wartime rape is painfully clear in this last quote, which portrays the African continent (we are led to understand that the movement of gravity analogizes movement southward) as characterized by 'Crap', in imagery that violently weaves together racist associations of a dark continent with the smell of faeces. In other words, in my reading of this statement, wartime rape is portrayed as an essentially African problem, and one that is productive of racist disgust, linked to well-established colonial imaginaries of filth and revulsion (Mertens 2019, 668; Bhabha 1994, 112).

My decision to reproduce this last particularly vile comment here was not taken lightly. I feel uneasy, both for re-enacting its violence as well as (admittedly somewhat paradoxically) for singling out for excoriation a single comment from an anonymous feedback form. Nonetheless, I feel an obligation to discuss the comment specifically, as it is indicative of more widespread, if often less explicitly articulated, logics. This statement demonstrates Sherene

Razack's point that when violence is presented through 'a decontextualized and dehistoricized narrative, the traumatized peacekeeper's story imports race into the very meaning of morality' (2003, 207). Training instructors sometimes make the effort to mention that wartime rape is not *only* an African problem—as they did in this Nordic training-of-trainers course, as well as in other courses I have observed. At the same time, such comments sit in tension with other statements made by—often the same—instructors who point out that CRSV is *mainly* a problem in African countries (statements sometimes also included in training curricula, see, for example, PSOTC 2014, 116). This tension does not transcend the regularity with which sexual violence is associated with the African continent. This much has been evident in a number of courses that I have observed, such as when a multinational group of European participants attending a gender course in the Western Balkans balked at the suggestion that sexual violence could occur in their home contexts, articulating their protest in the terms: 'This is not Africa!' Such statements emerge as particularly paradoxical, considering the wealth of evidence about sexual violence, including wartime rape, that occurs and has occurred in Europe.

Ahmed writes: 'how we recognize sexism or racism here can be a way of not recognizing it there. A location can be a reduction' (2017, 29). In this case, a similar logic applies, in amended form: how we recognize sexism *there* can be a way of not recognizing it *here*. How we recognize *sexism* there can be a way of not recognizing *racism* here. The location still does the work of reduction. In this case, the location of wartime rape in a geographically separated zone facilitates a movement *away* from the subjects of the film; and a script of 'horror and alterity' around CRSV persists (Mertens 2019, 669).

The pedagogic work that trainees' emotional reactions to the documentary does can therefore be described as ambivalent, or as producing contradictory movements. On the one hand, movements toward the scene of violence, either by identification with victims or with perpetrators, imply what Miller and Moskos (1995) describe as humanitarian strategies employed by peacekeepers, grounded in empathy and a desire to examine the problem from the point of view of peace-kept populations. On the other hand, movements away imply revulsion, and possibly apathy on the part of peacekeepers. Such movements of awayness imply Miller and Moskos' descriptions of warrior strategies, which rely on sustaining fundamental distinctions between 'us' and 'them'. In other words, emotional responses lend themselves to two different and mutually contradictory kinds of knowledge about sexual violence.

## Warriors and Humanitarians

The contradictory emotional responses of trainees to the topic of sexual violence suggest a need for the management of emotion at the pedagogical site of training. This training occurs in the context of broader policy shifts aimed at challenging the notion that sexual violence is an inevitable by-product of war, but rather a strategy or tactic of war, and one that can and should be addressed. The point of training is to convince peacekeepers that they can address sexual violence. Peacekeeping mandates, with their focus on protection of civilians and a responsibility to protect, involve humanitarian action. Rather than recoiling in disgust, or sinking into apathy, the aim of the training is to convince peacekeepers to act, to convince them to move toward the scene of violence. Accordingly, trainers speak to the broader humanitarian mandates of peacekeeping missions. For example, an instructor on the gender course I observed in the Western Balkans spoke about the military's response to CRSV, that it is, as his presentation slides declared: 'Morally the right thing to do!!! If we are not acting to Protect Civilian [sic]—why are we there?' This remark is in keeping with the aim of training to convince peacekeepers that they have a duty to prevent and respond to sexual violence. Viewed in this light, the incitement to talk about emotions can be read as a strategy to convince trainees to care about the issue. If trainees agree that sexual violence is horrible, this constitutes the first step in convincing them to act upon it. This is driven by a perception of training designers that what is needed for peacekeepers to address sexual violence in conflict is 'a switch in the mindset' (Cammaert 2019, 92).

This switching of mindsets is not, however, simply achieved through an appeal to humanitarian impulses. Peacekeeper training proposes martial action as the appropriate response to sexual violence, thereby smoothing over confusion about whether soldiers are emotional or stoic through an affirmation of warrior strategies. The incitement to express emotion is subsequently channelled to an understanding of the phenomenon as a military problem. For example, in the Nordic training-of-trainers course, the viewing of *The Greatest Silence* was followed by presentations. One trainer's presentation slide read: 'Conflict-related SGBV is used by our adversaries as: command

and control; strategic communication; and biological weapon/force generation'. He went on to explain that rape is a reward for soldiers, and thus a feature of the 'command and control' structure of the warring group. Further, it is used as 'strategic communication' to send out a message of fear to the civilian population in the conflict area as well as a message of control to adversaries. Finally, the spread of HIV/AIDS through rape is a 'biological weapon' used to decimate the affected community, whereas orphans and children born of rape can be recruited into the armed groups, and hence rape also serves the purpose of 'force generation' for armed groups. Another instructor on this course summarized: 'Armed terrorist groups are using an operational gender perspective to achieve their political and military goals'. In both cases, the trainers sought to domesticate the problem to the military by describing it through strategic terminology. This framing of wartime rape as a military strategy or tactic is dominant but not comprehensive. Many of the prescribed training materials and training practice do mention the consequences of wartime rape for the individual victim/survivors as well as for the society. Nonetheless, the dominance of the martial frame serves to emphasize that the *reason* peacekeepers are concerned about the phenomenon is a military one. In Cynthia Enloe's terms, the framing of rape as a martial problem works toward its '*remilitarization*' (2000, 109). The significance of this discursive move is, then, to channel the emotional impetus toward 'doing something' about wartime rape into martial action.

Further, the framing of wartime rape as a purposive and goal-oriented action by 'the enemy' serves to foster an understanding of gendered violence as committed by 'others', enabled by what is portrayed as a barbaric racialized sexuality in combination with illegal tactics of war. This frame serves to obscure the gendered violence committed by peacekeepers themselves, placing sexual exploitation and abuse outside the framework of CRSV. This learning outcome often requires disciplining the sense-making processes of the students, and is not always successful. In the Nordic training-of-trainers course, the lecture on sexual violence mentioned both sexual exploitation and abuse and sexual harassment committed by peacekeepers, but in very narrow terms. First, the instructor outlined that it is important to avoid sexual harassment, exploitation, and abuse in order to ensure that intervening actors would 'set a good example' for local forces. Second, he continued, these were separate matters and *not* CRSV. This discursive framing circumscribes the violence that can be discussed. It addresses reactions such as that mentioned in the previous section that witnessing the horror of wartime rape 'made me ashamed to be a man', by allowing the trainees to know (however unfounded the knowledge may be) that they are implicated in what they have seen only as protectors, not as complicit in the perpetration of sexual violence.

Framing wartime rape as a military problem, and one that is committed by enemies, is supported by prescribed solutions that accommodate the impulse to 'do something' about the problem. The goal of the training for the military is to use emotional responses to the phenomenon as a motivator for the troops to take *martial action* against warring parties, in keeping with a warrior strategy. As such, the emotion must be carefully managed, not necessarily to helping victim/survivors so much as to undertaking military action. The training therefore provides concrete but carefully circumscribed actions to undertake. The prescribed courses of action typically involve apprehending perpetrators; using military patrols to protect women and girls; devising early warning mechanisms; reporting; and liaising with other actors, including community organizations.[2]

One notable feature of this training is its focus on organigrams and reporting structures. Many training sessions on sexual violence dedicate a large portion of time available to reviewing organizational charts, detailing who (including the civilian and police components of peacekeeping missions, as well as humanitarian organizations and non-governmental organizations) does what and to whom different issues can be referred. The underlying point: the role of the military is to report, not to investigate. In this way, the training reels in the more proactive impulses of students, who often jump to conclusions such as, when encountering victims: 'They must tell us who did this to them so that we can catch them!' The disciplining of such impulses may be desirable, as few would argue that military personnel, mostly men, untrained in victim-centred responses to sexual and gender-based violence should be encouraged to interview victims. However, such moves also indicate how training serves to channel empathetic emotional responses to the production of military subjectivities that follow a martial logic. In other words, it resolves emotional discomfort by presenting martial action as the resolution.

The training also suggests more proactive measures than reporting, including measures that involve physical action for the peacekeepers. One such example is that of early warning mechanisms. In these, the peace-kept population and the peacekeepers devise ways for the population to communicate with the peacekeepers in the event of an impending threat, for example, through radio channels, drumming, or smoke signals. Such scenarios position military actors as ready to intervene with martial solutions in the event of an attack, and suggest that security is achievable through military patrols. In other words, it positions the peacekeepers in ways that enable them to use force to address the problem. Such strategies reassure peacekeepers that the emotional discomfort that they may feel as a result of witnessing sexual violence can be resolved through warrior strategies. Consider the remarks of Patrick Cammaert, a retired Dutch general who has been instrumental in the design and delivery of CRSV training for peacekeepers (2019, 90):

> you have to remain very unpredictable, very mobile and quick with a strong, robust posture. It scares people off and gives the impression of 'I have to be careful with those guys, because those guys are tough'.

In these remarks, Cammaert is responding to a question of how peacekeepers can prevent sexual violence. His framing positions peacekeepers who take action to prevent and respond to sexual violence as strong, as having a robust posture, and as generally tough guys; all attributes which are commensurate with traditional concepts of military masculinity. Cammaert then goes on to lament that many countries' peacekeepers are reluctant to act on sexual violence because they are 'risk-averse' (2019, 92). A binary opposition is thus reasserted between tough, manly peacekeeping countries whose peacekeepers are willing to take risks, and feminized peacekeepers who lack this courage or moral resolve.

Although the training prescribes responses in keeping with the logic of military engagement, training participants themselves often suggest solutions that are not grounded in the use of force. For example, in several courses I observed, some participants worked in the medical corps. Their first reaction was that they wanted to provide medical assistance to victims, and asked why they were not provided with post-exposure prophylaxis and other supplies needed to provide medical assistance to a victim of sexual violence. The instructors told them that providing medical care to the peace-kept was not part of their mandate; they were on the mission to provide medical care to the peacekeepers and the local population should be referred to non-governmental organizations in the area. The logic at work in restraining the desire to provide help to victims is not solely one of containment, but also one of serving larger protection goals. Instructors explained that because the military are legitimate targets according to the laws of war, their close involvement with peace-kept populations can expose civilians to martial violence. One participant succinctly summarized this learning in her student presentation: 'When military units provide direct assistance and engage in civilian activities they blur the line between civilian and military targets and can place civilians at risk'. By evoking both the military mandate of the peacekeepers as well as appealing to the safety of the population, the instructors sought to contain humanitarian strategies for peacekeepers by re-affirming warrior subjectivities.

## Excess Emotion: Knowing Otherwise?

The regulatory moves of training are how the military institution manages feeling through an emotional pedagogy. This regulatory pedagogy is, however, not always successful. Disagreements with the messages of the training curriculum—with the knowledge offered—produces ruptures in the discourse and an excess emotion endures. Against the backdrop of stoic masculinity, I described my encounter with Lasse as a disruption of dominant discourses. Lasse's introduction of feelings to the conversation can be described as the surfacing of excess emotion: that which exceeds the social boundaries of the organization, that which does not fit. Emotions are intersubjectively produced and regulated, social norms prescribe how one is supposed to feel in a given situation. After watching *The Greatest Silence*, we the viewers were *supposed* to feel upset and horrified. Feeling otherwise—for example, critiquing the representational politics of the documentary—would be in excess of the demands of the social situation and likely unwelcome. Feminist philosopher Alison Jaggar (1997, 396) describes emotions that do not conform to what is socially expected as 'outlaw emotions', whereas Ahmed describes the non-conforming emotional subject as an 'affect alien' (2010, 30). Jaggar and Ahmed's descriptions of emotions out of place are thus similar to how I characterize excess emotion. However, an important difference remains: both of these theorists are speaking about disavowed feelings that stem from the experience of oppression by marginalized subjects such as Ahmed's feminist kill-joys, unhappy queers, and melancholic migrants. This is a category which I feel ill at ease extending to describe uniformed peacekeepers, given the situational and material power they exercise. As such, I continue to privilege the term 'excess emotion' to describe disjunctures and disagreements with the dominant narrative.

## Enduring Excess

One way in which the regulatory techniques of training fail to provide resolution to emotional discomfort, at least for some students, is in the suggestion that the forms of violence committed by peacekeepers are entirely separable from those committed by warring parties. One participant in the gender advisers' course I observed in East Africa protested upon being told that addressing sexual exploitation and abuse committed by peacekeepers was not in the gender advisers' remit. She insisted that, from the view of the peace-kept, the distinction of whether they were attacked by a local armed group or by a peacekeeper was not the most salient factor of their experience and proclaimed: 'It cannot be that we encourage troops to violate the local population while we claim to protect them from abuse committed among themselves!' In a similar manner, in the Nordic training-of-trainers course, one student explained in her learning diary:

> There exists an internal-external continuum in the frameworks related to CRSV [conflict-related sexual violence], from harassment that happens inside missions to actual SGBV [sexual and gender-based violence] that happens external to the mission. Between these exists SEA [sexual exploitation and abuse], which relates to abuse by members of missions. Understanding the continuum and the fact that gender topics are not just related to mission activities, should be discussed in any training I will have on SV [sexual violence].

By locating sexual violence on a continuum, this training participant is rejecting a schema in which wartime rape could be understood as easily separable from violence committed by peacekeepers themselves. The conclusion presented here—that gender topics are not just related to mission activities—speaks distinctly against the dominant message of gender training. For these students, their commitment to keeping the violence committed by peacekeepers in their analytical vision appears to have contributed to an enduring feeling of outrage and responsibility. This emotion did not find resolution in the suggestion that the violence committed by 'us' could be decisively separated from the violence committed by 'them'.

Other training participants exposed how limitations imposed on them by institutional mandate were an insufficient resolution to their impulse to 'do something' to help victims. During the course of my observation, I heard several accounts from instructors themselves, in front of their classes, about how their military mandate did not accommodate their emotional reactions, and how they had stepped outside of their military role to pursue what they felt was the right course of action.[3] One military instructor on the multinational course in the Western Balkans, whom I call Mark, detailed how on deployment his task was to implement 'quick impact projects', which are small-scale development projects designed to help the local population in the area of operations and thereby win their trust and support. In one instance, Mark had to choose between allocating funds to support a school or to support an orphanage. He had been advised that he should support the school, because that would win over the parents of the school children (the orphans, by implication, had no parents whose hearts and minds needed to be won). Mark ruminated on this decision, lamenting that the choice to support the school over the orphanage 'wasn't the right choice morally, but it was the right choice tactically'. However, he had subsequently made a private donation and volunteered at the orphanage: 'I did have to go do something off my own back with the orphans because I felt guilty. The lesson of CIMIC [civil-military cooperation] is to not get emotionally attached, but that's impossible'. Mark's account exposed the ways in which his military mandate could not accommodate his desire to help. His emotional disposition was in excess of it. Indeed, numerous studies have demonstrated that soldiers join militaries for a number of reasons, one of which they report as a humanitarian desire to help populations in need (Whitworth 2004, 151).

While military organizations may not have the mandate to assist victims, police peacekeepers do, and at least some are trained in victim-centred responses. However, although police officers have the mandate to assist, they may lack resources. I observed one multinational police training course on victim-centred approaches to sexual violence in West Africa. Like much of military training, this training devoted large portions of time to examining institutional mandates, mainly in the form of referral pathways. This aspect of the training sought to clarify how the police work with victims' services: medical care, safe houses, social services, legal aid, and so forth. It outlined how police response was only one aspect of the response to cases of sexual violence, and that individual police officers should not be responsible for addressing all of the victim's needs. However, unlike military training, where NGOs and women's groups are often presented as a reliably present panacea to all otherwise unmet needs, this police training explicitly addressed the other organizations' lack of capacity, or even non-existence.

An instructor whom I call Angela noted, as she was presenting the referral pathways: 'but sometimes the institutions we are referring them to are even worse off', alluding to institutional resource shortages. She coupled this with examples of police officers exceeding their role within this formal division of labour, such as using a police vehicle to drive victims home from the hospital, even though this should be social services' role. A participant pointed out that using the police vehicle for this purpose was against organizational rules, to which Angela simply responded: 'This is where your humanitarian instincts kick in'.

Over the course of the two-week police training course, participants and instructors alike recounted stories reminiscent of Mark's, except what was transcended here were resource limitations as well as limitations posed by institutional mandate. Two students—both policewomen—mentioned that they currently had victims of sexual violence living with them in their homes, and were providing care in the form of food, shelter, counselling, and medical care. Both had undertaken to do so at their own initiative, albeit with the approval of social services, who lacked the resources to provide such care. One woman, who had taken in an eight-year old girl who had been forced by her mother to sell sex, reflected: 'You have to focus on the best interests of the child. We know it is not right [that I should take this child in], but we must protect the child'. At this juncture, Angela chimed in:

> Who here has not parted with some of his [sic] own money to help victims? Once they brought somebody to my office, she had been selling herself, she was not quite right in the head. She was in menses and her clothes were stained with blood. I have a whole suitcase of things in my office that I could give her. I have sanitary towels, I have clothes. We are not supposed to be doing this. But we are tormented by the plight of the victims. What are you going to do?

In other words, what was privileged in these accounts was the underlying institutional mandate of providing a police response to sexual violence that is centred on the needs of the victims. The officers who recounted these stories had transcended constraints of institutional resources and divisions of labour by taking on themselves the responsibility and often also the cost of providing for the needs of the victim. By recounting these stories, they brought into sharp relief the shortcomings of their own institution in providing needed assistance. Their excess emotion manifested in these stories of taking on personal responsibility in the face of institutional shortcomings.

## Knowing Otherwise?

It would be disingenuous to pretend that I was not deeply touched by the stories of Mark, Angela, and many training participants in their attempts to do whatever they could to help people in vulnerable situations. Nonetheless, I do not extend this admission to a claim that a humanitarian emotional orientation is ethically unproblematic nor that warrior responses are always misguided. My own emotional response to the West African policewoman recounting taking in a child victim of sexual abuse is informed by the gendered assumption that a girl child must be safe from further exploitation and abuse when placed under the care of a policewoman—an assumption I have no way of verifying. At a more foundational level, it is worth bearing in mind the dangerous political potential of emotions such as pity, sympathy, and empathy, given their selective application to those we deem deserving. These emotions are not politically unproblematic: they can serve the function of affirming our own sense of moral superiority while negating the need to examine our own complicities in structures of oppression (Boler 1999, 159; see also Razack, 2007; Sontag, 2004). What is more, it can hardly be read as surprising that military training prescribes military solutions. It is worth noting that the concerns, such as potentially turning civilians into military targets through close association with peacekeeping troops, are genuine and likely reasonable. In other words, I do not suggest that an empathetic emotional orientation is necessarily a normatively superior one.

This being said, I want to return to the question of what this excess emotion signifies, and argue that it exposes the limits of martial thinking. As detailed in the above examples, these admissions of exceeding institutional mandates and resources exposed the fundamental lack that underlies peacekeepers' interventions on CRSV. They cast a persistent shadow of doubt over any claims that the use of martial force could constitute a satisfactory response to this violence. The discussion around sexual exploitation and abuse also rejected efforts to remove peacekeeper violence from the field of vision when it comes to sexual violence. In other words, these discursive moves draw tentative linkages between the peacekeeping endeavour and, per Razack, 'peacekeeping violence, Western complicity, [and] the illusory foundations of the New World Order' (2003, 207). They provoke moments of instability in a discursive frame that insists on holding these questions apart. Through the pedagogical work that these emotions do, in exposing limits and shortcomings in prescribed solutions, excess emotion can provide the basis of knowing CRSV otherwise.

Further, the persistence in talking about emotion chips away at the hegemonic masculinity at work. That the military relies on ostensibly unemotional orientations was explained by one of my interlocutors:

> You can't talk about feelings, like what it means to shoot someone. If you did, the whole organisation would unravel. That's why so many of these guys have problems when they come home from deployments.

In other words, this destabilizing move has implications not only for how sexual violence is understood but it also exposes the silences that enable the exercise of military violence, and the consequences of post-traumatic stress disorder for those who wield it (Whitworth 2008). Enduring excess emotion therefore exposes the unstable foundations on which sexual violence training is predicated: it collapses firm distinctions between peacekeeper violence and conflict-related violence; it undermines the hegemony of unemotional military masculinity. Homi Bhabha (1994) has shown that colonial discourses are systematically constituted through ambivalence, that they are characterized by a simultaneous attraction toward and revulsion from an object. The contradictions at play in peacekeeper gender training similarly expose ambivalent relations between the desire to be or to foster stoicism/ emotionality and warrior/humanitarian subjectivities. What excess emotion does, then, is it exposes this vexed relationship. It resists attempts to smooth over the contradiction between peacekeepers as stoic warriors and emotional humanitarians.

If enduring excess emotion troubles the regimes of truth which training (re)produces, what does knowing otherwise do? Discussions of the shortcomings of institutional mandates and resources are characterized by both the admission of limitations and a sense of powerlessness to change them. The steps taken by Angela, Mark, and many trainees point toward the kind of action excess emotion produces: taking small, piecemeal steps to alleviate a situation where they can. In relation to conditions of life she calls 'slow death', Lauren Berlant proposes we think of small pleasurable activities such as over-eating as an exercise of lateral agency. This agentic action is not future-oriented, it is not geared toward producing structural change, but rather provides 'a relief, a reprieve, [but] not a repair' (Berlant 2011, 117). Similarly, individual police officers providing victims of violence with food, shelter and clothing at their own cost are carrying out immediate responses characterized by personal responsibility rather than structural change. These actions do not offer a coherent alternative to transcend the hegemonic logics of peacekeeping. Instead, what knowing otherwise does is that it reveals ambivalence and cracks in the discourse; it provokes moments of instability productive of new questions, but falls short of revolutionary vision. It takes away the sense of emotional resolution offered by framing the problem of sexual violence as one amenable to military solutions as it undermines the sense of clarity offered by a warrior stance, but offers little certainty in its place.

## Conclusion

This chapter began with a contradiction: the discussion of feelings in an environment of hegemonic masculinity. This contradiction suggested that stoic military masculinity cannot simply be taken as a given, but rather that its production must be analytically accounted for. In this analysis, I have interrogated emotions as a site of knowledge and a pedagogy that secures attachments to certain ways of knowing the world and one's place in it. Gender training evokes and attempts to manage discourses of emotion in order to smooth over the ambivalences of the expectation that peacekeepers are stoic but also emotional, that they are humanitarians as well as warriors. Its hegemonic discourse proposes warrior subjectivity and martial action as appropriate responses to gendered problems like that of sexual violence in conflict. Attentiveness to the role of emotion in pedagogical endeavours illuminates the politics of knowledge circulation through gender training: it provides insight into how the purportedly gender-progressive initiative of training the troops on CRSV is domesticated into the military context, and how this knowledge is transformed to serve the military institution in the process.

At the same time, this emotional pedagogy remains marked by ruptures in the dominant discourse and by moments of instability. Excess emotion exposes contradiction and ambivalence within the peacekeeping endeavour more generally, and in particular in relation to interventions against CRSV.

There is little to suggest that such excess emotion leads to a meaningful challenge or transformation of the structures of peacekeeping or the martial institutions that dominate it: excess emotion is not necessarily a transformative force. Nonetheless, it sustains the ambivalence of peacekeeping discourse, and resists a smoothing over of its discourses. The contradictory nature of the emotional discourses that circulate around peacekeeping attest to unresolved tensions within gender training. They suggest that the knowledge about gender that the curriculum puts forth is neither comprehensive nor ultimately fixed. They imply an ongoing struggle over meaning within the gender training classroom. At times these struggles emerge from ambivalence contained within the gender knowledge itself. At other times, these struggles are prompted by resistant subjects, who are the topic of the next chapter.

# 4
# Resistance

## Struggles for Meaning in The Classroom

When gender trainers gather in social settings—such as coffee breaks or workshop dinners—the conversation often turns to the question of resistant trainees. Trainers swap incredulous stories of training participants who disrupted training they conducted, the stories oscillating between outrage and bemusement. There is the jovial late-middle aged man who is friendly but who makes inappropriate jokes during the training. The agitated participant who asserts over and over again that women are simply fundamentally different from men, and hence not suited to the same tasks. There is the young man (or occasionally woman) who insists that they do not differentiate based on gender—that the institution sees only soldiers, not men or women—and hence no inequality can exist here.

These stories serve both as occasion to exchange on what the best ways of dealing with resistant participants are as well as providing the simple consolation of a sympathetic ear. This discussion of, or even preoccupation with, resistance is not limited to gender trainers and social encounters: several studies of peacekeeper training raise the issue as a potential impediment to effective gender mainstreaming (Mackay 2005, 267; Higate 2004, 18; Puechguirbal 2003, 117; see also Chapter 2). Many training manuals accordingly provide advice to trainers on how to overcome resistance from audiences (see e.g. Reimann 2013, 48; Johannsen 2009, 15). Nor is the issue of resistance confined to peacekeeper training: gender trainers in other institutional settings also highlight the question (Cornwall 2016, 77; Kabeer 1991, 192), and resistance is discussed at some length in the feminist pedagogical literature in reference to higher education settings (Bell, Morrow, and Tastsoglou 1999, 29; M. Lewis 1992, 168; Lather 1991, 123). This preoccupation with resistance stems from its ubiquity in training encounters. We have already touched upon the notion that trainees might be indifferent, sceptical, or even hostile to the message of gender training in previous chapters of this book. Recall, for example, Nadine Puechguirbal's call, described in

Chapter 2, for gender trainers to relate a happy affect and to foster a positive orientation toward the topic in order to overcome scepticism or even hostility on the part of training participants. In keeping with the prevalence of this theme, resistance came up in some shape or form in every pedagogical encounter that formed part of my research for this book.

This chapter is thus dedicated to exploring this pervasive phenomenon, asking: How is resistance performed in gender training? What does resistance tell us about the epistemic and political effects of this training? This line of inquiry extends the recognition, developed in the previous chapter, that gender training often produces pedagogic experiences and learning that exceed what is explicitly prescribed by training curricula. In Chapter 3, I examined training on conflict-related sexual violence to suggest that an emotional pedagogy underlies the curriculum and indicated that this training produces different sense-making processes and a range of options for understanding one's own subject position. I argued that training on conflict-related sexual violence is characterized by confusing demands on peacekeeper subjectivity with contradictory implications for being and acting in the world as a warrior/humanitarian. In addition to exploring the different political options that knowledges about sexual violence open up, this analysis speaks to the broader importance of paying careful analytical attention to what happens in pedagogical encounters, as opposed to only attending to what is prescribed in the curriculum. It confirms that the training enterprise cannot simply be understood as the transfer of knowledge from curriculum or trainer onto students, but rather attests to what pedagogical theorizing describes as the intersubjective constitution of knowledge through encounters among learners, instructors, and the text of the curriculum (Freire 2005, 73; Maher 1987, 94). Resistance not only offers a helpful vantage point from which to examine how gender knowledge is negotiated at the site of pedagogy, it also helps us see what articulations of gender knowledge are (more easily) accepted in the peacekeeping endeavour, and what forms of gender knowledge remain contentious. Resistance, in other words, exposes where the challenges to and limits of political possibility lie. In this chapter, I examine how resistance is performed in gender training settings, and how instructors respond to resistance. I argue that resistance is performed through a number of different scripts, not all of which involve explicit disagreement with the aims of gender training. Rather, resistance works in ambiguous ways through joking and laughter; it aims to limit understandings of gender to forms that are politically neutral, heteronormative, and founded in colonial difference. Resistance reveals that while many (though certainly not all) training participants recognize, in principle, the importance of gender, they contest an understanding of gender as embedded in patriarchal and racialized power relations.

This being said, a word of caution is in order before delving into how resistance plays out in gender training encounters. Here it is important to bear in mind that resistance is subtly but importantly distinct from refusal, and thus from a neat oppositional set-up of being for or against gender analysis or gender training. The word 'resistance' connotes friction and struggle rather than a dead end or clean break, meaning that resistance is best understood as a process rather than an outcome. Throughout the analysis that follows, I thus maintain a commitment to examining resistance as an ongoing struggle over meaning; as a process whose politics are constantly shifting. This is an analytical necessity because, as this chapter lays out, 'resistance' is a conceptually slippery term, where meanings and allegiances are only ever contingently fixed. Further, feminist pedagogical theorizing suggests that resistance is a common or even integral feature of learning. Offering a psychoanalytic reading of pedagogy, Deborah P. Britzman (1998, 11) explains:

> What education asks of students [is to] confront perspectives, situations, and ideas that may not be just unfamiliar but appear at first glance as a criticism of the learner's view. In all demands, education seems to be asking selves to risk their resistance even as educators have difficulty tolerating the forms working through resistance takes.

In gender training this is quite obviously the case: the training (sometimes) seeks to effect quite fundamental shifts in worldviews. In questioning traditional gender roles, the training challenges deeply held beliefs, and may seem like a criticism not just of trainees' views but also of how they live their lives. That participants might be resistant to the training is thus certainly unsurprising, probably inevitable, and perhaps not undesirable. This is why bell hooks (1994, 154) insists that we recognize that '[n]ot all pain is harm, not all pleasure is good'. The learning involved in gender training may be an experience marked by pain, but this pain may be necessary and generative. In contrast, an understanding of gender that prompts no resistance may alert a critical feminist observer to the fact that an understanding of gender is at play that does *not* seek to undo structures of oppression. Again, as hooks reminds us, not all pleasure (comfort?) is good. My analysis in this chapter thus departs from a concurrent recognition that resistance may demarcate the political limits of gender training, at the same time as resistance is not necessarily a bad thing.

## Conceptualizing Resistance: Politics and Performance

'Resistance' is a slippery concept. This much became clear to me when I spoke with a UN gender adviser whom I call Sandra. Sandra told me that she had attended a two-week-long military gender training-of-trainers course. She was impressed by the course and recounted how many participants had undergone a complete change in perspective on the course:

> Oh my God [laughter], they were so hilarious. They were so into gender at the end of the training. [In the beginning] I had guys in my group who were all these big military guys and all: 'Oh, I'm doing a *gender training*', and making a lot of jokes about it. And then towards the end they were just full-on gender: 'How can we do military without gender anymore?' ... And they started making jokes about being gender-force, almost being proud about it.

What stood out to me about this story is the fact that, in it, making jokes is an indication both of initial resistance to the topic—' "Oh, I'm doing a *gender training*", and making a lot of jokes about it'[1]—and of a change in perspective—'they started making jokes about being gender-force, almost being proud about it'. Is making jokes about being in gender training an indicator of dismissal and ridicule or a sign of appreciating the importance of the issues at stake? Clearly, it can be either, and resistance can become not-resistance through subtle changes to context and tone.

Not only does the meaning of jokes change from resistant to supportive through elusive changes, the meaning of the term 'resistance' itself depends on—and changes dramatically—depending on what is being resisted, by whom, and to what effect. The term in and of itself does not determine what part can be played by which actor: the training participant is not always the one doing the resisting and the trainer is not always the one being resisted. Neither does the term automatically denote progressive or regressive politics: depending on how the concept is used, the object of resistance may be colonial power structures or the feminist movement. The political meaning of resistance is likewise in flux: it may be a necessary (if painful) part of a learning process or an active impediment to liberatory politics. Some remarks are therefore necessary to narrow down the conceptualization of resistance that informs the analysis in this chapter.

## Political Ambiguity

The term 'resistance' is used in so many different senses that the word itself is characterized by a significant amount of political ambiguity. Consider, for example, the seeming discontinuity between gender trainers' descriptions of audiences hostile to arguments about gender equality as 'resistant', and my suggestion that feminist pedagogy or gender training might enact a form of subversive, 'resistant' feminist politics per Foucault and Butler. The term is used in the feminist pedagogical literature in two similarly contradictory senses. One use of the term refers to radical political movements—ranging from the French Resistance (Trimbur 2001, 9) to a 'mass-based feminist resistance struggle' (hooks 1994, 77). The other way in which the term is used is to denote student resistance *to* such radical political projects, and to the classroom practices these projects inspire. 'Resistance', in the latter sense of the term, involves the resistance of 'male students to the feminist teacher' (Trimbur 2001, 3), and manifests as ' "resisting" students who [do] not want to learn new pedagogical processes, who [do] not want to be in a classroom that [differs] in any way from the norm' (hooks 1994, 9). In other words, the term 'resistance' has been used both to denote the resistance of radical political movements to forms of oppression and to signify the resistance of students to critical ideas.

Highlighting the political ambiguity of the term 'resistance', Elizabeth Flynn (2001) argues that educators should differentiate between three different kinds of resistance: strategic, counter-strategic, and reactive resistance. Flynn explains that strategic resistance involves collective or individual resistance against structures of oppression, such as feminist protest or feminist pedagogical practice. Counter-strategic resistance, in turn, involves 'deliberate attempts by the group in power to oppose or undermine strategic resistance,' such as the concerted movement against feminist politics (Flynn 2001, 18). In contrast to these two deliberate types of resistance, Flynn (2001, 18) suggests that what is most often at stake in pedagogical encounters is reactive resistance: 'a spontaneous and emotional reaction which may have multiple and conflicting motivations and effects'. Flynn's typology is helpful in that it establishes political motivations and effects as a means of navigating the ambiguity of the term. Resistance itself is not inherently progressive or regressive; it can be an effect of different political motivations. In this chapter, I use the term 'resistance' in the sense that it is often used by gender trainers and feminist educators, to denote forms of resistance against feminist politics and feminist analyses, encompassing what Flynn describes as counter-strategic and reactive resistances. What is germane here is that these are forms of resistance that the feminist pedagogical literature characterizes as 'neither liberatory nor benign' (Prebel 2014, 535).

I agree with Flynn's contention that, while counter-strategic resistance is often quite hostile and deliberate, reactive resistance is not necessarily destructive—indeed, it may in fact be a generative dynamic in the classroom. I am nonetheless uneasy with the notion of drawing a neat distinction between deliberate counter-strategic resistance and spontaneous reactive resistance, for both methodological and epistemological reasons. First, my research method does not lend itself to making pronouncements about whether the performances of resistance in my research archive were produced by conscious and deliberate strategies to undermine the training or trainer, or spontaneous individual reactions. Working off what research participants articulated in gender training, I have no way of determining the authenticity of or level of deliberation underlying such statements, nor do I seek to make any claims in this regard. Second, a strict delineation between what is deliberate and what is reactive sits uneasily with the epistemological framing of this study. It implies a level of autonomy and voluntarism that does not quite fit with how resistance works in training settings.

## Scripts and Performance

Understanding resistance as *either* (counter-)strategic *or* reactive does not map onto the examples of resistance in my research archive. This is because, in my observations of training, even seemingly reactive forms of resistance follow fairly predictable scripts. The patterned nature of resistance was brought to my attention in an interview with a western European NGO trainer I call Alessia, who mentioned that training participants often make inappropriate comments during or after the training. Alessia said that she entertained the notion of keeping a record of these utterances, and cataloguing the types the comments she heard on a PowerPoint slide. When I asked her what she would this slide for, she explained:

> I mean, you don't want to open a workshop or training with it, but at some point, if something like that comes out, you might just come up with a nice slide with like, these are some of the things people might say. And they feel uncomfortable about it, and you're like 'Oops, yeah...' Just to show that... it's a pattern in a way. You know what I mean? That... there's some deeper reason for it. It's not just that you're being funny.

Alessia's impression that there is a pattern to the forms that resistance takes finds traction in research that examines resistance in training and educational endeavours. This literature charts forms of resistance, sometimes organizing them into typologies. Emanuela Lombardo and Lut Mergaert provide a succinct example, tabulating forms of resistance in gender training according to the following categories: denial of the need for gender change, trivializing gender equality, and refusing to accept responsibility (2013, 305). The feminist pedagogical literature likewise records forms of student resistance, including the repeated use of tropes such as insisting on hearing 'the other side of the story' in relation to feminist analyses, women students' anger at the suggestion that women as a group are oppressed, and the persistence of 'phallo-centric myth-making' (M. Lewis 1992, 184).[2]

I suggest that the patterned nature of resistant statements is significant, and that it can be understood with the help of the sociological notion of social interaction as scripted (Goffman 1990). Understanding resistant statements as drawing on broader interactional frames suggests that it is too reductive to interpret resistance that does not fall into the category of a deliberate, conscious politics (i.e., Flynn's counter-strategic resistance) as simply reactive and individual. Rather, the patterning of resistance attests to the availability of existent scripts that provide legible ways of articulating objections to feminist politics. They demarcate a site at which broader struggles over truth claims play out. Understanding resistant interactions as drawing upon, and producing, social scripts suggests that trainers and training audiences can be read as, extending the theatrical metaphor, *performing* certain roles within these encounters.[3]

The notion that resistance involves a performative element was also emphasized by some gender trainers I spoke with. In our interview, another western European NGO trainer I call Vincent recounted the following story about a training workshop he had facilitated in Latin America with security and justice sector personnel:

> As we were doing the introductions around the room . . . one of the prosecutors stood up and said 'Hello my name is such and such, I'm the prosecutor from such city, and I believe that if there are no scratches, it's not rape'. And that was his business card, the way that he introduced himself to everybody. I honestly don't think that he truly believed that. I think that he needed to establish his own place in the group, and say, you know, that I am a force to be reckoned with, and I demand respect, and I'm not going to sit here and have these people [the trainers] tell me how to do my job.

Without wishing to dwell on the (in)authenticity of resistant statements such as that described by Vincent—it is not possible to arbitrate here whether this prosecutor truly believed what he said—what is of particular interest in Vincent's analysis of the encounter is the suggestion that the resistant utterance is a performance of the self that serves a particular social function. When read in this light, resistance can be seen as a performance that establishes a subject position, and marks out where one stands in relation to struggles over truth claims. As such, resistant statements are social rather than purely individual. Reading resistance as performative has important implications for understanding its function: a performance has an intended audience and communicates how a person wishes to be seen. What this implies in a training context is that when trainers or participants engage with the group, they are not only convincing or failing to convince the individual who voiced the resistance to see another point of view but also involved in performing the interaction for the rest of the training audience. Again, this suggests that what is at stake in resistance is not only, or even primarily, the act of convincing a resistant individual but also the staging of broader struggles over truth claims.

My characterization of resistance as scripted and performative does not aim to negate the fact that individual responses and emotions in particular play a role in resistance. Indeed, and as I will explore in more depth in the next section of this chapter, I contend that the performance of resistance is importantly informed by (individual) efforts to grapple with what is experienced as 'difficult knowledge'—that is, knowledge that makes one question one's own role in structures of inequality (Britzman 1998, 19). Being asked to consider truth claims that challenge how we see the world and our sense of self—to unlearn what we know (Mehta 2019, 29)—may well involve, as hooks reminds us, a degree of pain. An account of resistance as scripted and performative does not amount to a negation of emotion or choice, nor does it rely on a wholly autonomous construction of the resisting subject. Rather, accounts of resistance and of emotional responses to training highlight how individual responses are produced within the context of social locations and particular regimes of truth. The articulation of resistance, importantly, is conditioned by what are socially legible scripts. These struggles over meaning are, in other words, both personal and political.

## Subjects and Objects

Much of the literature on both gender training and feminist pedagogy portrays resistance as performed by the student/training participant against the teacher/trainer. The image of resistance that these accounts produce is often that of the white, heterosexual, male student, who is resisting the feminist teacher. In other words, such accounts imply that counter-strategic or reactive resistance is performed only by those who enjoy structural power and privilege, but who find themselves in a position of diminished situational power given the classroom setting (see e.g. Boler 1999, 148; M. Lewis 1992, 181). However, an understanding of resistance as performative introduces some complexity as to who can be the resistant subject in gender training or the feminist classroom. First, it is important to note that resistance to feminist analyses may also be performed by women, or by other subjects in marginalized positions. As feminist pedagogy has noted, in continuity with broader feminist analyses, 'students may be expressing forms of dominant ideology . . . in which their practices are invested without necessarily being members of the dominant group' (Bell, Morrow, and Tastsoglou 1999, 25). Resistance to feminist analyses is not the sole preserve of those who enjoy structural power and privilege, but may also be performed by members of oppressed groups who reap certain advantages from aligning their performance with the interests of the dominant group (see e.g. Stoler 2010; Kandiyoti 1988). Second, a conceptualization of resistance as staging particular types of political claims means that resistance does not only find expression among students or trainees. As is hopefully evident from the analysis in preceding chapters, clearly not all gender trainers subscribe to or practise feminist politics (as also observed of the broader field of gender training, see, for example, Ferguson 2019b, 115; Sexwale 1996, 61). My research archive likewise points to the fact that trainers themselves may be resistant to more progressive elements found in some training, or to more intersectional approaches to gender. Accordingly, the resisting subject of my analysis is not always the white heterosexual man, or the training audience; what is germane in this analysis is what is being resisted rather than who is the resistant subject.

I have already introduced the object of resistance as feminist politics and feminist analyses. To add some specificity to what is resisted in gender training settings, in broad terms, forms of overt resistance that I observed in gender training settings resonate closely with the typologies of resistance identified in the literature on gender training (see e.g. Lombardo and Mergaert 2013; M. Lewis 1992). By way of example, a western European NGO trainer I call Malcolm described his understanding of resistance to me in an interview:

> People talk about gender equality as self-evident . . . For me, it is political, it is inherently political. It is a norm, and the resistance we're talking about is people who reject the worldview that women are fundamentally disadvantaged, and that they're complicit. At best complicit and at worst actively contributing to it.

In this description, Malcolm pointed toward a form of resistance to feminist politics that is grounded in the argument that feminism, or gender training, is irrelevant, because equality has already been achieved. Further, Malcolm pointed to trainees' resistance to seeing themselves as implicated in perpetuating systems of dominance, suggesting that the imperative to deny the existence of oppression is intimately linked to the refusal to question one's own position in hierarchical relations. As such, his characterization of resistance maps onto what Lombardo and Mergaert describe as denial of the need for change in gender relations, coupled with a refusal to accept responsibility (2013, 305).

In addition to questioning the persistence of gender inequalities, the concept of 'gender' itself can be the object of resistance. A trainer I call Johanna recounted a training in which she attempted to distinguish between sex and gender, and in which a participant rejected this framing, saying 'but this is simply, you know . . . God has made us differently'. What appears to be at stake in Johanna's example is a form of 'anti-genderism': the rejection of an understanding of gender as socially constructed, and an insistence on a stable and reliable distinction between men and women (Korolczuk and Graff 2018). Such an objection to a socially constructed understanding of gender, in the context of peacekeeper training, lends itself to what Magda Lewis describes as 'phallo-centric myth-making' in the classroom, re-asserting traditional understandings of gender roles (1992, 184). For example, an NGO trainer I call Aisha recounted stories of military officers declaring to her that women were not able to perform in the military, and that they would refuse to be led by a female officer. These military officers associated fixed and traditional understandings of femininity to women as a category, and thus re-inscribed the essentialism of sex categories against any suggestion of shifting and contested (and contestable) gender roles. In other words, an objection to feminist analyses of gender, and a re-assertion of biological dimorphism, serve to undermine any political challenges to the status quo.

Finally, sometimes the object of resistance is more total and less specific, as Alessia described: 'there's the very open one where they, you're starting a workshop on gender and they're like: "Can we leave? We don't want to be here"'. As likewise observed by Higate, sometimes the object of resistance is not specific to the content, but rather evoked by the mere mention of 'gender' (2004, 19). I suggest that what such statements imply is that the resistance to feminist analyses and feminist politics is assumed to be so commonly shared in the institutional or cultural environment that it need not be specified any further. A blanket resistance to gender indicates resistance in the form of trivializing gender equality work, and is so prevalent that it becomes a form of patriarchal common sense that does not require further explanation (Lombardo and Mergaert 2013; Zalewski 2006, 58).

## Resistance Scripts: Joking, Distancing, Projecting

While the examples I used to describe the object of resistance above involve overt articulations of resistant logics, in many cases resistance is couched in more indirect discursive manoeuvres. Further, a focus on resistance as denying inequality between men and women or the need to address it can obscure the ways in which colonial thinking and heteronormativity pre-empt resistance and secure attachments to narrow understandings of gender inequality. In this section, I discuss in more detail the operations of such forms of resistance, which I characterize as: joking and laughter, distancing from feminist politics, and projection of questions of gender inequality onto racialized others. In discussing these resistance scripts, I do not mean to propose an exhaustive or fixed typology of resistance. These were simply elements of resistance that emerged from my research archive, and which I believe shed light on the epistemic and political implications of the gender training endeavour.

In describing these scripts, I also discuss how trainers interpret and respond to them. Training manuals that address the question of resistance typically offer an array of counter-arguments, ways of either pointing out the fallacious logic of the resistant statement or providing additional information to undermine these claims (see e.g. Reimann 2013, 51–55). In practice, however, trainers and audiences practise a number of pedagogical strategies in response to resistant claims. Their responses are equally important to understanding how the struggle over meaning is staged; responses to resistance that go beyond countering arguments are significant for understanding the epistemic and political effects of struggles over truth claims in the training setting.

## Joking and Laughter

When I first asked Alessia about resistance she encountered in gender training, the first thing that she brought up was not overt resistance in the form of 'Can we leave?', but rather 'the little joke cracked at gender training, before, during, or after'. Accordingly, I suggest that one script that resistance follows is less the kind of overt disagreement that lends itself to counterarguments, but rather a subtler undermining of the message of training through humorous interjections. Alessia gave this example:

> You do the gender training with this group, and then in the end somebody comes up with a joke: 'You know why in Afghanistan women now walk in front of men?' You're like 'Oh, why?' 'Landmines.' And you're like 'Ha ha ha' [sarcastic]. Or even more inappropriate ones, but it's just like . . . why did you feel you had the need to share this after a gender training?

Many trainers I spoke with related similar stories of trainees joking about the topic of the training. These jokes, like the example provided by Alessia, bring to mind philosopher Paolo Virno's (2008, 119) formula, according to which:

> Jokes reside in a no-man's land that separates a norm from its realization in a particular case. The point of the witty remark lies in its ability to show how many different ways one can apply the same rule. Or, if you prefer: in its ability to show that no application agrees with the rule; nor, after all, does it contradict the rule, given that between one and the other there exists an overwhelming gulf.

Although Virno does not delve into the content or politics of jokes, he does hint at a multiplicity of political effects in stating that the content of a joke 'is not always irreverent to the establishment and to social hierarchies' (2008, 165). Indeed, in the case of joking as resistant performance in gender training, the content of the joke appears designed to uphold social hierarchies, and points to the futility of trying to change them. To return to Alessia's example, this joke is showing different ways that one can apply gender equality thinking, pointing out the supposed absurdity or impossibility of more equitable gender relations.

Further, joking serves to establish or reinforce communal bonds (T.E. Lewis 2010, 642). By sharing a laugh, a group is formed; laughter serves to demarcate boundaries of inclusion or exclusion in the group (consider, for example, the 'inside joke'). Because of the social function of the joke, the use of inappropriate humour by training audiences presents trainers with a dilemma. While it would be wholly appropriate to challenge sexist, racist, or homophobic humour in the classroom, doing so risks being seen as the person who spoils the fun for the group—the 'feminist killjoy', to borrow Sara Ahmed's evocative term (2017, 65). By taking up the position of the feminist killjoy, the trainer positions herself outside of the in-group, which could have problematic consequences for her ability to engage in dialogue and be heard. To avoid this situation, instead of directly pointing out the problematic politics of such jokes, some trainers encourage self-reflection by pointing toward a problem, disrupting the flow of laughter, but stopping short of naming the problem directly. Another trainer I call Aisha explained:

> I call people on crap. When [a] military officer for St Patrick's day decides to put up a huge poster in the classroom of a big-breasted woman dressed as a leprechaun with her tits hanging out, saying join us in this bar, [I ask:] 'Do you really want to use that as a motivator for a social activity? Because I don't feel very excited'. That's what I said, and the next day it was gone. But I didn't tell him to get it out, I made him think about the reason why.

Aisha noted that in other situations, she might pose the remark made to the class, asking the group for differing opinions, noting that what was important was:

> Finding the right people to convey the message, because maybe I'm not the right person to convey the message. Maybe the right person to convey a message to a guy like that would've been [a male trainer] ... The message is as important as the messenger, right? It's not finding just who you need to speak, but how many different people, also. Sometimes you need the message to come multiple times.

In other words, Aisha's account appears to be characterized by a desire to avoid taking up the killjoy position in relation to trainees with a direct challenge ('That's not funny!')—a position which would likely be interpreted through the derogatory trope of the humourless feminist; the woman who can't take a joke. Arguably, being framed as the feminist killjoy would play right into the joke and rob the killjoy trainer of her ability to disrupt its meaning-making process.

While Aisha's account was focused mainly on demonstrating to the resistant trainee the error of his ways, Vincent saw this strategy as having broader implications:

> As a facilitator, definitely the last thing you should do is confront them directly. But the very least you can do is make sure they don't ruin the whole group. What you do is, you have other members of the group from the same context, from the same cultural milieu, from the same religious group maybe, not challenge the person, but indicate that he doesn't speak for the whole culture, or for the whole religious group, or for the whole country. That there are different opinions. And at least he may come out of the workshop believing that there is diversity of opinion. He may agree or disagree, but there's diversity of opinion, he doesn't hold the absolute truth.

Like Aisha, Vincent is arguing that a trainer should not engage in a direct debate with a participant, as this would lessen their situational power and undermine their credibility. Two further observations pertain to Vincent's account. First, he is drawing attention to the performative element of resistance discussed above, suggesting that perhaps the most important issue at stake is not to convince the resistant trainee, but rather to manage the scene so that 'they don't ruin the whole group'. Virno (2008) reminds us that a joke is performed for an audience, and that laughter creates a sense of community and agreement. There is a sense in Vincent's account that it is important to challenge the joke, not to convince the resistant trainee, but rather to disrupt its ability to create shared meaning among the group. Second, Vincent is highlighting the importance of providing different opinions, to challenge the notion that the resistant trainee is privy to some 'absolute truth'. In other words, I read in Vincent's account a desire to prevent the joke from becoming the basis on which a resistant in-group identity is formed.

The performative element of joking was also highlighted by a Nordic military trainer I call Kalle. I asked Kalle why he thought trainees made such jokes, and he responded that they are looking for 'some form of relief, or they are trying to be manly, or they are observing each other's manliness'. What Kalle was suggesting was first that a form of relief was needed as a break, in order to create space to, as he explained, 'have a bit of a laugh, and to think back on the things that did happen to many of them, even though you don't want to remember them'. In this sense, Kalle was suggesting that laughter provided a break in the discussion, a break that was necessary for dealing with the difficult knowledges that gender training brings to light. In other words, Kalle was drawing attention to the emotional, reactive discomfort that training participants might be experiencing. Second, Kalle surmised that misogynistic humour provided a way of performing a certain form of manliness, of re-asserting a properly masculine subject position that was made vulnerable or insecure by participation in gender training. Kalle's account highlights the resistant nature of inappropriate jokes in gender training—through re-asserting their status as properly manly men, trainees are signalling to one another that their subjectivity has not been transformed by the training.

Kalle's strategy for managing this resistance script was somewhat different from the challenges that Vincent and Aisha suggested. Kalle suggested that because the element of relief provided by laughter was needed to be able to cope with difficult knowledge, he built jokes into his gender training session, starting with the introductory comment: 'This is the kind of topic that you have to lighten the mood a bit at the outset'. Kalle explained that he was offering his own humorous comments as a way of pre-empting participants feeling like they needed to volunteer their own, possibly offensive jokes. At the same time, though Kalle did not mention it, the effect of his jokes appeared to also secure his own masculine status in front of the all-male training audience.

That being said, the purposive use of humour is not the sole preserve of military men. A western European gender trainer I call Johanna explained to me that she likes using 'playful' methodologies in training. As an example, Johanna noted that she sometimes slips and makes gendered assumptions, and that trainees 'love calling me out when I'm being not gender sensitive'. Johanna explained that she encourages this type of banter because 'I don't want anyone to feel there's this, you know, this angry person, who looks down on me if I say anything. That closes every door'. Like Kalle, Johanna could of course be read as upholding a normative arrangement in refusing to perform the angry feminist. However, I contend that there are good pedagogical reasons to ease discomfort experienced by trainees so as to maintain an openness to learning. In making strategic use of humour, Kalle and Johanna appear to be enacting the suggestion made by Lucy Ferguson that sometimes the pedagogical role of a trainer is to be a joker; that lightening the mood is necessary in order to bring down defences and for trainees to be able to engage with new knowledge, rather than shutting it out (2019b, 104). 'Laughter,' in other words, serves as 'a political operator [that] reconnects the disconnected' (T.E. Lewis 2010, 642). Rather than attempting to curb laughter, Johanna and Kalle appeared to try to control the content of jokes, while at the same time establishing a sense of community in the group that did not position them as outside of or in opposition to the group.

In sum, joking and laughter can involve either a performance of resistance to gender training, trivializing and mocking the topic, *or* a pedagogical strategy that seeks to navigate the pain involved in confronting difficult knowledges. This diversity confirms Tyson Edward Lewis's argument that there exists, in political terms, a 'complexity of laughters' (2010, 638). The political effects of laughter are neither guaranteed nor are they stable. Rather, joking and laughter are implicated in ongoing struggles over meaning.

## Distancing from Feminist Politics

Another way in which trainers and trainees perform resistance in gender training is by distancing the concept from feminist analyses and feminist politics. In this script, resistant subjects do not contest the importance of gender (narrowly defined) per se, but they do maintain a vigilance that the approach must not go 'too far'. They voice agreement, in principle, on the need for better gender awareness or more equitable gender relations, but insist that this approach should be distanced from, or constitute a disavowal of, feminist politics.

A poignant example of this resistance script played out in the multinational gender course I observed in the Western Balkans. On this course, every morning a trainer would ask participants to recap what they had learned on the course so far. On the fourth and penultimate day of the course, one participant asked to show a video clip which, he said, summarized his learning. The video clip was a seven-minute-long YouTube film titled 'Modern Educayshun [sic]', produced in 2015 by comedian Neel Kolhatkar. In the clip, Kolhatkar (whose social media presence is characterized by misogynist and anti-feminist comedy) is shown in a dystopian school classroom, in which the laws of science and meritocracy have been suspended, and in which students are rewarded in inverse relation to their 'privilege points'. In the opening scene, a teacher asks what the answer to '1+1' is, and Kolhatkar's character is horrified to learn that the correct answer is not '2', but rather 'equality'. When Kolhatkar's character protests the absurdity of the exercise, he is violently assaulted by the teacher and other students, who shout: 'Stop violating me with your different opinions!' The clip, in other words, exemplifies the violently misogynistic fear-mongering of so-called men's rights activists, who contend that feminism poses a threat to societal order, and particularly to (straight) men (Ging 2017).[4] After showing this clip, the participant shared that what he had learned was that it was important 'not to take gender too far', and that the video served as a humorous reminder of the (for him) very real possibility of taking gender too far. I was taken aback by this presentation, as in my view it directly countered and belittled the key message of the course. I hoped that another participant would challenge this view and was disappointed when none did. I was surprized and dismayed when the instructors on the course likewise let this intervention quietly pass and did not address the deeply misogynistic politics that it dovetailed with.

My surprise was perhaps unwarranted, as many gender trainers—rather than confronting them—pander to such views. They seek to pre-empt such resistance against feminism and 'going too far' by assuring their audiences that the version of gender that they are presenting is uncontaminated by such influences. Kalle, during the course of the Nordic pre-deployment training I observed, at one point noted about gender perspectives to his exclusively male audience: 'I can't find any kind of feminist point of view in this, in case somebody's horrified that soon we [men] won't be anything'. This desire to assuage men's assumed fear of feminism was also deployed by the western

European military trainer I call Robert, who noted that in designing gender training:

> We had to demonstrate that it was a mainstream issue. Which was sort of divorcing from a particularly sort of feminist agenda and just sort of explaining why people should genuinely care about this stuff.

Implicit in this declaration is, of course, that feminist demands did not constitute something people need genuinely care about.

Not only were Kalle and Robert invested in presenting gender as something that was safe from what they implied was an excessive and misguided feminist focus on women but they also sought to protect a binary and heterosexual gender order. Kalle explained that trainees might also be worried about a 'homosexual, purple hue' to the topic, but insisted to me that there was no such content in gender training. In a similar vein, Robert noted that a problem with the term 'gender' was that it can be associated with women and also 'associated with transgender in a bizarre way as well'. Both were keen to disavow any such content in their training. In this way, these gender trainers sought to make gender a 'safe' concept, amenable to hetero-patriarchal logics. By insisting that gender training should not be too focused on women, and especially not related to feminism, they were denying the ways in which gender works as a structure of power to create hierarchy and inequality. Rather, they sought to reduce gender to equivalent difference by, for example, concluding from the fact that men are also victims of sexual violence that there is no gender hierarchy. Further, the effort to rule out transgender subjects from discussion signals an unwillingness to question the normative framework of gender as fixed and given, rather than fluid and performative. These discursive moves are in no way unique to these individuals, but rather exemplify commonly voiced critiques of gender mainstreaming as a depoliticizing exercise which secures binary and essentialist understandings of gender (see e.g. Otto and Heathcote 2014, 10; Whitworth 2004, 121). Nonetheless, I suggest that we can also understand Kalle and Robert's approaches to training as a performance of resistance to feminist ideas, by seeking to make gender a safe concept, devoid of feminism, and reliably binary, cis, and straight.

While gender is typically emptied of critical feminist content in this way in training, some trainers clearly communicate that this a strategic choice rather than a personal conviction. Puechguirbal, for example, notes a need 'not to antagonize or "lose" the audience', signalling that what is at work is a strategy for managing discomfort (2003, 118). Similarly, Malcolm explained that creating a pedagogically productive space often required him to self-censor:

> Not only do I not come out as a feminist . . . I also present things in a less extreme way than I might otherwise. I don't use words like patriarchy, because it's not conducive, and . . . also within work I limit the scope of my activities to things that are more acceptable in the mainstream than my political opinions.

Malcolm related how he managed his performance in the classroom, not only as a feminist but also as a gay man:

> Usually I don't come out before I give sessions . . . I think there's a certain element of performance when you work as a gender trainer, and if people label you as gay you're somehow feminized. And you become less credible to some audiences. . . . There's a stereotype, and then there's a sense of betrayal, maybe, that they might see. That the gay man betrays their gender somehow. I think I'm comfortable being open once they've reflected on how they are also restricted by their own gender roles, but I think at the beginning, you might be seen as co-opted into some kind of female-led feminist agenda.

Malcolm, similarly to Puechguirbal, did not himself disavow feminism or insist on heteronormativity in training. In fact, he communicated his personal commitment to the feminist and LGBT movements. What was at stake in his account was a strategic distancing from stereotypes in an effort to maintain a connection with the training audience, in a bid to, as feminist pedagogical theorizing puts it, 'lessen the red flags' (Bonnell 1999, 216).

The strategic distancing of gender training from feminism nonetheless aims to introduce feminist ideas into the training when audiences are deemed receptive to it ('once they've reflected', as Malcolm put it). The trainers I encountered differed on when and how to push feminist analyses, indicating differences in strategy and their ability to transgress norms. Johanna, for example, related:

> Yeah, I do [disclose that I'm a feminist], and actually I enjoy, let's say I enjoy confusing people with that, because they think I'm too happy to

be a feminist [laughter]. And so kind of owning it and challenging the preconceptions that people hold.

While Johanna sought to challenge conceptions of feminism through her own performance, other trainers put up contentious questions for explicit discussion. On the West African course I observed, one participant asked during a group activity: 'Nature has made a man different from a woman. Rather than equality, why don't we talk about gender complement?' In response to this comment, Angela, one of the West African police instructors on the course, came back the next day with an addition to the programme: a forty-five-minute discussion on patriarchy. Angela described gendered issues such as female genital mutilation and son preference, and explained: 'At the root of this is the master's hand; patriarchy'. She described how patriarchy 'affects the way we are taught to act and exist in the world', and cited extensively from bell hooks' work. Angela clearly did not shy away from introducing feminist concepts to her training. In the face of student resistance, rather than distancing herself from feminist analysis, she drew upon its concepts and theories to articulate a stronger case for gender equality. When I spoke with her after the session, she admitted that 'patriarchy' is a difficult word for men, suggesting that it is hard for men to admit its existence because they often do not see it. Angela's training therefore appeared to be practising a form of what Megan Boler (1999, 175) calls a 'pedagogy of discomfort', demanding that students examine structures of inequality that they are implicated in. Contrary to what one might have expected, Angela's intervention did not provoke further resistance from the trainees, who quietly acquiesced. I do not believe this outcome to be a given, but rather a reflection of the personal authority Angela commanded in the classroom. The ability of trainers to practise a pedagogy of discomfort doubtless stems not only from their own political strategies but also from the position of situational and social power from which they are speaking.

What is clear from these examples is that the resistance script of distancing gender from feminist politics can dovetail neatly with deeply misogynistic and homophobic 'men's rights' agendas. This resistance script is performed by (some) training participants and trainers alike. However, interviews and observation of training practices also indicate first, that such distancing is sometimes strategic, and second, that gender trainers sometimes embrace the label of feminist and feminist analytical concepts such as patriarchy. Indeed, in continuity with one of the broader argumentative threads

I advance throughout this book, an examination of the resistance script of distancing gender from feminist politics reveals that gender trainers have complex and varied relationships to feminism.

## Projecting Gender onto 'Others'

If distancing from feminist politics constitutes one way in which feminist understandings of gender and their political potential are contained in peacekeeper gender training, then the projection of gender onto racialized others constitutes another. Like distancing, this resistance script is covert, insofar as it takes the form of agreement, in principle, on the importance of gender, accompanied by a simultaneous move to ensure that gender does not implicate the self in any uncomfortable knowledge. There are countless examples of how this projection works. I described in Chapter 2 Robert and Lasse's comments in which they positioned themselves, as Western men, as already gender aware, but noted that African peacekeepers needed instruction on the question. Similarly, in Chapter 3, I discussed the stubborn association of conflict-related sexual violence with the African continent. Both gender trainers and training participants often frame gender along the lines of the well-rehearsed Spivakian trope of 'white men saving brown women from brown men,' in which the problems of gender are reliably located in another geographical space (Spivak 2010; Pratt 2013).

However, this is not the only form that this projection takes. In contrast to the saviour narrative, one oft-heard comment in training settings, typically articulated as a resistant statement to the trainer, takes some form of: 'We have to be careful not to impose Western values on these societies' (this particular phrasing was used by a participant in the western European gender course I observed). While this statement appears to be challenging the white saviour narrative, it also constitutes a retreat to 'cultural essentialism', where manifestations of gender inequality are explained as inherent and immutable characteristics of 'other' societies (Duncanson 2013, 121; see also Narayan, 2000). Projection is therefore best understood as a script that is performed through a number of articulations, all of which have the effect of displacing the problems of gender onto the bodies of racialized others. These scripts are rehearsed by trainers and training participants alike.

Some gender trainers I spoke with recognized the displacement of gendered violences onto other geographical locations as a problem and characterized the move to do so as a form of self-preservation. Johanna explained:

> People like to talk about gender when it's 'over there', they like to talk about gender inequality in a faraway conflict-affected country. But when you talk about how actually their own understandings of gender, their identities, gender relations, influence the work; how there's power imbalances in the relations that they're in with partners or local contacts, I mean, that's when it gets really uncomfortable. Where it's challenging what you think, how you live your own life, and how maybe that, you prize yourself on being kind of a modern liberal citizen, and realise that in your daily life there's a lot that's not quite as 'modern' and 'liberal'.

Johanna's account of the desire of training audiences to locate gender inequality elsewhere, and to avoid critical self-reflection, attests to the well-established colonial mode of thought which projects undesirable qualities of the self onto racialized others (Bhabha 1994, 238). In a similar manner, Malcolm spoke about the problem of displacing gender issues elsewhere: 'It means you're stuck in the sympathy bracket, where we're just going to be crying about how sad it is that women in the Congo get raped, because we can all agree that's terrible'. Malcolm explicated that focusing solely on 'other' places in Global North training contexts is problematic because it fosters sympathy rather than empathy. Sympathy is problematic, as Megan Boler argues, because it elides questions of complicity. It allows trainers and trainees to 'exempt themselves from the category of the oppressor ... by saying that we too were nauseated' (Boler 1999, 186).

Some trainers and training audiences do then attempt to bring questions of complicity into view. Recall the frustrated declaration by a training participant described in Chapter 3: 'It cannot be that we encourage troops to violate the local population while we claim to protect them from violence committed among themselves!' Further, some trainers I observed sought to disrupt the dehistoricized and decontextualized discourses of gender training, which are operative in occluding questions of complicity from view. For example, in the training course I observed in West Africa, a West African police trainer I call Samuel talked back against the 'colonial aphasia' (Stoler 2011) that characterizes so much of Global North discourse. Samuel delivered a session on gender and security sector reform (SSR). Training on SSR typically focuses on political challenges and technocratic solutions, where the need for SSR is premised on the assumed mismanagement and/or incompetence of those countries deemed in need of reform (Hudson 2016; Kunz 2014). Contextualization in this training—as is the case with conflict-related sexual violence training—is typically limited to conflicts in the immediate past and recent political developments, which in turn effectively portrays countries targeted by SSR interventions as inherently corrupt and violent. In contrast, Samuel began his session by asking his audience of West African police peacekeepers: 'Why do we have these problems?', referring to corruption and police misconduct. The answer: 'Colonial histories'. Samuel spoke of the police services instituted under colonial rule and explained that their function was to protect those in power—'the colonial masters'. He argued that this was a common feature of police forces of the time in Europe as well as in the colonies. Samuel thereby gave police corruption and brutality a history; denying an ahistorical reading that would fix these as characteristics of West Africa in need of no further explanation. His insistence on historical context enabled him to speak back to colonial tropes that portray countries in need of reform as somehow inherently deficient. His exclusively West African training audience nodded approvingly to the lecture but did not volunteer further analysis. In a dynamic that echoed Samuel's point, it is entirely possible that the training participants' responses were muted by the presence, in the back of the room, of European guest trainers and a researcher.

In the multinational course in the Western Balkans that I observed, a trainer from the region whom I call Maja directly challenged especially the western European participants on the course to consider their own positionalities and complicities in peacekeeping operations. Maja facilitated a session on gender stereotypes. This type of session is fairly standard in gender training, and usually involves laughter and joking, as training audiences enjoy the opportunity to make jokes out of stereotypical ideas such as 'men are strong' and 'women are vain' with impunity. These sessions are often a source of mirth but end up doing little to demonstrate why such stereotyping may be harmful. To the contrary, they often run the risk of reinforcing notions of essentialized gender difference. Maja's session began with similar light-hearted exchanges, accompanied by cartoons that play on gender stereotypes projected onto the screen. The session then took a turn toward the serious. Maja showed the group a photograph of a graffiti, telling them that the photograph was of a wall in the Dutch peacekeepers' compound in Srebrenica.[5] The graffiti reads:

No teeth?
Moustache?
Smel [sic] like shit?
Bosnian girl!⁶

Maja asked the group to reflect on the fact that this graffiti was written by peacekeepers, who were ostensibly there to protect the local population. How would Bosnian women and girls, many of whom lived in refugee camps where getting nutritious food and maintaining personal hygiene was a daily struggle, feel knowing that their 'protectors' so callously mocked their plight? How could we expect peacekeepers to adequately protect civilian populations if they demonstrated such lack of respect? The atmosphere in the class became sombre—no doubt partially in recognition of the pain Maja appeared to be feeling in relating this example. At the end of the session, Maja noted that the training audience, especially those who came from outside the region, may hold certain preconceptions about what this post-conflict space would be like. Maybe especially the western European participants had certain notions of blindly aggressive men and violated women. She said that she hoped their week in the country would help challenge some of these stereotypes, and that they would get to know real people who lived there, perhaps coming to see them differently. With this example, Maja challenged Western peacekeepers' sense of self as an inherently benevolent and gender-aware presence and invited them to see the peace-kept population in a deeply humanizing light.

While the central involvement of local trainers, speaking from an understanding of their own context, is a particularly powerful way of challenging colonial discourses of projection, efforts to do so are also undertaken by some Global North trainers. Eric, a western European NGO trainer, spoke in our interview about consulting anthropological literature to deepen his understanding of the sociocultural spaces he worked in abroad. Katie, a western European military trainer who directed the course I observed in East Africa, told me that she now incorporates visits to a local women's organization into the course programme, both for her and training audiences to gain a better understanding of the local context, and to demonstrate the value of consulting women's groups. Other Global North trainers bring up examples of violence and inequality in their home contexts in order to underscore that gender violence cannot simply be written off as a characteristic of 'other cultures'. Such moments in training represent, I argue, a postcolonial pedagogical practice that seeks to disrupt forms of national stereotyping that present some countries (and peacekeeping contingents) as already gender equal, and other countries and contingents as pathologically disposed toward corruption and violence.

The script of projection, in sum, works to resist the notion that an examination of gender might require critical self-reflection. Instead, it follows a colonial logic, projecting any gender problems onto racialized others. This is a common resistance script in training, performed by training developers, trainers, and trainees alike. What is being resisted is not the concept of gender or gender training per se, but rather readings of gender that bring an 'intersectional analytical sensibility' into play (Cho, Crenshaw, and McCall 2013, 795). However, a number of gender trainers and training audiences identify this projection as problematic and seek to challenge the script by speaking back to colonial stereotypes, and by insisting on locating the peacekeeper self within history and power relations. As with the scripts of joking, and distancing from feminist politics, the performance of the resistance script of projecting marks a site of struggle over meaning; a meaning that continues to be contested, and thereby resists an attempt to fix its political effects.

## Conclusion

I began this chapter with the suggestion that an examination of resistance in gender training provides a way of seeing the political contestation at work in gender training for peacekeepers. Though resistance in and of itself is neither politically regressive or progressive, in this chapter I conceptualized it as resistance to certain types of intersectional feminist politics. I characterized resistance as scripted, pointing to the mutual implication of personal emotional responses and the availability of broader interactional frames, meaning that resistance cannot be adequately understood as a purely individual response. Resistance is performative, and it is staged in front of and for an audience, meaning that it marks an attachment to (or disinvestment from) truth claims that others are invited to share in. Accordingly, I have argued that resistance matters because it serves as a kind of weathervane for where struggles over the meaning of gender and the aims of gender training play out.

While overt contestation of the concept of gender, of the existence of inequalities, or of the desirability of addressing them, are certainly present in gender training classrooms, these are well documented in the literature on gender training and feminist pedagogy. I have chosen to focus here on subtler forms of resistance, which I characterize as following scripts of: joking and laughter, distancing gender from feminist politics, and projecting gender issues onto racialized others. These particular resistance scripts demonstrate that acceptance of the term 'gender' is often purchased at the price of intersectional feminist politics. Participants of gender training may be willing to accept the term 'gender', insofar as it is separated from feminist politics and non-normative sexual subjects. They may be willing to accept gender as long as the definition sustains colonial difference. Resistance, in other words, is not necessarily against gender in and of itself, but against attempts to make gender 'unsafe'; against having the term implicate the peacekeeper self.

In describing how these scripts function, I also examined strategies trainers and training audiences use to deal with them. The overarching observation of this discussion is that struggles over meaning are complex and dynamic. Trainers as well as trainees may take up a resistant position. Joking and laughter may constitute an attempt to mock or trivialise the topic of gender, or it may be part of a pedagogical effort to help students manage difficult knowledge. Distancing from feminist politics may echo deeply misogynistic agendas, but it may also be part of a deliberate strategic move, designed to introduce feminism or feminist concepts when the audience is more likely to be receptive to them. Projecting the problems of gender onto racialized others may produce either a desire to save 'others' or an unwillingness to challenge relations of domination. The logic of projection is disrupted by moments in training where trainees are invited to see peace-kept populations differently, or where they are asked to confront their own complicities in oppressive structures. These dynamics of struggle echo the argument I put forth in the introduction to this chapter: resistance is best understood as a process of negotiation, in which meaning is only ever contingently fixed.

While active resistance to intersectional feminist political projects may take on some rather jarring forms (I certainly felt a rush of anger and frustration when watching the video clip 'Modern Educayshun'), this does not mean that resistance is necessarily bad. If not all pleasure is good (such as laughter at misogynistic jokes), as hooks (1994, 154) reminds us, then neither is all pain harm. To the contrary, feminist work on pedagogy and gender training insists that 'for there to be learning, there must be conflict within learning' (Britzman 1998, 5). Indeed, Malcolm told me: 'I would be very disappointed to have a long training session where there was no resistance,' explaining that he understood resistance to be an indicator that training audiences have had to grapple with how the topic of gender affects them personally; that the training has unsettled or at least disturbed some established understanding. An instructor on the western European course I observed likewise expressed satisfaction that trainees were verbalizing their doubts, as this indicated, in his assessment, a willingness to work through these questions. Resistance, in other words, opens up a possibility for negotiation. After all, while hearing resistant statements may be uncomfortable from the point of view of practising feminist politics, it is not as if—pace Virno (2008)—these statements are introducing any new knowledge. Misogyny, homophobia, and colonial thinking are widely available as systems of meaning making, and often circulate freely in martial institutions. When they are evoked in a gender training setting, this resistance suggests that a struggle over meaning is being staged, not that some new meaning is disturbing a pre-existing feminist consensus. The outcome of such struggles is uncertain, but I suggest that the existence of this struggle has political worth in and of itself. The next chapter takes up these questions of feminist pedagogical practices and their uncertain politics.

# 5
# Small Subversions
## Feminist Pedagogical Moments

My account of peacekeeper gender training so far has emphasized the incommensurability of intersectional feminist political commitments with the militarized logics of peacekeeping operations. This analysis has highlighted how gender, in the context of such training, gets framed as a tool that benefits the operations of violent institutions, and how sexual violence is conceptualized as a martial problem that can be addressed through the use of force. I have further argued that peacekeeper training reproduces heteronormativity, and constructs gender along 'the colonial difference' (Lugones 2007). Gender, as the subject of peacekeeper training, gets figured as something that is reliably binary, straight, and normatively white, and any attempts to disturb this figuration provoke resistance. In sum, these analytical threads expose the different ways in which gender training serves the status quo of patriarchal protection, colonial difference, and heteronormative gender.

That being said, such framings may be dominant, but they are not the whole story of what happens, politically speaking, in gender training. In Chapter 3, I described the contradiction contained in the demand that peacekeeping soldiers care about sexual violence and protecting civilians, highlighting ways in which trainers and training audiences recognized that military action is insufficient and imperfect as a remedy to sexual violence in conflict, interpreting their acting on their 'humanitarian instincts' beyond their military mandate as an exercise of 'lateral agency' (Berlant 2011, 95, 117). In Chapter 2, I suggested that gender training is haunted by colonial difference and non-normative sexual subjects. Chapter 4, in turn, demonstrated that these hauntings produce a need to continually reassert the disavowal of such analytics, taking the form of resistance to feminist politics. I argued that the ubiquity of resistance signifies that these are ongoing struggles over meaning rather than secure conclusions. In other words, my analysis has sought to draw attention to the persisting ambivalence in the politics of gender training. Homi Bhabha (1994, 160) has shown that discourses of colonialism always contain contradiction and ambivalence, and that this internal contradiction provides an opportunity to destabilize and rework their meaning. Like all hegemonic discourses, the colonial and heteronormative logics of gender training are never *only* that thing but are also internally contradictory and unstable. In this chapter, I focus attention on how this ambivalence might be worked in the service of resistant feminist politics, asking: What does feminist pedagogical practice look like in gender training? What epistemic and political effects does such practice produce?

Deborah P. Britzman (2013, 112) writes of educational endeavours: 'All of this is a gamble with meaning, against the tide of predetermination'. In exploring the possibility that some peacekeeper gender training might involve feminist pedagogical practice, my intention is to provide an analysis that goes against the tide of predetermination. What do I mean? From a critical feminist point of view, that training in martial institutions robs gender of its radical political potential is not wholly surprising. In the analysis that I undertake in this chapter, however, I seek to highlight that this is not the whole story. Against a critical feminist analytical impulse (the tide of predetermination), this task requires an analytic mode in which bad conclusions are not fixed from the beginning, but rather in which it is 'realistic and even necessary to experience surprise', as Eve Kosofsky Sedgwick described it in her influential and evocatively titled essay 'Paranoid Reading and Reparative Reading, or, You're so Paranoid You Probably Think This Essay Is about You' (2003, 146). This is important, because to focus only on critiques and bad outcomes would risk producing what Sedgwick describes as a paranoid reading.

A paranoid mode of analysis can be characterized as a critical analytical stance that assumes that the nebulous workings of power are omnipresent and is determined to expose them in any object of analysis. Sedgwick's point of departure in describing paranoid reading practices is a conversation with her friend and colleague Cindy Patton about conspiracy theories that the HIV epidemic was engineered and intentionally spread by the U.S. Military. Patton, in Sedgwick's rendition of their conversation, voiced little interest in investigating the truthfulness of such claims, asking instead: 'Suppose we were ever so sure of all of those things . . . *what would we know then that we don't already know?*' (Patton quoted in Sedgwick 2003, 123, emphasis added). We *know* that Black and gay lives are devalued by the U.S. government; we *know* that military research is centrally involved in the business of killing. In a parallel move, critically inclined readers of my exploration of peacekeeper gender training might reasonably remark that *of course* the military militarizes gender knowledge, and, echoing Patton, ask: What have we learned that we didn't already know? Critical analytical practices may just confirm what we know, and in doing so they veer toward tautology. Such analyses become paranoid when they anticipate negative effects. Paranoia creeps in in the form of an anxious concern: '*There must be no bad surprises*' (Sedgwick 2003, 130, emphasis in original). Driven by this anxiety, paranoid analysis 'can't help or can't stop or can't do anything other than prove the very assumptions with which it began' (Sedgwick 2003, 135). Paranoid analysis, then, predetermines bad outcomes and closes off the possibility of surprise and learning something new.

The limitations of paranoid reading practices are political as well as analytical. Critical analyses often imply that exposing problems will spur action to address those problems. A singular faith in exposure, Sedgwick highlights (2003, 138), is a problem because:

> [P]aranoia for all its vaunted suspicion acts as though its work would be accomplished if only it could finally, this time, somehow get its story fully known. That a fully initiated listener could still remain indifferent or inimical, or might have no help to offer, is hardly treated as a possibility.

A reliance on exposure alone rests on a cognitivist paradigm that if only we *knew*, we would be compelled to act. However, critical scholarship has grown increasingly 'unsure of the self-authorising thesis that has given political motive to decades of scholarly work: that *knowing* is the means for knowing *what to do*' (Wiegman 2014, 7). Placing all critical faith in the practice of exposure, in other words, does not guarantee different political outcomes.

Paranoid analyses may not be wrong per se (after all, just because you're paranoid doesn't mean they're not out to get you), but they do have political and analytical limitations. Accordingly, if we work with an epistemology that locates possibilities for change in disruptive practices at the margins of hegemonic discourses (as I do), and if we take seriously the political possibility opened up by ambivalence and hybridity (as I argue we should), then it is imperative to remain open to, as Bhabha put it, moments that might 'alienate our political expectations and change the terms of our recognition of the moment of politics' (1994, 37). Hence why it is realistic and necessary to experience surprise. In that interest, this chapter takes up Sedgwick's call for producing reparative readings in addition to critical ones.

The notion of 'repair', stemming from the psychoanalytic work of Melanie Klein, signals the construction of a whole from part objects. It results in 'a guilty, empathetic view of the other as at once good, damaged, integral, and requiring and eliciting love and care' (Sedgwick 2003, 137). In other words, a reparative reading is determined to see the good as well as the bad in an object. It admits that in addition to uncovering problems, critique may also reveal desirable qualities in an object. Neither negates the other, and two opposing claims can be true at the same time. In the context of my inquiry, reparative reading means that, though I provide a critical account, I seek to account for the good as well as the damaged. Reparative reading insists on seeing the whole picture—not picking out only the problems or the positive aspects. This kind of repair is not a naive practice—it does not replace a determination to find only the bad with a determination to see only the good. Rather, a reparative critique is one that remains open to the possibility that an object (gender training) may be both good and bad feminist politics at the same time. It provides, in other words, a means for working with the ambivalent politics of gender training.

To that end, in this chapter I argue that gender training (sometimes) involves discernible moments in which trainers appear to be enacting the promise of liberatory pedagogy to function 'as a decentering, displacing, and transforming force in a project aimed at pursuing social justice'—that is, moments where feminist pedagogical practices appear to be at work (Peters and Lankshear 1996, 33). Examining elements of feminist pedagogical practice in gender training, I seek to provide an account of the politics of such practices—what, in other words, does feminist pedagogy in gender training 'do'? How might we think about its effects? In the latter part of the chapter, I suggest that feminist pedagogical moments constitute moments of instability, or 'small subversions', rather than an assured programme for structural or cultural transformation. I argue, however, that the smallness of these subversions does not render them without political worth. Rather, picking up on Britzman's (1998, 112) notion of 'a gamble with meaning', I suggest that feminist pedagogical practice in gender training might be thought of as a project that does not come with a teleological programme for feminist transformation so much as it is a series of destabilizations and delinkings for hegemonic logics. The gamble inheres to the notion that this a politics which fails or refuses to put forward a coherent alternative vision. It makes a mess of things without proposing a clear alternative. I further argue that this can nonetheless be understood as political work; as work that has meaning.

While this type of epistemic and political project does not guarantee a transformed future, it does highlight the importance of continuing to partake in struggles over the meaning of gender.

## Identifying Pedagogy as Feminist

My aim in this chapter is to acknowledge, describe, and reflect on moments in gender training that I argue amount to feminist pedagogical practice. In short, I want to draw attention to training practices that align with certain feminist politics and ethics. In order to do so, a few words are in order on what makes a particular training practice feminist. I do not wish to be too definitive or overly prescriptive here: feminist pedagogical thought covers an impressive array of thinkers, disciplines, and political and intellectual traditions. A common point of departure for many theorizations of liberatory pedagogy,[1] in which feminist pedagogical thought is often located, is Paulo Freire's groundbreaking work in *Pedagogy of the Oppressed* (1970) and *Education, The Practice of Freedom* (1976). Feminist pedagogies have been developed within women's and gender studies, and within the educational literature (Luke and Gore 1992, 8). Feminist theorizing on pedagogy draws on and reflects the many political and epistemological commitments of feminist theories more broadly, including but not limited to Marxist feminism (Maher 1987); Black feminism (Smele et al. 2017; hooks 2009, 2003, 1994); postcolonial feminism (Mehta 2019; Dunlop 1999); and queer feminism (Quilty 2017; Allen 2015; Britzman 1995). Feminist pedagogical theorizing has drawn insights from care ethics and Womanism (Beauboeuf-Lafontant 2002; Noddings 1988); postmodernism (Lather 1991); the study of emotion (Boler 1999); and psychoanalysis (Britzman 2013). Indeed, there are at least as many approaches to feminist pedagogy as there are strands of feminist thought.

Just as there is no one 'feminism' that works as a yardstick against which to measure the political credentials of any activity or intervention, there is no singular model of feminist pedagogy that serves as the template against which to assess gender training interventions. Nor is it my aim to establish such a model here. The goal of this exercise in reparative reading is a more open-ended one: it is to highlight how certain training practices draw from and/or align with traditions in feminist thinking on epistemology, politics, and ethics. In particular, I highlight how training practices can reflect feminist epistemological commitments to understanding knowledge as always situated within particular social, political, and historical locations, and how a feminist ethical concern with care is enacted in gender training settings. Before delving into the details of how such pedagogies are practised in gender training, I want to situate these practices within traditions of feminist theorizing, and outline whom I identify as the subjects of feminist pedagogy.

## Political, Epistemological, and Ethical Commitments

At the core of feminist pedagogical thought is the assumption that pedagogy is an inherently political exercise, imbued with power relations. Michel Foucault (1991) famously identified educational institutions as key apparatuses of power, and contemporary observers continue to posit that 'it is almost impossible to separate the arguments over social engineering, nation building, and economics from the wishes and institutions of education' (Britzman 1998, 2). Education is seen in critical scholarship as a traditionally repressive enterprise, geared toward the production of docile bodies and obedient subjects. Against the observation that there is in education 'a will to power' (Britzman 1998, 3), critical thinkers of various lineages have sought to envision a different kind of education: a transgressive education that works for social justice rather than for systems of domination (hooks 1994). This political orientation is unmistakable in feminist accounts of gender training: while military trainers and experts may argue for the need for gender training on the grounds of efficiency and organizational performance, many feminist gender trainers see training as a form of liberatory political practice, and advocate for its closer alignment with feminist pedagogical praxis (Ferguson 2019b, 71; Enderstein 2018, 52).

In terms of political commitments to social justice, a quintessential premise of feminist pedagogy is that it should be devoted to improving women's lives (hooks 1994, 61; Maher 1987, 94). On the one hand, the underlying policy rationale of gender training for peacekeepers is to better address the needs and priorities of the 'Woman-in-conflict' within the framework of the international Women, Peace and Security agenda. As such, gender training could be understood as ipso facto invested in ameliorating women's lives. However, a closer examination of how this commitment plays out in gender training underscores that the terms on which training concerns itself with improving women's lives is of crucial import. As we have seen, rather than centring the perspectives and experiences of women in conflict, gender training consistently marginalizes them in its episteme, constituting the Woman-in-conflict as an object of knowledge rather than as multitudinous knowing subjects. Further, the racialized frames of gender training allow peacekeepers to understand themselves as innocent protectors of the Woman-in-conflict, rather than being themselves implicated in the structures that produced her insecurity in the first place. Neither of these are particularly liberatory outcomes for actual women in conflict. A feminist critique of the politics of gender training thus requires not only looking at the extent to which it centres the goal of improving women's lives but also examining the terms on which these women, and the peacekeeper selves, are interpellated into the knowledge production scenario. While the political injunction for pedagogy to qualify as feminist may still be the goal of improving women's lives, the application of this principle in peacekeeper training underscores the importance of asking: on whose terms?

Indeed, an uncritical concern for the plight of the Woman-in-conflict can lend itself to politics that reinscribe unequal relations of power. Here, feminist epistemic commitments demand that feminist pedagogy foster the development of critical self-consciousness, in which the self is understood as relationally bound, as existing in and through webs of interdependence with others. I have already alluded to the problematic politics of empathy for women victimized in conflict and cautioned that empathy is not necessarily a normative good in gender training. Megan Boler devotes sustained attention to this question in her account feminist pedagogy, and urges us to ask: 'Who benefits from the production of empathy in what circumstances?' (1999, 164). If we think back to Malcolm's sarcastic comment, introduced in Chapter 4, of training scenarios where 'we're just going to be crying about how sad it is that women in the Congo get raped', we can see that the injunction to focus on ameliorating women's lives is not so simple. Rather, as Malcolm's example lays bare, there are many ways of addressing women's victimization which facilitate an imperial gaze, in which the 'self is not required to identify with the oppressor, and not required to identify her complicity in the structures of power' (Boler 1999, 160). In the face of this political problematique, I suggest that Boler's invitation to move from a practice of 'spectating' to a practice of 'witnessing' provides a critical understanding of how feminist pedagogy might be practised in gender training (1999, 184). Through the practice of witnessing, Boler urges us to 'undertake our historical responsibilities and co-implication', and learn to sit with discomfort; not to foster paralysing and unproductive guilt, but rather to construct '*genealogies* of one's positionalities and emotional resistances' (1999, 186, 178). This practice of witnessing constitutes a 'pedagogy of discomfort', and Boler concludes: 'Learning to live with ambiguity, discomfort, and uncertainty is a worthy educational ideal' (1999, 198). Accordingly, what I take from Boler's argument is that a feminist pedagogical praxis in the context of peacekeeper training must not only include a concern for ameliorating women's lives but must also be informed by a feminist epistemological stance, which involves a critical interrogation of positionalities at play.

These commitments to feminist politics, informed by feminist epistemic perspectives, require additionally an attentiveness to feminist ethics. Freirean understandings of liberation have been the subject of not only adulation but also a sense of unease for the ways in which they position critical educators as an enlightened vanguard in the Marxist sense (Lather 1991, 134). By doing so, these educational practices are liable to re-inscribe hierarchies in knowledge production. Post-structuralist feminist analyses in particular emphasize that even liberatory educational paradigms are susceptible to a will to power, both in terms of the prescriptiveness of their vision for social justice and their inevitable involvement with 'the essentially paternalistic project of education' (Ellsworth 1989, 306). No discourse, however emancipatory, is innocent; education must be understood as an 'interference' with its subjects' sense of self and psychic lives (Britzman 1998, 5). This attention to tension within liberatory pedagogical discourses has produced a call for constant reflection on the *ethics* of pedagogical interventions (Gore 1993; Ellsworth 1989). Such an ethics should not be premised on an assumption of the innocence of liberatory politics, but rather grounded in a recognition of their inevitable failures—'an ethics of failure' (Britzman 1998, 9). This insight complicates the call for a feminist practice of gender training, insofar as it demonstrates that feminism is not an inherently innocent politics, as its ethical practice also requires theorizing (Prügl 2016). Overall, the discomfort with a desire for mastery prompts many theorists of feminist pedagogy to refuse to articulate their pedagogical goals in terms of fixed knowledge, characterized by 'rationality, certainty, measurement, and control', and rather to locate ethical feminist pedagogical praxis in encounters that seek to undo relations of oppression (Britzman 1998, 2). Like much of feminist ethical thinking, this praxis is often grounded in consideration of how to do so with an attentiveness to care. There is, in sum, no paint-by-the-numbers approach to assessing the feminist credentials of a pedagogical approach, but rather this is a question of ongoing, contextual judgments over interrelated questions of politics, epistemology, and ethics.

## Practising Feminist Pedagogy

Context and positionality, as always, matter to how and on what terms these pedagogical commitments are deployed. Here it is worth reflecting on the subjectivities of those involved in peacekeeper gender training as potentially involved in feminist pedagogical practice. For Freire, a liberatory pedagogy enables people to 'develop their power to perceive critically *the way they exist* in the world *with which* and *in which* they find themselves; they come to see the world not as a static reality, but a reality in process, in transformation' (2005, 83, emphasis in original). This description captures the spirit of critical consciousness-raising, which is an ambition common to liberatory pedagogical approaches and many feminist gender training approaches. Critical consciousness-raising, of course, implies an active role for students in learning, and affirms that their experiences and perspectives are valid and important to the learning process. What is, however, notable about this vision of feminist teaching is the extent to which it is derived from experiences of teaching women's/gender studies classrooms and premised on the assumption that students share an experience of oppression that feminist theory speaks to. Consider, for example, hooks's characterization of her engaged pedagogy: 'When our lived experience of theorizing is fundamentally linked to processes of self-recovery, of collective liberation, no gap exists between theory and practice' (1994, 61).

This view of pedagogical practice, however, is by no means blind to differential power dynamics in the classroom, and has consistently interrogated who is authorized to speak, about what, and on behalf of whom (Mehta 2019, 26; Ellsworth 1989, 317). These forms of attentiveness to power relations within the classroom 'dispel the misplaced notion that feminist teachers merely facilitate a process emerging from a class that gives equal validation to any and all student values and attitudes' (Schniedewind 1987, 27–28). This attentiveness to power is particularly important in the context where 'our students are no longer necessarily already committed to or interested in feminist politics (which means we are not just sharing the "good news" with the converted)', implying that '[f]eminist scholars must change ways of seeing, talking and thinking if we are to speak to the various audiences' (hooks 1994, 111). The feminist pedagogical literature therefore offers a nuanced theorization of questions of student voice, political confrontation, and power in teaching and classroom practices. These questions are particularly germane for efforts to theorize teaching gender in the context of peacekeeper training, where students are typically not members of marginalized groups, nor do they (often) enter the classroom with a commitment to feminist politics. Accordingly, questions of voice and experience are of particular importance in thinking about how feminist pedagogy might be practised in institutional settings saturated with power and privilege (Ferguson 2019a; Cornwall 2016).

The recognition that students bring different experiences and values to the classroom—and not always ones predisposed to liberatory projects—does not negate the fact that these experiences and values inform how they engage with the material presented and their colleagues in the first place. Hence, questions of student experience and voice cannot simply be dismissed because they do not necessarily serve feminist political projects. Even if we are of the political view that not all students' voices need empowering, I suggest that feminist pedagogical theories' grounding in a politics of difference offers helpful analytical tools to navigating questions of voice and experience in the classroom (Ellsworth 1989, 322). This, however, is no small ask of gender trainers working in martial institutions. A politics of difference requires a double epistemic shift away from traditional modes of education. First, it requires taking students' experiences and feelings seriously, seeing learners as complex subjects with pre-existing histories and desires rather than as empty vessels to be filled. However, fostering student voice in this way risks giving in to a kind of tyranny of experience, in which student experiences cannot be challenged (i.e., 'I have not experienced discrimination, so discrimination does not exist'.). The second epistemic shift required then is to historicize experience and treat any knowledge deriving from experience as inescapably partial. Coming to see experience as valuable, but also as partial and situated, requires a willingness to listen to and take seriously the experience of others. It requires a capacity to entertain the notion that two contradictory views may both be true at the same time. This recognition of situated and partial knowledge amounts to nothing short of an epistemic revolt in a world characterized by liberal scientific rationalism. It precipitates 'poststructuralist crises of truth' in that it 'denies the reader's desires for certainty' and 'replaces coherence and resolution with vulnerability and ambiguity'

(Boler 1999, 169). What this means is that teaching gender in a feminist pedagogical sense is less about establishing a new regime of truth to replace an old one, and more about disturbing the notion that any one thing alone is true. It is not about replacing 'X' with 'Y' so much as it is about insisting on also seeing y, a, z, b, and an infinite number of other possibilities in addition to 'X'.

Creating the conditions to practise a politics of difference requires an attentiveness to operations of power within the classroom. Feminist pedagogical theorizing has typically focused on moderating the unequal power relations both between students and between student and teacher in a quest to create a more democratic and participatory classroom setting (Ellsworth 1989). However, when dealing with students who enjoy a socially privileged position, and draw upon classed, raced, and gendered forms of power in the classroom, the dilemma becomes 'how to acknowledge male students' "voices" without validating the racism and sexism inherent in their positions' (Bell, Morrow, and Tastsoglou 1999, 29). It is at this juncture that the consistency between feminist teaching practice and the insistence on attention to political context becomes germane. 'Because', as Elizabeth Ellsworth reminds us, 'all voices within the classroom are not and cannot carry equal legitimacy, safety, and power in dialogue at this historical moment, there are times when the inequalities must be named and addressed by constructing alternative groundrules for communication' (1989, 317). Accordingly, feminist pedagogical theory affirms the importance of using the teacher's situational power in the classroom to interrupt ideologies of domination: 'Feminism is a politic that is both historical and contingent on existing social relations...justifying the use of... institutional power to create the possibility for privilege to face itself and own its violation publicly' (Lewis 1992, 181). In other words, a key feature of teaching in feminist pedagogical theory is a constant attentiveness to operations in power—both in the classroom and in attending to the relationship between classroom power dynamics and broader social structures. Power is, in this analytic, both situational and structural.

If the student or trainee's positionality in the pedagogical encounter requires consideration, so too does the teacher or trainer's. Who can implement feminist pedagogy? First, I contend that in order to qualify as feminist pedagogy, there is no need for the practice to explicitly derive from or reference feminist theory. As Gayatri Chakravorty Spivak argues: 'When you practice... you construct a theory and irreducibly the practice will norm the theory, rather than be an example of indirect theoretical application' (Spivak et al. 1990, 44). In other words, in identifying instances of feminist pedagogical practice, I do not mean to posit a linear understanding in which theory must always be neatly separable from, and prior to, practice. Rather, I suggest that it is possible to engage in pedagogical practices that enact or create feminist pedagogical principles without being self-consciously involved in the elaboration of feminist pedagogical theory.

Flowing from this understanding of feminist pedagogical practice, I locate feminist pedagogy in moments of practice and specific reflections provided by gender trainers. While I refer to trainers who self-identify as feminist and who reflect on the relationship of feminist political commitments to gender training as 'feminist gender trainers', this fixing of political subjectivity should be understood as contingent and provisional. Though gender trainers have varying relationships to 'feminism'—with some using the term to name their political commitments, and others pointedly disavowing it—I do not wish to suggest that there is a linear connection between claiming feminism and consistent feminist pedagogical practice (see also Holvikivi 2019). Further, Sara Ahmed has shown that those working on questions of diversity in institutions typically have ambivalent relationships to institutions, simultaneously working 'for' and 'against' them, lending themselves to different forms of engagement (Ahmed 2012, 15). Accordingly, in this analysis, my epistemic approach aims to create space to understand individuals as inhabiting multiple and contradictory subjectivities, meaning that the politics of an individual are not understood as structurally predetermined, nor do I demand that they be consistent and unchanging. This perspective allows for people to be 'discontinuous, divided subjects caught in conflicting interests and identities' (Bhabha 1994, 42). As such, identifying a particular trainer's practice as feminist does not entail a fixing of a subject position. Indeed, throughout this inquiry, I try to resist fixing subject positions—whether that of the feminist, or the racist, or the homophobe—onto individuals, even while I interrogate what kinds of logics any practice or utterance aligns with. In other words, I identify feminist pedagogical practice through a reading of the politics and effects of the practice itself, rather than as flowing automatically from individual identifications or structural positions.

Finally, a word on the outcomes of feminist pedagogical moments. Many approaches to feminist and critical pedagogies (especially those produced prior to feminism's turn to post-structuralism in the 1990s) describe as their key ambition to prompt students to take concrete political action to enact change. For example, Ellsworth describes teaching a course that involves students undertaking protest action against racist school structures, and laments that in the broader field 'there have been no sustained research attempts to explore whether or how the practices [critical pedagogy] prescribes actually alter specific power relations outside or inside schools' (1989, 301). Such accounts suggest that the aim of feminist pedagogy is to produce a 'feminist revolutionary subject' (Hutchings 2013, 20–21). The expectation that critical education produces observable, explicitly political action, can be read as a variant of the question: Does gender training work? This, as I highlighted at the outset, is not the question that drives my research. My inquiry is instead interested in the epistemically distinct question: What work does gender training do? This question is informed by a post-structuralist understanding of knowledge as productive of ways of being and acting in the world, and training as a discourse that 'makes possible particular identities, fixes categories of things and people, and makes various forms of conduct thinkable' (Prügl 2010, 4–5). In this vein, I do not assume that in order for pedagogy to qualify as feminist, it needs to result in directly observable, explicitly political action. In this way, my reading of pedagogical practices through a post-structuralist understanding of knowledge departs from certain strands of feminist pedagogical theorizing. Rather, my interest in pedagogy is characterized by the more diffuse ways in which knowledge provides 'a grid of intelligibility' that determines the range of possibilities of who or what I can be in a racialized and gendered global order (Foucault 1998, 93). My inquiry is interested in questions similar to those Sherene Razack asks, seeking to understand 'who people think they are and how this informs what they do' (2004, 8) and examining 'how people are educated to participate in the social, how they are interpellated into practices that leave the trails of violence in their wake' (2004, 57). My designation of a particular pedagogical moment or practice as feminist in what follows is thus not contingent on a particular outcome or action taken by the student, but rather on how I interpret its political and epistemic effects.

## Moments of Feminist Pedagogical Practice

Against the backdrop of the militarizing dynamics of gender training for peacekeepers, several gender trainers I encountered during my research described and enacted practices in the classroom that align with the commitments of feminist pedagogy. In what follows, I describe such instances of feminist pedagogical principles at work, with a particular focus on two features of gender training practice: theorizing from experience and practising an ethic of care in the classroom. Some gender trainers seek to disrupt hierarchical classroom practices by emphasizing the importance of personal histories and lived experience as a basis for knowledge. They recognize their training audiences as individuals with needs and desires that exceed the learning interaction and relate to them in a caring fashion. Throughout, these pedagogical practices demonstrate an attentiveness to context, to the ways in which the positionalities occupied by trainers and training audiences have been historically and politically shaped. These endeavours are grounded in a recognition of the complex (dis)empowering effects of coloniality and patriarchy for men and women in different locations of the world. In this way, these approaches are involved in constructing the kinds of critical genealogies of positionality that Megan Boler describes as crucial for moving from spectating to witnessing. Through an attentiveness to complex subject positions occupied by training audiences, these approaches combine elements of a Freirean 'pedagogy of the oppressed' with a 'pedagogy for the powerful' (Cornwall 2016), or a 'pedagogy for the privileged' (Ferguson 2019a). Importantly, the trainers describe their pedagogies as aiming at liberatory politics rather than at enhancing the effectiveness of martial institutions.

## Theorizing from Experience

I argued in Chapter 4 that one way in which resistant training audiences and gender trainers attempt to ensure that gender is a 'safe' concept is by ensuring that it does not implicate the peacekeeper self in any unflattering self-reflection. In most peacekeeper training, gender is understood as a property of peace-kept populations and located in another geographical location. However, as also mentioned in the previous discussion, some gender trainers view this tendency to project the problems of gender onto racialized others as problematic. In response to such othering epistemic perspectives, Malcolm, for example, explained that his approach 'is always to try and get them to connect with a personal experience'. Trainers like Malcolm thus seek to expose to training audiences their—our—own complicities in the maintenance and reproduction of structures of power, in a training practice reminiscent of what Andrea Cornwall terms a 'pedagogy for the powerful' (2016, 76).

It is interesting to note that in these trainers' accounts, the quest to make training personal is often explained through the trainer's own relationship with feminism. Trainers I spoke with recalled feeling that something was out of joint as they encountered gender norms and discrimination when growing up. Johanna mentioned being excluded from the games that boys were playing in school because she was a girl; Malcolm related being forced to cut his hair at age eleven because his school deemed his hair too long for a boy. They recounted, in other words, events when they had felt something was wrong, long before they could name that injustice. Both talked about how, in their encounters with feminism in university curricula, they found the conceptual vocabulary to express what they had already felt and experienced. Their accounts aligned perfectly with a moment that countless feminists, including Ahmed, have described: 'In finding feminism, you are finding out about the many ways that feminists have tried to make sense, already, of the experiences you had, before you had them; experiences that left you feeling all alone are the experiences that lead you to others' (2017, 31). Both Johanna and Malcolm linked their own experiences of finding feminism to the reason that they wanted their gender training to feel personal. As Malcolm explained, he sought in his training practice to cultivate an awareness of gender dynamics in the everyday lives of the people he trained: 'I think perhaps fundamentally that was what got me into the field, was that once you see it in one instance in your daily life, you can't stop seeing it everywhere'. This pedagogical desire maps onto Ahmed's account of the development of feminist consciousness: 'once you become a person who notices sexism and racism, it is hard to unbecome that person' (2017, 32). I suggest that this desire to get trainees to see gender as playing out in their own lives is linked to feminist pedagogical projects that foreground critical epistemologies of location and interconnectedness. Insisting that gender is not something that is a problem 'out there' but that it also fundamentally shapes the lives and conditions of liveability of those in the Global North goes against the grain of much of gender training and its racializing and colonizing impulses.

This desire, which I interpret as a desire to foster a feminist consciousness, was coupled with an acknowledgment of the potentially colonizing dynamics of imposing understandings of gender, especially in transnational contexts. Malcolm reflected:

> What we're doing is we're providing a lens for analysis, and a language. And drawing attention to everyday interactions . . . and this is where I feel OK

about being a Westerner going to different contexts. [It is about] saying that I found these tools to be useful for better understanding my daily life; I'd be curious to see what these tools give you. I think pedagogically that's what we're doing: we're providing a framework for analysis and a language that enables individuals in your training audience to engage with both the training and with others.

The sentiment that comes through in Malcolm's statement is, I argue, linked to a feminist suspicion of universalizing, totalizing accounts of gender which, as I suggested in Chapter 2, appear to inform the design of gender training curricula in institutions of global governance. Such practice is commensurate with a feminist epistemology grounded on a 'foundation of difference', a position which 'suggests that we cannot claim single-strategy pedagogies of empowerment, emancipation, and liberation' (Luke and Gore 1992, 7). Malcolm's training practice implies a commitment to taking the context and life experiences of those he trains seriously.

His practice, I contend, reflects a feminist pedagogical ethic that resists totalizing statements and a desire for certainty. Indeed, his approach brings to mind the orientation of the '"queered" gender adviser' Marjaana Jauhola advocates for. This subversive figure queers the notion of expertise insofar as they refuse the technocratic demand to provide certainty and prescriptive solutions to problems. They do not assert a singular definition of gender as universal but remain alive to the messiness of contextual meaning. 'Instead of "knowing gender"' the queered gender adviser takes on 'the task of interrupting the processes of knowing and subverting the normalized understandings of gender' (Jauhola 2013, 174). In other words, I suggest that feminist pedagogical practice, while provoking moments of 'unlearning' established understandings of gender, remains cautious of the oppressive potential of seeking to replace old thinking with new and authoritative forms of knowledge. This pedagogical project is more aptly described as taking up the epistemic task of 'messing things up' for dominant knowledge paradigms (Zalewski 2000, 126).

In a similar fashion, Johanna recounted using training activities that encouraged trainees to share their personal experiences with the group, emphasizing the importance of 'listening to each other's ... struggles'. She explained: 'I feel that helps ... rather than me trying to give examples and definitions, helping them talk about it amongst themselves'. Taking students' experiences seriously as a source of knowledge is attuned to the feminist pedagogical critique which insists on recognizing students as subjects of their particular material, cultural, and political histories, and authorizing experience as a way of knowing. In other words, I suggest that Johanna and Malcolm's accounts are underwritten by a feminist pedagogical practice that is committed to fostering student voice, disrupting hierarchical norms of the classroom, and taking personal experience seriously. They involve ceding the epistemic authority of the trainer, and thereby enabling collaborative knowledge production practices. They seek to create the space for new questions, rather than replacing one dominant knowledge paradigm with another. Importantly, these endeavours are coupled with a desire to foster an understanding of the world as 'reality in process'—to enable trainees to formulate critiques of the practices they witness and partake in (Freire 2005, 83).

However, this feminist desire to centre student voice requires, as feminist pedagogical theorizing has pointed out, an attentiveness to context and power relations: 'to do this when we perceive a student's voice to have been marginalized based on their social location is clearly easier than when we are dealing with students whose "realities" we most wish to challenge (i.e., those of dominant social groups)' (Bell, Morrow, and Tastsoglou 1999, 36). Like feminist theorists of pedagogy, feminist gender trainers observe that the problem with validating experience is that doing so may also validate myths about gender equality. For example, Malcolm explained the dilemma he grappled with when women in his training group claimed that there was no gender discrimination:

> With women it's slightly more complicated and arguably, if people feel equal, it's not that nice to make them feel unequal, because you're making them feel less empowered... But I think it's also about suggesting that perhaps what they accept from society should be questioned.

Gender trainers have to grapple with the ethics of dispelling gender equality myths among audiences who may be personally invested in them; a question that ties in with the concern over whose experience is validated in classroom discussions. Concern over the politics of amplifying student experience is germane in peacekeeper training, which typically involves groups who occupy positions of relative power and privilege, given their position as soldiers or police officers. There are clearly limits to the extent that blindly affirming student voices and experiences can be considered a desirable outcome of gender training for peacekeepers, from the point of view of feminist politics.

One way of navigating this tricky dynamic between granting epistemic authority to experience emerged in Vincent's account, introduced in Chapter 4. Vincent highlighted that he sought to gather a diversity of opinions from among the training audience in order to demonstrate that no-one held the absolute truth. Vincent's pedagogical approach, I suggest, bears the markings of a feminist politics of difference, aimed at demonstrating the situatedness and partiality of knowledge claims.

Not only do gender trainers seek to demonstrate to training audiences the partiality of each individual's point of view but also they create moments that resemble Boler's description of a 'pedagogy of discomfort' (1999, 175). A western European NGO trainer I call Sarah recounted facilitating a session on men and masculinities:[2]

> It's something that a lot of the men, particularly the ones from a more military kind of background, would tend to, in the first instance, really kind of engage with: 'Oh, ok, you're talking about men. You're acknowledging that I have gender too, and that my experiences are relevant, and that we don't have to just talk about women all the time'. And so in that sense, they would be energized by it, but then when I started to unpack the ideas around militarized masculinities, and that being something problematic, suddenly walls would go up, and some of them would start interrupting me when I was talking.

Sarah further explored this discomfort, noting that with Western audiences 'it's important not only to problematise masculinities of others in conflict-affected countries but also Western, white men who are members of the army, or perhaps making policy'. Similarly to Malcolm pointing to training audiences who were happy to agree that women being raped in the DRC was horrible; here Sarah was alluding to Western training audiences who are all too ready to marvel over the supposedly monstrous masculinities of Congolese men as perpetrators of gender violence while never turning that critical gaze on male violence inward. In contrast to this impulse, the example Sarah used was U.S. President George H. W. Bush's decision to invade Iraq in 1990, and how a performance of militarized masculinity was implicated in that decision. Sarah surmised that the trainees' resistance to this framing was a response to their 'personal investments in notions of masculinity' being challenged. In this sense, Sarah asked her training audience to confront uncomfortable questions about the problematic politics of their own investments. While Sarah sought in our conversation to construct genealogies of their 'positionalities and emotional resistances', what the effect for the training audience was remained unclear (Boler 1999, 178). In this particular example, in Sarah's account, the resistant trainees sought to defend their investments indirectly, by arguing that 'the First Gulf war was a good war, it was an important war, it was justified'.

In other instances, trainers sought to get training audiences to recognize the politics of their own investments through activities that were separated from historical events, in what appears to be a strategy to pre-empt the conversation veering into the politics of whether a certain war was justified. For example, in the course I observed in the Western Balkans, a trainer from that region whom I call Dalia facilitated the 'King and Queen' activity. In this activity, the trainer tells the training audience a short, fictional, and purposely decontextualized story:

> A queen and king live in a castle. One day the king goes on a business trip. Before he leaves, he orders the queen not to go out of the castle until he returns. Nevertheless, moments after he leaves, the queen flees to a nearby village to see her lover. After spending several hours with him, the queen returns to the castle. However, the castle guard does not want to let her in because the king ordered him not to allow her to return if she left. At this point the queen returns to her lover to ask for his assistance. He tells her that he does not think they have a serious relationship, and he does not want to help her. Then the queen goes to see a friend in the village and asks for assistance. The response is that, unfortunately, the friend cannot help her because she is also friends with the king and does not want to destroy this relationship. The queen becomes desperate and again returns to the guard to ask him one more time to let her in, but the answer is still solidly 'no'. As a last resort the queen remembers there is a man with a boat in the village: she asks him to sneak her behind the castle (which is surrounded by water) so she can at least take her belongings and then leave again. The boatman agrees to this but charges the queen 500 euros and insists that the money is paid up front. This is not possible for the queen because her money is in the castle. Now desperate, the queen decides she will run into the castle, take her belongings and then run out. She attempts this, but as she runs, the guard shoots and kills her. The end.

In summary, after a number of twists and turns in the narrative—which involves controlling behaviour in a relationship, infidelity, seeking assistance from bystanders, and following orders—the queen of the story is killed by a palace guard. After closing the story, the facilitator lists the six characters of the story on the blackboard: the king, the queen, the lover, the friend, the man in the boat, and the guard. Training participants are then asked to rank, in order of culpability, who they believe to be responsible for the death of the queen. The trainer facilitates a discussion around the different rankings that participants come up with (for a detailed explanation of this activity, see Pepper 2012, 44).

I have observed and facilitated this exercise numerous times, and the ranking provided by participants is always varied, though typically with many assigning blame to the queen herself. The activity highlights the disjuncture between trainees' disavowing victim-blaming and following obviously illegal orders in the abstract; and their application of patriarchal sexual morality in their assessment of a particular case (the queen deserved to be shot, because she was unfaithful and disobeyed her husband). The differences between rankings are usually sufficient to spark a debate in the classroom. The trainer may intervene with further questions to encourage participants to reflect on their reasoning. What if the queen had left to see her sick mother, instead of a lover? Would our understanding of culpability change? What about if the king had gone to see his mistress? Why do we assume that the king, and not the queen, is the sovereign? And of course, the favourite of military audiences: Was the king's order an obviously illegal order? (Referring here to a soldier's obligation under international humanitarian law to disobey obviously illegal orders.) Was it the duty of the guard to carry out the order or not?

In this instance, Dalia focused on the illegality of the order, and practised a pedagogy of discomfort by pointing out to the trainees after the discussion that the point of the exercise was to show that: 'When we think something is morally wrong, we find excuses for actions that are illegal'. Dalia ended the session on an empathetic note: 'When I was introduced to this exercise, I gave the same answers as most of you because I come from a patriarchal family, and I've worked for the military for seventeen years. But as I've done this exercise many times, I've changed my mind'. I read Dalia's statement as fostering a critical awareness of the ways in which patriarchal modes of thought inform our thinking, but also providing a hopeful indication that it is possible to question these ways of perceiving the world. In this sense, Dalia was not simply fostering unproductive feelings of guilt but rather attempting to give her audience the tools with which to critically interrogate their own positionalities.

Finally, while the examples I have provided here primarily demonstrate how gender trainers develop feminist pedagogical approaches that combine elements of a pedagogy for the oppressed with a pedagogy for the powerful or privileged, it is worth highlighting that to understand peacekeeper training audiences as singularly privileged would be an oversimplification. Although soldiers and police officers doubtless wield power conferred upon them by both uniform and weapon, it is also the case that many of them join these services from situations of economic deprivation. Further, while Global South/majority world peacekeepers count for the majority of troops and police contingents deployed, gender expertise and gender training are dominated by actors based in the Global North/minority world. Power and privilege thus operate in complex ways in the gender training scenario.

Indeed, trainers I spoke with were attentive to complex positionalities and multifaceted relations of power in the classroom. For example, Malcolm recalled a training course held in Southern Africa with a majority Black audience. A male trainer from a local NGO had asked a group of around fifty service men and women to reflect on who had been a male role model in their lives. Many trainees were troubled by the question, and several told the trainer that they could not think of anyone. A few participants shared stories of growing up with fathers who were absent, abusive, or alcoholic, and one young man reported that he was his own role model because he had provided for his family from an early age after his father left. Malcolm raised this example out of a wish to recognize that many military personnel come from socially or economically deprived backgrounds where a history of dispossession and oppression contributes to ongoing economic marginalization. In recounting this incident, Malcolm sought to recognize that racist patriarchy has complex (dis)empowering effects for men as well as women. I suggest therefore that what these trainers' practice demonstrates is that it is ethically suspect to assume that training audiences in peacekeeper gender training are singularly privileged subjects, and that a feminist pedagogical practice should be attentive to shifting and uneven relations of power in the classroom.

## Care and Classroom Dynamics

Feminist pedagogical theorizing has long been attentive to the fact that asking students to share personal experiences in the classroom can involve the evocation of 'difficult knowledge' (Britzman 1998, 11). While some gender trainers, as we have seen in Chapter 4, seek to avoid discomfort in the first place by, for example, assuring trainees that there is no feminist or homosexual agenda at work in the training materials, others, as described above, practice a 'pedagogy of discomfort' (Boler 1999, 175). The latter is a process that requires a great deal of care—in two senses of the word. First, introducing such conversations to the classroom requires an attentive handling of the topic for instrumental reasons. Care must be taken to ensure that students feel comfortable sharing experiences, and that the conversation is facilitated in a way that allows for self-reflection instead of defensiveness and the hardening of already established opinions and self-perceptions. Second, facilitating these kinds of conversations also often involves care as an *ethic*; as a normative commitment. Care as instrumental concern and care as ethic are of course not mutually exclusive, but often emerge as intertwined concerns in feminist pedagogical practice in training.

Martina, a civilian faculty member at a multinational security studies institution in western Europe, spoke of the need to attend to students' experience in a holistic manner. She reflected that students need time and space 'to become familiar with a topic, or to feel safe with a topic, or to become interested in the topic, and curious about the topic'. For Martina, the emotional aspects of learning are of particular significance in the context of gender training:

> For gender you need the space even more... If you've never thought about this in your whole life, it has so many implications for your private life, for your family, marital relationships, with your friends, so many different aspects... [You need to create] the space for an opening, for rethinking their own relationship with the world.

Martina's assertion that her students require time to think through questions of gender was posed in juxtaposition to the neoliberal demands for efficiency so often made of gender training, which result in restrictions on the amount of time available (see also Mukhopadhyay 2014, 362; Sexwale 1996, 61). She complained that in her training institution, students' schedules were filled with activities, and that empty space in the schedule was seen as wasted time. Her complaint was echoed by the Nordic military trainer Kalle, who likewise noted:

> You could easily spend [more time] on this, we could discuss and mull over questions, doing small group work and talking about things. That would be a good thing. There's a lot of experience in the classroom, that we could ask about from those people . . . we could use that as the basis for the session. But then there isn't enough time. That's a challenge.

Kalle and Martina's sense of not having sufficient time to delve into questions of gender is common in the world of gender training (as also documented by Alaga and Birikorang 2012, 17). Instead, gender training becomes subject to, per Foucault, 'a theoretically ever-growing use of time: exhaustion rather than use; it is a question of extracting, from time, ever more available moments and, from each moment, ever more useful forces' (1991, 154). Against this regime of temporal regulation, Martina developed ways to carve out time and space for her students to rest, enjoy themselves, and let the ideas that their academic programme provided sink in. Martina explained that she tried to create more space for them by organizing a city tour, and releasing students early on Fridays, recognizing that they had travelled from far and had spent substantial time away from their families, and needed to 'buy presents for their children'. By doing so, she challenged the military organization's view that the subjectivity of students could be reduced to their function as knowledge acquirers. She recognized them as individuals, with needs, hopes, and desires that exceeded their student role. Martina was thus demonstrating a caring orientation in her approach to pedagogy.

In a similar display of attentiveness, many of the gender trainers I observed took an active interest in the training participants as individuals. This attentiveness was evident in how instructors paid attention to the energy levels of the participants, and to how much each participant contributed to conversations. They put a lot of thought into the composition of small working groups, ensuring that shy or reserved participants would not be paired to work with someone who was likely to dominate them in conversation. For example, Katie, a western European military officer and gender adviser, who was the course director of the training I observed in East Africa, constantly shared observations with me about levels of participation in the training group and introduced fun activities such as tossing a ball around the classroom when she felt energy levels were waning. She subtly monitored each trainees' classroom participation, seeking to understand and address any barriers to participation, such as gendered interaction dynamics, language issues, shyness, or any other inhibiting factors. Katie was consistently observing classroom interactions and asking herself questions that are familiar to feminist observers: 'Who speaks? For what and to whom? Who listens? Who is confident and comfortable and who isn't?' (Lather 1991, 144). This type of caring activity extended beyond the classroom as well. All the course directors I observed were constantly engaged in making sure participants were comfortable and supported, through activities that ranged from personally ensuring that all participants' accommodation during their stay on the course was satisfactory, to writing letters of support for them to their superior officers, trying to help students in their career progression.

While a strand of feminist pedagogical theorizing argues that care is both a feminine quality and a feminist ethic, as with feminist pedagogy's advocating theorizing from experience, this pedagogical commitment requires careful contextualization in practice (Maher 1987, 92; see e.g. Beauboeuf-Lafontant 2002; Noddings 1988). As Laura Duhan Kaplan (1994) warns, the idealization of care as feminist ethic can support patriarchal militarism. First, associating care with femininity risks affirming the essentialized gender difference—of women as innocents and carers of children and the home front—that animates patriarchal militarism. Second, caring activity is easily recruited to the service of an imagined 'us' (who are deserving of care) over an imagined 'them' (who are devalued and not cared for) (Kaplan 1994, 123). Kaplan's critique reveals that in order for care to qualify as feminist pedagogical practice in gender training, a careful contextualization is in order.

I am actually relatively less concerned by Kaplan's first critique of care ethics reproducing gender difference in the context of peacekeeper gender training. I contend that this type of care is not an essentially feminized characteristic in the context of martial institutions. This is because the type of camaraderie that is often observed in military units and thought to foster 'cohesion' can also be understood as maintained by caring activity (Whitworth 2004, 159; see also; King 2013; Furia 2009; Titunik 2008). For example, while the course directors who were making sure that the course participants had adequate lodgings, food, and access to healthcare when they needed it can be understood as performing care work, it is worth noting that these are also the typical responsibilities of a commanding officer. Seen in this light, we may understand care as an integral feature of the functioning of martial institutions and recognize that these institutions have figured out ways to incorporate it into their culture, potentially amounting to a re-gendering of care as an attribute of military masculinity. Care in this context does not, then, necessarily reproduce the 'woman as caretaker' ideology that Kaplan critiques.

The potential of care to contribute to the devaluing of others, in contrast, is an important concern in martial institutions. Extending Kaplan's argument, I suggest that care is closely related to love as an emotion that binds together groups. Such love, in turn, is predicated on distinguishing members of the group from those who are excluded. Ahmed provides an example of this dynamic, famously arguing that white supremacist groups—groups often understood as hate groups—draw on the emotion of love rather than hate to produce a sense of group belonging: 'those who love this nation . . . anyone who loves liberty', and so forth (2014, 122). Bearing in mind this warning, I contend that care is not inherently or necessarily a feminist ethic. Rather, care can be an activity that demarcates those who belong from those who do not. As was the concern with validating personal experience and voice in the discussion above, the *politics* of caring depend as much on *who* is cared for and *on what terms*. Care as feminist ethic requires recognizing the complex positionalities and multidirectional power dynamics at work in this setting. It involves making choices and taking a stand.

In the East African training course I observed, Katie demonstrated how such care ethics are negotiated in practice. During a session on cultural competence, facilitated by another western European woman military instructor, a particularly uncomfortable exchange unfolded. When the instructor asked the group whether cultures can change, a West African military officer offered the example of female genital mutilation (FGM) in her home country. Another West African military officer added to this, speaking about how in her generation cutting was the norm, but how this is changing, and how she would not allow anyone to cut her daughter. Strongly implied in both women's comments was that FGM was a practice they knew intimately. At this juncture, a western European military officer, a young white man, asked the two women whether they knew where the tradition of FGM came from. When they referred him to culture and religion, he launched into a historical explanation of Arab trading routes that nobody asked for, describing how these facilitated the spread of the custom of FGM. This display of 'mansplaining' was interrupted by a loud snort from Katie in the back of the room who interjected: 'It's amazing that you think you should explain

FGM to our West African sisters. I think you have just given us a pretty good example of how *not* to do cultural awareness'. Katie's interruption of this conversation demonstrated that the politics of the classroom require an ongoing attentiveness to power relations, and affirmed that 'it may be necessary to exercise teacher authority and interrupt relations and ideologies of domination in the classroom' (Bell, Morrow, and Tastsoglou 1999, 40). In other words, Katie as the course director had to choose between allowing two Black women to be talked over and condescended to and embarrassing a white man. Katie's choice demonstrates the need to complicate our understanding of care as feminist ethic; it reveals that refusing to embarrass a training participant is not straightforwardly the most caring choice. Practising care ethics requires instead an attentiveness to relations of domination in the classroom.

Katie's interruption of relations of domination in the classroom provides one example of the political considerations underlying care ethics in training. However, to develop an account of feminist care ethics as part of peacekeeper gender training, it is essential to also consider the politics of caring for peace-kept populations. Recalling the moment in which Maja asked her audience to consider the significance of the graffiti disparaging Bosnian women, described in Chapter 4, provides an example of a gender trainer extending an ethics of care toward the peace-kept population. In showing that peacekeepers themselves were implicated in the harm experienced by peace-kept women, Maja made her audience uncomfortable. Again, this pedagogical strategy required an assessment of who our caring energies should be directed toward. I argue, based on the examples provided by Katie and Maja, that an ethics of care should foreground a consideration of relations of power and domination. In other words, for a pedagogical practice to qualify as feminist, it needs to be contextually grounded and informed by relations of power between the beneficiaries of caring labour.

## Strategizing at The Margins: Small Subversions

The examples detailed above offer a reparative reading of peacekeeper gender training insofar as they demonstrate the possibility of practising feminist pedagogy within this endeavour. In short, they reveal that not all training simply reinforces martial thinking. In fact, feminist pedagogical practices appear to subvert martial logics. They challenge uniformity by affirming the importance of personal histories and lived experience; by making the training personal. They trouble the saviour narrative in which peacekeepers are portrayed only as protectors, not perpetrators of gender violence, by suggesting ways of knowing our own complicity in unequal structures of power. They destabilize military modes of caring by disrupting relations of domination. They create a space that contains the possibility of unearthing contextual, situated knowledges that reveal the historical and social contingency of peacekeeping interventions. All of which goes against the grain of what I have identified in earlier chapters as the militarizing dynamics of gender training. And yet these subversions take place within military institutions; institutions of hegemonic masculinity. So how do these gender trainers get away with it? Perhaps one of the reasons that feminist pedagogical practices manage to fly under the radar, so to speak, of these institutions is because though their pedagogical practices are subversive, these subversions are small. Which raises the question: What does this ambiguity *mean*, politically speaking? How might we think of the significance of such subversions? These are not large, paradigm-shifting changes; they are best characterized as moments of instability and disruption.

## Strategically Feminist

Feminist gender trainers and gender experts are often characterized (and self-represent) as 'Trojan horses' who smuggle feminist knowledge into martial institutions under the guise of technical-neutral gender expertise, including through gender training (see e.g. Kunz 2016, 103; Prügl 2013, 60; Woodward 2001, 3). Gender trainers who named their politics as feminist noted that the Trojan horse strategy was enabled by the fact that their work was not perceived as challenging the institution in any significant way. Johanna, for example, identified not only an obstacle but also an opportunity in the fact that gender remains a marginal question in peace and security work:

> By gender never being taken, or often not being taken seriously, I've had a lot of space to do things that worked. And gender not understood as being something so political, and going to the core of everything, I was given that space to do quite a lot of things. So, I guess, that has worked for me in many ways too.

Johanna thus described a Trojan horse strategy of taking advantage of the fact that her work was seen as unthreatening, as something not 'political', to carve out space for creative feminist interventions. Key to this strategy, I argue in this section, is carefully managing the pedagogical encounter of gender training so that the exchange does not upset audiences to the extent that they disengage from dialogue, or that it does not reveal the full extent of the subversive nature of the exercise.

In order to understand how the Trojan horse strategy works, how feminist gender trainers manage to keep doing what they are doing, it is important to recognize that the instances of feminist political practice identified in the previous section take place within institutions of hegemonic masculinity. In this environment, hegemonic 'norms of recognition determine what can be read, heard and understood as intelligible and legible' (Dhawan 2012, 47). Trainers who subscribe to a transformative feminist political agenda are therefore constrained both by what can be said in the institution and by what can be heard by their audience. Even if feminist pedagogical practice does not necessarily entail an unwavering commitment to being the 'happy gender trainer' (as introduced in Chapter 2), singularly committed to not upsetting the audience, gender trainers practising feminist pedagogy do nonetheless have to be strategic as to how far they can push their analysis before it causes such an irreconcilable break with the trainees' ways of being in and understanding the world that the conditions for genuine dialogue dissipate.

Martina explained the importance of easing training audiences into the topic slowly, for them to feel 'safe so that they don't feel it's this feminist thing so I have to [shut down]'. In other words, she worked with what gender trainer Lucy Ferguson describes as a 'calculated ambiguity', designed to not push training audiences (or the institution commissioning the training!) so far that possibilities for being heard would disappear (Ferguson 2019b, 30, 33). Malcolm reflected on an instance in which his training audience included individuals who identified as feminists, and who vociferously disagreed with their colleagues:

> I agree with what you're saying, but by shouting at people and calling them chauvinists, which did happen in [one training], and saying you need to read books, you're very uneducated in this topic, I've done a Master's degree in gender studies and I'm tired of this bullshit, I think that can be kind of difficult.

The exchange Malcolm describes sounds like the situation Ahmed (2017, 187) calls 'feminist snap'; a moment in which one finds the demands of the situation too much, and refuses to bear them any longer: 'I'm tired of this bullshit'. Feminist gender trainers themselves sometimes teeter close to snapping. I described in Chapter 4 how Johanna said that she enjoys confusing audiences who believe her to be 'too happy to be a feminist'. At the same time, Johanna reflected on the stereotype of the angry feminist: 'No wonder that you're being made out as a feminist for being a difficult and angry person because it *does* make you very angry about a lot of things'. While acknowledging the reasons for feminist anger, both Johanna and Malcolm argued that in the pedagogical encounter, being angry or confrontational was unlikely to be productive. Gender training, as a strategic enterprise, does not allow for feminist snap among its practitioners.

Gender trainers who practise feminist pedagogy regulate not only their affective performance but also the concepts and terms on which they speak. In contrast to Malcolm's feminist trainees who insisted that their colleagues should pick up a book and educate themselves, Johanna described her practice as a work of translation:

> I can't make my colleagues read *Gender Trouble*... they're not going to do a PhD in gender studies, so if I want to see change then I kind of need to translate slightly what is happening, you know, what the thinking is in academia and what we can take from that, and make that kind of come into our work.

Johanna's characterization of her work relates to an understanding of gender training as a practice that involves 'working across epistemological contexts' and that thus requires the work of translation from one epistemic register to another (Mukhopadhyay and Wong 2007, 13). Her reflection not only describes strategies employed by gender trainers to ensure that they can be heard but also offers a useful reminder for the grounds on which academic critiques of gender training should be formulated. It calls attention to her 'contextual entanglements' (Chappell and Mackay 2021, 324). She suggests that maintaining theoretical purity is not feasible in her work. Johanna recognizes that her colleagues who work in this field have neither the time nor inclination to develop the kind of understanding of academic debates on gender that would allow them to grasp the nuances of gender theory. Nonetheless, Johanna maintains that the insights of this work can inform practice. In other words, her reflection reminds us that academic critique of gender training should not be based on how closely its conceptual vocabulary resembles that of feminist works, but rather on how their ideas are being made to work through translation.

In taking up this work of translation, feminist gender trainers pick up both the vocabulary of the institution they are working in and its discursive frames. For example, gender trainers often deploy the language of operational effectiveness, or remain silent about their feminist political commitments, in a bid to be taken seriously by the institutions they are working in. Vincent provided an example of adapting to the frameworks of the audience, describing a training he was involved in where participants consisted of military and police officers from a number of African countries. Vincent noted that many of the participants' home countries have in place the kinds of anti-sodomy laws used to persecute homosexuals, and reflected on his decision to work within that framework:

> If you're working with a group of police officers, no matter how repugnant the idea of LGBT being illegal is to you, you cannot ask police officers to break or ignore the law. [But] I think you can introduce other ideas that make them think a little bit deeper. My point was clear: that you perceive a person to be gay doesn't have anything to do with their rights as a citizen, their rights as a victim of a crime, their reliability as a witness of crime. Has nothing to do with it... You're not directly challenging the law directly, but you're asking them to consider their [LGBT subjects'] humanity.

In other words, Vincent described how he both worked within the frameworks and the vocabulary of the institutions he was working with (by not challenging the law directly); as well as how he sought within that frame to prompt his training audience to examine the question from another angle. His personal disagreement, expressed in terms of anti-gay laws being repugnant to him, informed his decision to try and frame the question differently; while the invitation he received to work with the institution in the first place dictated that he could not simply work against its norms. In his attempt to reframe the question, Vincent is both repeating a norm (accepting legal persecution of gays) as well as introducing a slight difference to that norm in its very repetition (considering their humanity).

Vincent's strategy of speaking within the normative framework of the context can be usefully thought of through Bhabha's conceptualization of mimicry (1994, 121). Mimicry involves the colonized adapting to and adopting the norms, language, dress, and mannerisms of the colonizer. However, this adoption is not simply an imitation; it involves 'an ironic compromise' in the form of a 'double articulation' where the repetition of the norm is never a faithful replica of the original (Bhabha 1994, 122). This deliberately imperfect repetition of the norm produces the effect of mocking the norm, exposing its ambivalence, and thereby resisting its power. I cede of course that there are ways in which Bhabha's analytic resists application to this example: Vincent, as a western European NGO employee, hardly occupies the position of the colonized in relation to the African police and military officers who make up his audience. Nonetheless, as a gender trainer invited into a martial institution, his presence is contingent upon his ability to play by the rules of the organization. The anti-gay laws that Vincent is attempting to subvert, in this scenario and in the limited context of the gender training, constitute a hegemonic discourse. The relations of power that enable the comparison to mimicry are therefore situational rather than structural.

Though it has subversive potential, mimicry is a politically risky strategy: irony has notoriously unpredictable political effects. One of these risks is that the ironic element of mimicry can be misunderstood or even lost. I suggest that when feminist gender trainers are consciously employing the strategy of mimicry, we can think of them as articulating a lie. I do not mean this in a derogatory sense: as Adrienne Rich (1995) explains, lying is a strategy commonly used by those in marginalized positions to ensure their own survival. Women have long been lying to men—laughing at inappropriate jokes, politely brushing off unwanted advances—in an attempt to keep themselves safe from violence. In the case of feminist gender trainers, they are lying insofar as they speak the language of martial institutions in order to be heard, even when they do not personally subscribe to these logics. Importantly, Rich cautions: 'There is a danger run by all powerless people: that we forget we are lying, or that lying becomes a weapon we carry over into relationships with people who do not have power over us' (1995, 189). I bring up Rich's warning as a way of highlighting that in order for mimicry to be an effective Trojan Horse strategy for feminist gender trainers, there is a need for a constant vigilance; to remember what are lies, what is mimicry. Remembering what are lies is important because 'in order to be effective, mimicry must continually produce its slippage, its excess' (Bhabha 1994, 122). Mimicry can be 'at once resemblance and menace', but in order to do so, it must remain an imperfect repetition of the norm: 'almost the same, *but not quite*' (Bhabha 1994, 123, emphasis in original). Vincent's subsequent reflections on his strategy of trying to push the norm slightly from within provides some clues as to how the effect of mimicry can be maintained. Vincent admitted:

> I don't know if this is the cowardly way out ... I've always felt very unsatisfied by that solution and have doubts about whether it's the correct thing to do or not.

Vincent's account testifies to enduring unease with his strategy. I suggest that this unease is generative because it serves as a reminder that this strategy is as imperfect as it is resistant. It prompts the feminist gender trainer to ensure that their repetition of the norm continues to produce the slippage which is essential to their discourse doing the work of resistance, to menacing the hegemonic discourse.

What I suggest feminist gender trainers can learn from Bhabha's concept of mimicry, then, is the need to sit with tensions, and to keep alive the discomfort that Vincent expressed, that feeling of being very unsatisfied. That dissatisfaction is constitutive of the slippage or excess that guards gender trainers who are acting strategically from forgetting that they are lying, that keeps alive the possibility of being a menace while navigating the hegemonic norms of martial institutions. Under these conditions, feminist pedagogy is possible in gender training for peacekeepers. And if feminist pedagogical practice is possible, then perhaps, as Cynthia Enloe puts it, '[t]here is also the possibility that patriarchal state elites have initiated something they cannot control' (2000, 287).

## A Gamble with Meaning

I call this type of strategizing at the margins subversive rather than transformative, because it is less a programme for radical, foundation-shifting change, and more a series of moments which destabilize hegemonic narratives. Indeed, in interviews with gender trainers, when asked what the goal of their training was, what success looked like to them, many gave vague answers. Johanna, for example, said: 'Success for me is not a complete, total, world-changed thing. I'm happy to see little steps along the way'. In gender training, she noted that this might take the form of 'a frank discussion among participants about what they *really* think about gender sensitivity, and how they understand gender, and kind of getting them to understand gender as being something that they live and do'. Johanna's understanding of success is shared by many gender trainers. Mckay (2005, 277–278) proclaims:

> We should not count converts but rather take sustenance from the participants who, at the end of the day, have gained a glimpse of recognition, who will continue to think about the subject, who are more sensitized to the world in which they carry out their duties than they were when they came in.

Mckay, in this assertion, is clearly not suggesting that the success of gender training be measured by the number of feminist revolutionary subjects it produces. In an even more modest assessment of the value of gender training in the military, Malcolm quipped that all funds spent on gender training were funds not spent on weapons; every hour of gender training was an hour away from training in acts of violence. In other words, these trainers did not explain their pedagogical goals as constituting a calculated and linear progression toward transformed individuals or institutions, but rather drew sustenance from moments which destabilized martial logics. These trainers' accounts echo characterizations of other liberatory projects such as decoloniality as 'not a master plan for liberation, but a myriad of delinkings' (Mignolo and Nanibush 2018).

The emphasis on destabilizing moments that I read in these gender trainers' accounts resonates closely with the broader literature on the practice of gender expertise. Elisabeth Prügl sets out to describe a feminist ethic for gender experts and gender trainers and argues that such an ethic should be focused on process rather than outcomes (2016, 30). Despite this focus on process over outcomes, accounts of gender training that recognize the feminist pedagogical potential of the practice typically rely on the implication that such gender training finds causal application in an overall project of transformation, forming a kind of slow drip of change that will ultimately flow over (Brown 2020; Ferguson 2019b, 49; Bustelo, Ferguson, and Forest 2016, 168). In contrast to such assessments of feminist pedagogical moments as cumulatively amounting to large-scale transformation, I propose we understand them instead as small subversions that do not necessarily amount to a master plan for liberation. I believe such a consideration to be necessary: as Butler reminds us, 'subversiveness is the kind of effect that *resists calculation,* [because such acts] continue to signify in spite of their authors, and sometimes against their authors' most precious intentions' (1993, 29). Thinking, for example, about the political effect of mimicry, its subversive potential lies in its exposure of ambivalences in colonial discourses, a process of disturbing truth claims, rather than a vision of a different future. In other words, I suggest that we examine the political worth of small subversions through an epistemic lens that admits a degree of indeterminacy to the meaning of small subversions and an unknowability of their cumulative effects.

Small subversions, in this analytic, represent 'a gamble with meaning' (Britzman 2013, 112). I evoke Britzman's phrase here in two senses: feminist pedagogical practice both gambles with the meaning of what constitutes gender and this gamble is meaningful. I outlined above that I do not think it possible to assign causal effects to the subversions that feminist pedagogical practice performs, hence there is a gamble to the meaning of these moments. Here, I would like to suggest that this gamble nonetheless has political worth. Instead of looking for guaranteed pathways to transformation, it may be useful to think of feminist pedagogical practice as a form of what Spivak calls 'a practical politics of the open end'. In Spivak's explanation of political labour, she points to the interplay of large ideological acts with the everyday work of maintenance, comparing the latter to the activity of brushing one's teeth (in Spivak and Harasym 1990, 105):

> When we actually brush our teeth, or clean ourselves everyday, or take exercise, or whatever, we don't think we are fighting a losing battle against mortality, but in fact, all of these efforts are doomed to failure because we are going to die. On the other hand, we really think of it much more as upkeep and as maintenance rather than as an irreducibly doomed effort. This kind of activity cannot be replaced by an operation. We can't have a surgical operation which takes care of the daily maintenance of a body doomed to die. The operation would be identical with death.

Spivak's analogy helps inflect our thinking into a different mode of political thought; one in which the worth of acts such as small subversions are not solely determined by their proven capacity to produce a transformed future. Even though the point of these acts is not a linear programme for change, paradoxically, as Aaron Belkin suggests, such transformation may not be the point (Spade and Belkin 2021). The point is to destabilize hegemonic discourses from the margins, to work their ambivalences in an attempt to carve out new modes of thinking and to resist the smoothing over of contradictions. This is the tooth-brushing variety of political labour: contesting heterosexism and coloniality as logics of meaning-making, even when this labour does not promise to rid the body politic of these for good. The point, in other words, is to continue to contest what political and epistemic work the concept of gender can be made to do. Developing and nurturing ways of thinking about gender in liberatory and intersectional terms sustains the *possibility* of different modes of being and acting in the world, at the same time as it does not guarantee that such a transformation will happen.

## Conclusion

What this chapter has sought to highlight is that while gender training for uniformed peacekeepers can, and often does, involve the domestication of gender knowledge to serve the purposes of martial institutions, this dynamic is not reflective of all gender training, all of the time. To demonstrate this point, this chapter has taken an analytical approach that focuses attention on moments of feminist pedagogy at work in gender training. This analytical exercise was inspired by a recognition of the limits of 'paranoid' analytical practices, most notably formulated by Sedgwick (2003). Thinking in a reparative mood, I have sought to highlight the ways in which training (sometimes) involves feminist pedagogical practice. The identification of moments of feminist pedagogical practice goes 'against the tide of predetermination', which would suggest gender training in martial institutions is inevitably bound to be a militarist and colonial exercise (Britzman 2013, 112). In this endeavour, I have drawn upon principles identified in the feminist pedagogical literature, notably the practices of theorizing from experience, and an ethics of care in the classroom. Through an examination of these principles at work, I have sought to highlight that the particular power dynamics of gender training classrooms for uniformed peacekeepers demand a contextually informed application of feminist pedagogical principles, attentive to relations of domination within and beyond the classroom. I have drawn attention to the ways in which feminist gender trainers navigate experience and notions of the self in training, and the ways in which they practice an ethics of care in the classroom. Such practices, I argue, represent moments of instability and disruption for hegemonic martial logics in peacekeeper training.

Having identified moments of feminist pedagogical practice in gender training, this chapter has considered their political and epistemic effects. I have sought to draw attention to the ways in which feminist strategizing is both enabled and constrained by its marginal position in institutions of power. Under these conditions, moments of feminist pedagogy amount not necessarily to an overarching programme of feminist transformation, but rather to small subversions of the meaning-making apparatuses of martial institutions. In the final discussion in this chapter, I argued that the political worth of such small subversions should be understood not as a failure to produce large-scale structural change, but rather as, following Spivak (in Spivak and Harasym 1990), a 'practical politics of the open end'. To invest feminist energies in continuing to contest what political work gender can and cannot be made to do through gender training constitutes a gamble with meaning. This gamble, I suggest, is meaningful. In the next, concluding chapter, I situate this gamble within a broader consideration of feminist political strategizing, examining what the implications are of attaching political worth to feminist pedagogical practice in the project of training uniformed peacekeepers on gender.

# 6
# Conclusion

## Practising Paradoxical Politics

What happens when the concept of gender is taken up by institutions of state violence? This has been the abiding concern of this book. This inquiry shares many concerns with feminist scholars working on a range of fields, from international development to academic feminism and the institution of the university, around exploring the 'entanglements', as Srila Roy (2022, 167) puts it, of feminisms with relations and institutions of power (see also Eschle and Maiguashca 2018; de Jong and Kimm 2017; Wiegman 2016; Ahmed 2012). The case of peacekeeper gender training has provided a particularly poignant example of such dynamics. Over the past two decades, gender training for uniformed peacekeepers has evolved into a wide-reaching transnational practice, involving significant numbers of military and police personnel deployed to conflict areas. This is in many ways a surprising development, and one might reasonably expect that introducing feminist concepts to martial institutions would set the stage for a significant political and epistemological contestation. The whole premise of training the troops on gender, based on what we know so far, sounds like mixing oil and water, potentially with a match involved. This volatile set-up provokes some persistent feminist curiosities, such as: How is it that these institutions of hegemonic masculinity come to accept gender as a necessary training topic? What happens to the concept in the process? What do they think gender is and does? These are the questions that have driven the investigation in this book, which takes a detailed look at what happens, epistemologically and politically speaking, in gender training classrooms. This investigation tells us something about what happens to a concept like gender when it travels across different institutional spaces—what potential and perils such travel involves. This, in turn, matters not only for critical debates over peacekeeping but also for feminist debates over whether and how to engage with institutions of state power.

## CONCLUSION: PRACTISING PARADOXICAL POLITICS

What happens to the concept of gender as it travels, as this book has aimed to capture, is rarely straightforward. On the one hand, the institutionalization of gender training itself represents a major victory for feminist practitioners and advocates of gender mainstreaming. As one watches gender training sessions unfold, however, one's political expectations are often confounded. It may be that one sees a gender training exercise and, as a feminist, groans, expecting it to confirm essentialist and heterosexist views, only to be surprised by the nuanced discussion that the exercise prompts. At other times, one might be pleasantly surprised to hear a speaker complicating understandings of victimhood by challenging us to think about why we always assume victims are women, only to hear that the follow-up to this questioning is the extraordinary claim that women, in fact, are the primary perpetrators of sexual violence. Similarly, sometimes training participants will resist feminist messaging in gender training, and at other times they will contest regressive claims made by trainers. Gender training, in other words, involves many contradictory epistemic and political strands, which often weave together in the same training session.

This book is an attempt to unpick those messy politics that make up gender training. I have sought to expose the contradictory pedagogies that underwrite gender training and lay out the complex ways in which training practices simultaneously affirm and contest hegemonic logics. In the process, I have drawn on the conceptual vocabularies of postcolonial and queer feminisms to develop a mode of analysis that specifically attends to ambivalence in the training enterprise, rather than trying to gloss over contradiction in favour of pronouncing gender training, once and for all, either good or bad feminist politics. Indeed, this book insists on continued attention to the fact that gender training simultaneously serves martial logics and subverts them. It constitutes, in other words, a paradoxical practice from the point of view of intersectional feminist commitments. Homi Bhabha (1994, 365) argues that what critical analyses need are 'an idea of action and agency more complex than either the nihilism of despair or the utopia of progress'. Attending to ambivalence and thinking about gender training as specifically paradoxical poses important questions for feminist political strategizing, including how to think in a political register that resists both the nihilism of despair and the utopia of progress. These questions implicate both feminist engagements with the global governance of peace and security and gender training as a strategy for feminist engagements with institutions of power more broadly. In this concluding chapter, I draw together the different strands of analysis that emerge from the account this book puts forward and discuss their implications for feminist strategizing.

## Training The Troops on Gender: A Contradictory Practice

The point of departure for this inquiry has been the theoretical conviction that what exactly gender is and does is produced rather than given: gender can be understood in different ways, and different understandings of the term have divergent epistemic and political effects. Critical feminist analyses have pointed out that ostensibly progressive feminist interventions, such as gender mainstreaming of peacekeeping, can produce deeply problematic politics which sustain patriarchy, militarization, coloniality, and heteronormativity (Henry 2024; Pratt 2013; Razack 2004; Whitworth 2004). The inquiry of this book is located within this body of scholarship, which interrogates the politics of deploying the language of gender in the governance of international peace and security. Informed by a feminist poststructuralist approach, I contend that training matters because it produces knowledges, which in turn are productive of different ways of being and acting in the world. These theoretical insights gesture toward the importance of posing the question: *What political and epistemic work does gender training do in martial institutions involved in peacekeeping?*

This epistemic stance further suggests that what gender training is and does is an empirical question, not automatically deducible from the concept itself. The first task for the analysis was therefore to establish an understanding of what exactly gender training involves. Chapter 2 examined how training curricula are constructed, and mapped varying understandings of what gender training does or should cover in different geographic contexts. It further traced how gender, in the context of peacekeeper training, is rendered a knowable object. This chapter suggested that the dynamics and politics of training cannot be reliably deduced from policy mandates or training curricula alone. In order to assess the epistemic and political work gender training does, it is important to examine questions of how gender is learned, who is authorized to know it, and what processes of translation, negotiation, and resistance are involved in this process. In other words, it requires a research archive that extends beyond scrutinizing what is prescribed in training curricula and heeds attention to what happens in the intersubjective encounters involved in learning.

## CONCLUSION: PRACTISING PARADOXICAL POLITICS

On the one hand, the story that unfolds across this book about what happens in gender training classrooms resonates with critical feminist literature on gender training as well as that on peacekeeping which cautions that feminist concepts, when deployed in institutions of state power, often come to serve the interests of the status quo (Zalewski 2010; Väyrynen 2004, 138). The status quo involves: unequal relations of power in global politics, colonial thinking, martial logics, and heteropatriarchal assumptions.

We have seen that the political economy of knowledge production privileges expertise in the Global North: training curricula are designed through processes which render conflict-affected women objects of knowledge rather than knowing subjects. Global North–based gender trainers dominate the field, reaping material and reputational rewards from their positioning as experts on the matter, as the ones who hold knowledge and not just experience. Epistemic authority—who can know gender—is consequently framed as male and military, in ways which mute other perspectives. This political economy of knowledge thus reaffirms the status quo of unequal relations of power along a global colour line.

The knowledge about gender that training produces is likewise informed by colonial thinking. This is a finding that emerges in different articulations across this book's examination of gender training. The understanding of gender that is deployed in training, as discussed in Chapter 2, simultaneously denies 'colonial difference' (Lugones 2010, 746), *and* renders race hyper-visible in ways that facilitate colonial thinking. Supported by this interpretive frame peacekeepers come, as we have seen in Chapter 3, to interpret conflict-related sexual violence through the lenses of colonial scripts of racialized difference. These scripts manifest in different ways in peacekeeper training: they either invoke a paternalistic desire to save women in the Global South or they prompt recourse to cultural essentialism that denies a responsibility to challenge structures of oppression. In the face of challenges to this framing, many training participants and trainers seek to ensure that the colonial difference is upheld, projecting gender onto the bodies of racialized others to ensure that gender thus understood does not implicate the peacekeeper self.

This mode of thinking through colonial difference is also inflected in militarized terms. Conflict-related sexual violence produces contradictory demands on peacekeeper subjectivity by evoking both warrior and humanitarian identities. I argued in Chapter 3 that this training compels peacekeepers to speak about their feelings of discomfort, upset, horror, and disgust in relation to wartime rape, and that training then proposes to resolve this emotional unease by evoking warrior subjectivity: the training positions peacekeepers as 'tough guys', ready to use force to address problems of sexual violence. Training thereby domesticates the problem of gender into military logics and modes of acting. It subordinates any feminist desire to transform a gendered system to that which is considered to bolster military goals and operational effectiveness.

Finally, this book has uncovered that gender training typically works to sustain heteropatriarchal assumptions. Most gender trainers and curriculum designers avoid addressing questions of non-normative sexual subjectivity, claiming that the topic of sexuality is 'too complex' for them to address, or that their audiences would not be receptive to it. Not only is gender framed as reliably binary, cis, and straight but also training typically evades any questions that might challenge peacekeepers' own performances of masculinity. In Chapter 3, I argued that the separation of peacekeeper sexual exploitation and abuse (SEA) from training on sexual violence serves to protect peacekeepers' understanding of themselves as protectors rather than perpetrators. Further, trainers and training participants sometimes use male victimization as a way to frame gender as a question of equivalent difference, thereby evacuating from view questions of male complicity in violence.

In sum, the pedagogical project of training uniformed peacekeepers on gender clearly works to affirm martial logics, colonial thinking, and heteropatriarchal subjectivities. Although gender training as an enterprise historically derives from feminist knowledge and feminist political projects, much of peacekeeper gender training actively resists intersectional feminist analytics and politics. Such defanging of gender knowledge demonstrates the dexterous nature of power, and its ability to fold in demands for transformation.

However, to note that collusion between feminism and imperialism is taking place is not the same as to posit that the tension between them is resolved. The story about gender training that unfolds in this book reveals that feminist knowledge is not fully co-opted into martial logics by practices of gender training; collusion with imperial politics is neither total nor final. A parallel analytical thread that runs through this account suggests that the pedagogical project of gender training sometimes precipitates productive (from the point of view of feminist politics) moments of crisis for hegemonic logics, and that some gender trainers strategically exploit these crises.

First, gender training exposes the contradictions and anxious features—the ambivalence—of martial logics themselves. While it is true that many gender trainers seek to avoid addressing non-normative sexual subjectivity (too complicated, they claim) in their training practice, a closer look at training encounters reveals that queer subjects continue to haunt training discourses, rendering the heteronormativity of the exercise ever contingent and insecure. Similarly, I noted in Chapter 3 that training on conflict-related sexual violence proposes warrior subjectivity and martial action to peacekeepers. At the same time, I called attention to the numerous contradictions contained in this demand. The (unevenly enforced) omission from such training of sexual violence committed by peacekeepers (SEA), and the confinement of peacekeeper responses to military action, produce moments of cognitive and affective dissonance in the training setting. These contradictions provoke moral crises among some trainees, and expose the ambivalence contained within the demand that peacekeepers care about and take action on sexual violence. In other words, gender training is disruptive for hegemonic logics because it exposes the ambivalence and contradiction which inheres to them.

Second, some gender trainers engage in feminist pedagogical praxis, and thereby subvert martial logics. These gender trainers consciously and strategically smuggle feminist analytical concepts and intersectional commitments into gender training. Such small subversions involve practices that disrupt martial time; make the training topic personal, exposing shared complicities in structures of oppression; and insist on the examination of problems through the prism of colonial histories. These trainers are aware that they are involved in a strategic contestation: they thus see resistance as an inevitable dynamic in an inherently contentious political project and welcome its occurrence as an indicator that the training is (as they argue it should be) challenging the trainees' world views and sense of self. They do not shy away from 'difficult knowledge' (Britzman 1998, 11), and see a 'pedagogy of discomfort' (Boler 1999, 175) as necessary for their politics. Many trainers who practise feminist pedagogies thus describe their strategy as that of sneaking feminist concepts into martial institutions as feminist 'Trojan horses' (Prügl 2013, 60).

In sum, these disruptive and subversive dynamics of gender training demonstrate that efforts to discipline gender knowledge are not (pun intended) uniform. This book thus, contradictorily, also argues that gender training can provoke moments of disruption, instability, and even crisis for martial knowledge. Considering these two analytical threads together reveals that gender training for peacekeepers is *both* a practice in which feminist concepts collude with martial logics *and* a pedagogy that brings imperial knowledge to crisis. In many ways, the epistemic and political effects of gender training resist calculation. This is not a dynamic that lends itself to a straightforward cost-benefit analysis in which *either* feminism *or* imperialism comes out on top. For feminist political strategizing, this poses a paradox. Joan Wallach Scott explains that the technical definition of a paradox is: 'a proposition that is both true and false at the same time' (1996, 4). From the point of view of feminist politics, gender training is both good and bad at the same time. In an attempt to push our thinking beyond the eminently reasonable but analytically and politically unsatisfactory conclusion of 'it is both', in this concluding chapter, I want to reflect on what thinking about gender training as a specifically paradoxical pedagogy might mean for how we understand what work gender training does, and what this implies for feminist political strategizing.

## Thinking with Paradox

Under the conditions of liberal thought, Wendy Brown warns us, paradox is 'a political condition of achievement perpetually undercut . . . a state in which political strategizing itself is paralyzed' (2000, 239). The question for feminist and postcolonial thinkers who critique liberal thought has therefore been to consider how paradox might be thought of productively, beyond such political and epistemological paralysis.[1] In continuity with broader queer feminist (and) postcolonial projects of critiquing liberal epistemology, I suggest that thinking about the productive nature of paradox is implied by a broader epistemic challenge to liberal progress narratives.

Indeed, feminist scholars examining gender and security politics invite us to abandon such teleological narratives of constant historical progress in favour of a politics of the present (Otto 2014, 158). The first analytical move that thinking with paradox suggests, then, is a certain disinvestment from futurity, contesting the notion that feminism's political worth is solely determined by its ability to perform as 'a future-producing epistemology and politics' (Wiegman 2004, 164; see also Rao 2020, 16–18). Such a disinvestment from futurity speaks to a mode of political thought that views politics as a process in which there are no guarantees, and that concedes: 'the outcome of our efforts . . . can never be known in advance' (Wiegman 2016, 85). This mode of thought is suspicious of grand narratives that would either reassure us that feminism is on its way to meaningfully transforming the peacekeeping enterprise through gender training or, conversely, that would declare gender training as a fatally flawed practice, consigning it to a scrap heap of misguided, and ultimately lost, feminist causes.

While this suggestion to disinvest from futurity may be unsettling for those committed to the pursuit of social justice, I suggest that thinking about this move with queer and postcolonial theorizing also provides an element of relief, perhaps even hope, insofar as it suggests a cautiously positive response to Bhabha's question: 'Can there be life without transcendence? Politics without the dream of perfectibility?' (Bhabha 1994, 88). What I mean by this is that it enables us to recognize that activities such as gender training may have political worth, even when they do not promise a transformed future. It alerts us to examine the ways in which gender training produces a form of hybridized knowledge about gender, which is neither properly feminist nor reliably imperial. This hybrid knowledge interrupts dominant scripts and shifts the terms on which the social is produced. While there is no guarantee that the practice of training will deliver knowable, better futures, paradoxically, per Aaron Belkin (in Spade & Belkin 2021), transformation is not (always) the point. Gender training opens up a space for small subversions, a place from which to contest misogynist logics and from which to exploit ambivalences within colonial scripts. It constitutes a form of politics that recognizes that while transformation may be elusive, resistance is imperative. A teleological path to transformation, in this mode of thought, is not the only politically worthwhile vision. It is an exhausting business being a feminist in a world that is so deeply structured by oppression, where each small victory has to be won time and again. Rather than only lament collective failure in the face of anti-feminist politics and enduring injustice, we need to find moments of sustenance, and to locate political possibilities in the micrological workings of power. This is both political and analytical necessity. Thinking with paradox, in other words, suggests that an analysis of gender training as colluding with empire need not end in the nihilism of despair.

Pointedly, in arguing for a recognition of resistant politics, I am not suggesting that we ignore the very real and harmful ways in which feminist concepts are deployed to forward martial ends. To the contrary, understanding these engagements as resistant rather than transformative highlights the need, as Otto argues, to produce forms of engagement 'that are less amenable to institutional capture' (2014, 165). Such forms of engagement take the inevitability of failure as their point of departure, and involve embracing strategies that are inherently 'flawed, imprecise, and corruptible' (Rodríguez 2014, 8). They can be understood as 'optimistically cruel', per Wiegman's reworking of Berlant's famous 'cruel optimism'. In a similar spirit, I contend that gender training in martial institutions will not deliver on a promise of a transformed future, but that the consequence of this argument is not that training is useless, that it is without political worth. Even an imperfect promise can be worked—as Ahmed (2012, 110–111) points out: 'If organizations invest in diversity or equality, even as shiny veneers, we can "do things" with their investments'. The optimism of this attachment stems from a recognition of this worth, this opening for 'doing things'; rejecting Bhabha's (1994, 365) nihilism of despair. This worth cannot and should not be premised on reassurances of transformed futures, but rather must attend to the cruelty of this attachment. This cruelty lies in the recognition that gender training is an inherently flawed enterprise. This cruelty is necessary in order to avoid Bhabha's (1994, 365) utopia of progress: the shortcomings of this approach must be recognized if it is to support the development of forms of engagement that are less amenable to capture. Thinking of an optimistically cruel attachment in these terms points to ways of engaging with paradox that are neither politically paralysed nor analytically stunted. It does not propose an ultimate resolution of the terms of the paradox, but suggests a need to keep this tension alive, and to sit with the tension.

## Feminist Political Strategizing

Reflecting on the paradoxical nature of gender training for peacekeepers leads me to suggest that there *is* political worth in tracking where and how feminist concepts travel, and in continuing to contest what political and epistemic work these concepts can be made to do, including through gender training. In other words, I identify political potential in cultivating resistant pedagogies, and developing ways of practising them. Such engagements must not come at the price of ignoring the ways in which such approaches are inevitably flawed, but must instead be grounded in a recognition that such projects are always messy, imprecise, and corruptible. What, then, are the implications of this theoretical argument for feminist political strategizing?

## CONCLUSION: PRACTISING PARADOXICAL POLITICS

In Chapter 5, I suggested that we read the subversive nature of feminist pedagogical praxis in gender training through the lens of Spivak's 'practical politics of the open end' (1990, 105). I drew on Spivak's analogy of brushing one's teeth to characterize subversive pedagogies as the everyday labour of maintenance for resistant politics. What is important to note about Spivak's analogy is that she maintains that there are occasions on which 'surgical operations', or large ideological acts, are necessary. However, these surgical operations are not a substitute for daily upkeep, which remains vitally important. Thinking with Spivak's theorization of resistant politics here, I want not only to suggest that subversive practices in gender training can be thought of as a practical politics of the open end but also to signal that my argument does not in and of itself disavow large ideological actions. It is not my intention to make a prescriptive claim for feminist strategizing, that working with paradox and exploiting ambivalence should be the only, or indeed the preferred, feminist political strategy. Asserting such totalizing truth claims is, in fact, contraindicated by the epistemological perspective that gives rise to my analysis in the first place. My argument is a more modest one, suggesting that there is political worth to resistant politics, and that there is opportunity opened up by gender training to engage in subversion. This strategy may be flawed, but, to borrow from Spivak again: 'That's the thing that deconstruction gives us; an awareness that what we are obliged to do, and must do scrupulously, in the long run is not OK' (1990, 45). This recognition does not imply that political worth may only be found in one form of feminist strategizing, nor does it contraindicate other forms of political action such as anti-militarist feminist organizing.

As one among many political strategies, the strategy of exploiting ambivalence and provoking instability and crisis in hegemonic discourse is, I contend, one that is particularly suited to powerful state institutions as a site of political contestation. In formulating this argument, I have drawn heavily on Bhabha's (1994) conceptualization of resistant, hybridized politics that exploit the ambivalences of dominant discourses. It is interesting to note at this juncture that Bhabha's work has been critiqued for its inability or unwillingness to attend to the fact that such forms of hybrid politics are typically produced from relatively privileged postcolonial positions associated with class/caste privilege, migration, and diasporic identities. Critics of his work have argued that this location renders the strategies of hybridity of limited use to postcolonial politics, and that they fail to account for properly subaltern resistance (Biccum 2007, 147; Huddart 2006, 151). While my ambition here is not to make a pronouncement on the political import or lack thereof of hybridized discourses to overall projects of decolonization, what I do want to highlight is the ways in which these critiques point also to the limits of the argument that I am making, limits which I very much accept. This book is concerned with martial institutions and forms of gender expertise—both of which produce subject positions which are privileged, albeit on different terms. It deals, in other words, with a site imbued with power and privilege. My reluctance to make transformative claims about the political worth I identify in gender training stems from a recognition of the limits of this site—there is little indication that contestations staged in this space have the ability to transform broader structures of militarism, heterosexism, and coloniality. While I insist that there is political worth to this form of political strategy in this institutional location, its political purchase at other sites remains an open question.

Circumscribing the scope of the argument thus still leaves open the question of where feminist political energies are best spent. Would it not be more worthwhile to invest in feminist anti-militarist activism, rather than to develop subversive forms of engagement through gender training? The response, of course, depends on context—whose energies and where we are speaking about. In the case of the gender trainers I met who practised forms of feminist pedagogy, this framing presents a false binary. Some gender experts engage in both gender training and feminist, anti-racist, and queer activism. One does not substitute for the other; activism and expertise are not mutually exclusive forms of engagement. Others only came to gender because of this job requirement, and for them the choice would be to work on gender training or work in other areas of military or development activities that do not deal explicitly with gender. In their case, feminist activism is ruled out from the outset—albeit some may discover it precisely through engaging in gender training. In the case of feminist academics, this question is slightly more complex. Here, I am not suggesting that we should privilege the study of gender training over other types of feminist strategizing. My point is, again, more modest, amounting to a plea not to write off the practice as doomed to failure and therefore to be written off without analytical engagement. My aim has been to demonstrate that feminist theory can inform feminist pedagogical approaches that have subversive potential, and that those who engage in feminist theorizing can both support and learn from the practice of gender training.

Finally, in terms of considerations for feminist political strategizing, is the question of whether there is a risk that engaging with martial institutions strengthens these institutions and the imperial projects they are engaged in. Are gender experts and gender trainers, and scholars who take seriously their perspectives and support their work, feminism's 'native collaborators' with martial power? Are they doing the work of what Belkin (2012, 31) describes as smoothing over the contradictions of empire? There is always the risk that feminist rhetoric is deployed to justify martial action (as we have seen with the U.S. invasion of Afghanistan in 2001), and that feminist analyses are used to military ends. Further, gender mainstreaming efforts such as gender training can help create a public image of the military as an essentially benevolent peacekeeping organization, thereby normalizing and legitimizing the funding and use of military violence. Not wishing to understate this concern, as I remain troubled by this potential to cause harm, I do want to point out that there is a risk of exaggerating the importance gender equality norms play in shoring up the public legitimacy of martial institutions, and the relative influence making demands of martial institutions has on bolstering militarism. I wonder, given the pervasiveness of militarization across the state system, and the persistence of these murderous institutions despite their well-documented involvement in attacks on civilians, sexual abuse, and other atrocities: Can we imagine a location in the historical present where a refusal on the part of military authorities to speak the language of gender would provoke a mass-based anti-recruitment movement, or better yet, a refusal to pay our taxes to fund military institutions? This example is of course reductive, and my intention is not to brush away concerns about feminist collusion with murderous institutions. My point is to draw attention to the importance of understanding militarism, as Kimberly Hutchings (2018) insists we should, as a pervasive and resilient condition. Militarism extends beyond the boundaries of martial institutions, weaving its influence through popular culture and the economy, implicating us all. This is not to detract from the importance of considering what it means to engage in feminist anti-militarist or pacifist politics, and whether and where attempting subversion from within, such as in the form of gender training for peacekeepers, may be harmful or counterproductive to such politics. To the contrary, it suggests a need to remain troubled by this question, opening up avenues for further inquiry. To remain uneasy with this question means to not only remain suspicious of collusion with murderous institutions, it also denies the possibility of claiming a purity or an innocence which is founded solely on a categorical refusal to engage with questions around peacekeeping practices carried out by martial institutions.

## Implications for Institutional Engagement

A recognition of the political worth of gender training for feminist strategizing alone does not translate straightforwardly into a prescription as to what feminist scholars and gender trainers should be advocating for when they (as most working in this field are apt to be) are asked for their 'policy recommendations'. Advocating for a feminist politics of disruption and subversion to policymakers is clearly an absurd proposition (although this idea does find traction with some feminist-identifying gender trainers in private conversations). Providing recommendations that are palatable to mainstream policymakers has not been a specific aim this book, but that is not to say that some suggestions for how to respond to the inevitable demand for such recommendations are not suggested by its findings. In keeping with the feminist post-structuralist account of political engagement that the book engages with, these suggestions privilege process over outcomes.

First, a cautionary note. There is a tendency within the literature on gender training to lament the poor standardization of gender training across institutional settings, the lack of coherent professional standards for gender trainers, and the absence of meaningful evaluation mechanisms in relation to gender training (Bustelo, Ferguson, and Forest 2016, 2). I am deeply sympathetic to the fact that the demand for more standardized training practices stems from a concern about the prevalence of training practices that often—as this book provides ample evidence toward—affirm logics of misogyny, heteronormativity, and racism. Nonetheless, my enthusiasm for standardization and systematic monitoring of training practices is limited. It is, I contend, specifically the lack of oversight that allows for more radical interventions; for ambivalence to be exploited. As Johanna pointed out in Chapter 5, it is precisely the undervaluing or underestimation of gender work that provided her with the latitude to develop creative feminist interventions. Accordingly, I worry that any set of standards that policymakers and trainers could agree on would curtail the space for resistant politics. While standardization could reign in some of the more flagrant displays of white heteropatriarchy, it is also the case that such discourses already enjoy wide purchase and are authorized to circulate freely within martial institutions. Would the benefit of suppressing them in a gender training setting really outweigh the benefits of what is a relatively free hand for subversive gender trainers to introduce more radical concepts into the discussion?

Introducing more robust evaluation mechanisms—in effect, developing the means to answer the question 'Does gender training work?'—likewise has double-edged potential. On the one hand, such an exercise would provide insight into the relative stability of any discursive shifts introduced by gender training, allowing scholarship to track how crises of meaning precipitated by gender training play out beyond the classroom, and what forms the negotiation of these crises take. Nonetheless, a cautionary note is also due in advocating for this. There is always the possibility that such evaluations would find gender training does not in fact 'work' on the terms it is expected to, which could have the effect of shutting down these conversations altogether. At the less extreme end, such findings could facilitate a process of quality evaluation that further consolidates the dominance of Global North gender experts of this field, portending parallel risks as standardization. In other words, I caution those called upon to provide recommendations to those in power to carefully consider the risks of standardizing this pedagogical exercise, and developing measures of success that may end up rather narrowly and conservatively defined.

The concern about the many forms of political work that gender training does, and the role of trainers and curricula in this work, can be addressed through different forms of engagement, not only through standardization and evaluation. The practice of critical friendship offers one such alternative. Feminist researchers often work in partnership with feminists working within institutions—acting as 'critical friends' who engage in ongoing dialogue on institutional approaches to gender, offering advice, critique, and support (see e.g. Chappell and Mackay 2021; Holvikivi 2019). Critical friendship, with its commitment to debate and to considering the contextual entanglements of feminist work in institutions, may offer a more productive route to developing feminist pedagogies in gender training than advocating for policy changes and structures or issuing recommendations from the outside and in a unidirectional mode. The transnational community of gender trainers is an economy of knowledge production, where knowledges and ideas circulate. Over the course of my research, I came across the same arguments and same learning activities across different geographic contexts, suggesting that the ability to introduce changes to training practices in one context has a good chance of travelling. This knowledge economy is, I contend, potentially less impacted by bullet pointed lists of recommendations or policy briefs, than by the subtle nudges of 'Have you considered posing this question?' or 'I saw an exercise recently that seems to work well for this topic' issued over coffee breaks during training courses. Opening up collegial dialogue with those who deliver gender training not only creates the conditions for exchange rather than direction but also, through this dialogic process, allows those engaged in research to gain a fuller understanding of the logics that inform any training intervention. Such contextual understanding is important to learning how to do the work of translating feminist thinking into a mode of enunciation that stands a chance of being heard by those who do not subscribe to feminist politics, or who do not have the theoretical grounding to engage with the conceptual vocabulary of feminist thought. Indeed, such processes may offer a more productive (and epistemologically consistent) route to 'policy engagement' than issuing recommendations and advocating for specific regulations for this practice.

While my reflections on policy engagement are marked by an epistemological and ethical discomfort with the notion of blanket recommendations, there are two related areas in which I am comfortable suggesting that our policy engagement advocates for specific action: time and expertise. As discussed in Chapter 5, the time devoted to gender training remains limited in most institutions. Indeed, some reports cite 'gender briefings' that are allocated ten minutes (Lackenbauer and Langlais 2013, 36). Clearly, if subversion is to stand a chance, more time is needed for gender training. This lack of time devoted to the topic is also a concern in relation to how the expertise required for gender training is acquired. To my knowledge, the most expansive preparatory course for gender trainers is a two-week long gender training-of-trainers course. This is hardly sufficient to prepare trainers to engage in nuanced discussions of gender concepts, and often leaves them unable to field questions posed by training participants. Questions, I might add, which often exceed the scope of the prescribed curriculum, including questions related to sexuality, the navigation of cultural difference, and the ethics of imposing understandings of gender equality in different contexts. I therefore see value in policy engagement aimed at advocating for the allocation of additional time and resources for gender training; a commitment which would reflect a valuing of gender expertise.

Finally, I want to suggest that expertise should not simply be considered a property of individuals, a property that can be infinitely increased by more time and training. As Sandra Harding reminds us: 'communities, not primarily individuals, produce knowledge' (1993, 454). This book critiques the ways in which the political economy of knowledge production in gender training concentrates epistemic authority in martial institutions in the

Global North. Accordingly, I advocate for a diversification of the voices that can speak in and through gender training. There is an urgent need to recognize gender knowledge produced in the Global South as expertise and to challenge the unidirectional knowledge transfer scenario in which Global North experts travel to the Global South but not vice versa.[2] Further, gender training interventions should not treat the needs and experiences of conflict-affected women (plural, lower case 'w') as already-known, but rather needs to create ways of hearing their voices. In the spirit of practising critical friendship, I suggest that feminist academics, civil society representatives, and military and police gender trainers have much to learn from one another and can collaborate productively on developing gender training practices. The final recommendation I am at ease offering is therefore: gender training must draw on different forms of expertise and create space for a variety of voices to be heard.

# Notes

## Preface
1. On gender 'experts' and expertise, see Kunz, Prügl, and Thompson 2019.

## Chapter 1
1. Feminist debate over engaging institutions of state power predates the question of military training—notably in the field of development policy and feminist activism (see e.g. Roy 2022).
2. 'Peacekeeping' as a term originates from interventions conducted under the auspices of the United Nations. While UN peacekeeping is typically described as being impartial, deploying troops from neutral countries and involving the consent of countries intervened in, the term has also been used to describe much more interventionist incursions by, for example, the North Atlantic Treaty Organization (NATO) in Afghanistan (Bergman Rosamond and Kronsell 2018; Duncanson 2009). While acknowledging NATO's more expansionist politics, critical analyses of peacekeeping have drawn attention to the fact that '[b]oth the UN and NATO converge in respect of their normative aspiration to facilitate the liberal peace' (Higate and Henry 2009, 21). Accordingly, the analysis in this book uses an expansive understanding of peacekeeping, including—in addition to UN peacekeeping—missions undertaken by regional organizations such as NATO or the African Union. Peacekeeping missions typically involve military, police, and civilian components. I focus on military and police peacekeepers, using the term 'uniformed peacekeepers' to refer to them, and characterize the police and military as martial institutions.
3. For an example of this line of argumentation, and a reference that is eagerly taken up by many gender trainers, see Hudson et al. 2014.
4. While much of this literature has focused on military masculinity, this does not necessarily preclude police, including police peacekeepers, from performing militarized masculinity (see e.g. Fassin 2013; Bevan and MacKenzie 2012).
5. Details of this research archive are stored by the UK Data Service: Holvikivi, Aiko (2021). *Peacekeeper Gender Training, 2017.* [Data Collection]. Colchester, Essex: UK Data Service. https://doi.org//10.5255/UKDA-SN-855287.

## Chapter 2
1. These materials are available on the UN website: https://research.un.org/revisedcptm2017 [Accessed: 26 April 2021]. For an account of how this training package was developed, see Curran 2013.
2. Consider, for example, the professional biographies of well-known gender experts such as Clare Hutchinson or Rachel Grimes, who have both served as both UN and NATO gender advisors. Biographic details available at: https://www.nato.int/cps/en/natohq/who_is_who_156598.htm and https://www.economist.com/international/2021/04/24/female-soldiers-are-changing-how-armed-forces-work [Accessed: 26 April 2021].
3. For an overview of such policy mandates, see Holvikivi 2021.
4. For an example of how this process is conceptualized, see Holvikivi and Valasek 2016, 84.
5. See, for example, training materials developed by DCAF (Johanssen 2009).
6. Some of the gender experts involved in this undertaking are keenly aware of the overrepresentation of the minority world in these processes, and invest in mediating this imbalance by inviting actors from the Global South to participate in the consolidation of such expertise (see e.g. Pepper 2012). However, such efforts remain marginal and do not amount to any radical reconfiguration of the knowledge paradigms that constitute gender training for peacekeepers on a transnational scale.
7. Róisín Read has drawn attention to the circulation of so-called killer facts as a common form of knowledge production on sexual violence (Read 2019).

## Notes

8. A similar observation of pre-emptive action to address presumed homophobia is made by Belkin (2012, 101).
9. See UN Women press releases on this course (UN Women 2015, 2013).

### Chapter 3

1. As discussed in Chapter 2, trainers often seek to manage this sense of shared responsibility for male violence. Some do so by screening documentaries that depict male rape victims, such as the 2011 documentary *They Slept with Me* produced by the Refugee Law Project. Discussions with trainers suggests that they seek to highlight the existence of male victims both to add to the gravity of the problem (it is not 'only' a women's issue) as well as to assuage male guilt by allowing them to know themselves not only as perpetrators but also potential victims.
2. For a detailed enumeration of suggested courses of action, see DPKO/DFS 2010, Anderson 2012.
3. Such strategies were also observed by Miller and Moskos (1995).

### Chapter 4

1. Reminiscent of the 'genderman' discussed by Matthew Hurley (Wright, Hurley, and Gil Ruiz 2019, 92).
2. It is worth noting that these characterizations of resistance also rightly highlight the significance of non-linguistic forms of resistance, such as silence and withholding strategies enacted by students, as well as the under-prioritization and under-resourcing of gender training and feminist educational programmes. However, my focus here is primarily on verbalized or active forms of resistance, and the patterns that they take.
3. In reading resistance as performative, I draw on Paul Higate and Marsha Henry's characterization of peacekeepers as engaged in performances of different types of peacekeeper subjectivity, according to established scripts and enacted in specific 'interactional frames' (2009, 100–105).
4. Kolhatkar's comedy is eagerly taken up by online communities of 'men's rights activists', for example, on the online discussion site Reddit: https://www.reddit.com/r/MensRights/comments/4hp932/check_out_the_short_films_made_by_neel_kolhatkar/ [Accessed: 4 July 2019].
5. Srebrenica was the site of a notorious massacre in 1995 of an estimated 8,000 Bosniak men and boys in the context of the war in Bosnia-Herzegovina (Baker 2015). The evacuation of Dutch peacekeepers from the town prior to the massacre has been widely criticized, with legal cases subsequently brought against the Dutch government (Ryngaert 2017).
6. This photograph, along with other graffiti, is available on the website: https://srebrenica-genocide.blogspot.com/2008/06/dutch-graffiti-in-srebrenica-sickening.html [Accessed: 5 July 2019]. It was also featured in the 2005 BBC documentary 'Srebrenica: Never Again?' (Wollaston 2005) and adapted through the artwork of Šejla Kamerić: https://sejlakameric.com/.

### Chapter 5

1. These types of pedagogical practices are also described in the literature as 'engaged pedagogy' (hooks 1994, 13), 'liberatory pedagogies' (Bell, Morrow, and Tastsoglou 1999, 24), 'pedagogy of critique and possibility', 'pedagogy of student voice', 'pedagogy of empowerment', 'radical pedagogy', 'pedagogy for radical democracy', and 'pedagogy of possibility' (Ellsworth 1989, 286).
2. While the topic of men and masculinities is notably absent from UN- and NATO-level official curricula (as also observed by Laplonge 2015), in practice, some of the training courses I observed incorporated such sessions.

### Chapter 6

1. On the question of contending with paradox, see also Holvikivi 2023.
2. Following similar observations about scholarly feminist research and work on the related field of women, peace, and security: Haastrup and Hagen 2021; Henry 2021; Medie and Kang 2018.

# References

Abu-Lughod, Lila. 2013. *Do Muslim Women Need Saving?* Cambridge, MA: Harvard University Press.
Ahmed, Sara. 2010. 'Happy Objects'. In *The Affect Theory Reader*, edited by Melissa Gregg and Gregory J. Seigworth, 29–51. Durham, NC: Duke University Press.
Ahmed, Sara. 2012. *On Being Included: Racism and Diversity in Institutional Life*. Durham, NC: Duke University Press.
Ahmed, Sara. 2014. *The Cultural Politics of Emotion*. 2nd ed. Edinburgh: Edinburgh University Press. 2004.
Ahmed, Sara. 2017. *Living a Feminist Life*. Durham, NC: Duke University Press.
Alaga, Ecoma, and Emma Birikorang. 2012. *Integrating Gender in Peacekeeping Training: An Approach from the ECOWAS Subregion. Fahamu*. Cape Town: Pambazuka Press.
Allen, Louisa. 2015. 'Queer Pedagogy and the Limits of Thought: Teaching Sexualities at University'. *Higher Education Research and Development* 34 (4): 763–775. https://doi.org/10.1080/07294360.2015.1051004.
Anderson, Leticia. 2012. *Addressing Conflict-Related Sexual Violence: An Analytical Inventory of Peacekeeping Practice*. 2nd ed. UN Women (New York). http://www.resdal.org/wps/assets/04dananalyticalinventoryofpeacekeepingpracti.pdf.
Axmacher, Susanne. 2013. *Review of Scenario-Based Trainings for Military Peacekeepers on Prevention and Response to Conflict-Related Sexual Violence*. UN Women (New York). http://stoprapenow.org/uploads/advocacyresources/1394227122.pdf.
Baker, Catherine. 2015. *The Yugoslav Wars of the 1990s*. London: Macmillan Education/Palgrave.
Barrett, Frank J. 1996. 'The Organizational Construction of Hegemonic Masculinity: The Case of the US Navy'. *Gender, Work and Organization* 3 (3): 129–142. http://dx.doi.org/10.1111/j.1468-0432.1996.tb00054.x.
Baruah, Bipasha. 2017. 'Women Should Be as Entitled to Peacekeeping Jobs as Men Are, without the Burdens of "Civilizing" and Improving the Missions' Operational Effectiveness'. *Policy Options*, 2017. Accessed 16 March 2018. http://policyoptions.irpp.org/magazines/november-2017/short-sighted-commitments-on-women-in-peacekeeping/.
Bastick, Megan, and Claire Duncanson. 2018. 'Agents of Change? Gender Advisors in NATO Militaries'. *International Peacekeeping* 25 (4): 554–577. https://doi.org/10.1080/13533312.2018.1492876.
Bauer, Delphine, and Hélène Molinari. 2017. 'ONU: Permis d'abuser?' In *Impunité zéro, violences sexuelles en temps de guerre: L'enquête*, edited by Justine Brabant, Leïla Miñano, and Anne-Laure Pineau, 159–195. Paris: Editions Autrement.
Beauboeuf-Lafontant, Tamara. 2002. 'A Womanist Experience of Caring: Understanding the Pedagogy of Exemplary Black Women Teachers'. *Urban Review* 34 (1): 71–86. https://doi.org/10.1023/a:1014497228517.
Belkin, Aaron. 2012. *Bring Me Men: Military Masculinity and the Benign Façade of American Empire 1898–2001*. London: C. Hurst & Co.
Bell, Sandra, Marina Morrow, and Evangelina Tastsoglou. 1999. 'Teaching in Environments of Resistance: Toward a Critical, Feminist, and Antiracist Pedagogy'. In *Meeting the Challenge: Feminist Pedagogies in Action*, edited by Maralee Mayberry and Ellen Cronan Rose, 23–46. London: Routledge.

Bergman Rosamond, Annika, and Annica Kronsell. 2018. 'Cosmopolitan Militaries and Dialogic Peacekeeping: Danish and Swedish Women Soldiers in Afghanistan'. *International Feminist Journal of Politics* 20 (2): 172–187. https://doi.org/10.1080/14616742.2017.1378449.

Berlant, Lauren. 2011. *Cruel Optimism*. Durham, NC: Duke University Press.

Bevan, Marianne, and Megan H. MacKenzie. 2012. '"Cowboy" Policing versus "the Softer Stuff"'. *International Feminist Journal of Politics* 14 (4): 508–528. https://doi.org/10.1080/14616742.2012.726095.

Bhabha, Homi K. 1994. *The Location of Culture*. London: Routledge.

Biccum, April R. 2007. 'Exploiting the Ambivalence of a Crisis: A Practitioner Reads "Diversity Training" through Homi Bhabha'. In *Derrida: Negotiating the Legacy*, edited by Madeleine Fagan, Ludovic Glorieux, Indira Hašimbegović, and Marie Suetsugu, 143–158. Edinburgh: Edinburgh University Press.

Blanchard, Eric M. 2003. 'Gender, International Relations, and the Development of Feminist Security Theory'. *Signs: Journal of Women in Culture and Society* 28 (4): 1289–1312. https://doi.org/10.1086/368328.

Boler, Megan. 1999. *Feeling Power: Emotions and Education*. New York: Routledge.

Bonnell, Cheyenne Marilyn. 1999. 'FreshMAN Composition: Blueprint for Subversion'. In *Meeting the Challenge: Feminist Pedagogies in Action*, edited by Maralee Mayberry and Ellen Cronan Rose, 215–228. London: Routledge.

Britzman, Deborah P. 1995. 'Is There a Queer Pedagogy? Or, Stop Reading Straight'. *Educational Theory* 45 (2): 151–165. https://doi.org/doi:10.1111/j.1741-5446.1995.00151.x.

Britzman, Deborah P. 1998. *Lost Subjects, Contested Objects: Toward a Psychoanalytic Inquiry of Learning*. Albany, NY: State University of New York Press.

Britzman, Deborah P. 2013. 'Between Psychoanalysis and Pedagogy: Scenes of Rapprochement and Alienation'. *Curriculum Inquiry* 43 (1): 95–117. https://doi.org/10.1111/curi.12007.

Brown, Vanessa. 2020. 'Locating Feminist Progress in Professional Military Education'. *Atlantis* 41 (2): 26–41.

Brown, Wendy. 2000. 'Suffering Rights as Paradoxes'. *Constellations* 7 (2): 208–229. https://doi.org/10.1111/1467-8675.00183.

Brown, Wendy. 2015. *Undoing the Demos: Neoliberalism's Stealth Revolution*. New York: Zone Books.

Bustelo, Maria, Lucy Ferguson, and Maxime Forest. 2016a. 'Conclusions'. In *The Politics of Feminist Knowledge Transfer: Gender Training and Gender Expertise*, edited by Maria Bustelo, Lucy Ferguson, and Maxime Forest, 157–174. London: Palgrave Macmillan.

Bustelo, Maria, Lucy Ferguson, and Maxime Forest. 2016b. 'Introduction'. In *The Politics of Feminist Knowledge Transfer: Gender Training and Gender Expertise*, edited by Maria Bustelo, Lucy Ferguson, and Maxime Forest, 1–22. London: Palgrave Macmillan.

Butler, Judith. 1986. 'Sex and Gender in Simone de Beauvoir's Second Sex'. *Yale French Studies* 72: 35–49. https://doi.org/10.2307/2930225.

Butler, Judith. 1993. 'Critically Queer'. *GLQ: A Journal of Lesbian and Gay Studies* 1 (1): 17–32. https://doi.org/10.1215/10642684-1-1-17.

Butler, Judith. 2004. *Undoing Gender*. New York: Routledge.

Butler, Judith. 2007a. *Gender Trouble*. New York: Routledge.

Butler, Judith. 2007b. 'Preface to the 1999 Edition'. In *Gender Trouble*, by Judith Butler, vii–xxviii. New York: Routledge.

Butler, Judith. 2009. 'Melancholy Gender—Refused Identification'. *Psychoanalytic Dialogues* 5 (2): 165–180. https://doi.org/10.1080/10481889509539059.

Butler, Judith. 2014. *Bodies That Matter: On the Discursive Limits of 'Sex'*. New York: Routledge.

Butler, Judith. 2016. *Frames of War: When Is Life Grievable?* London: Verso.

Cammaert, Patrick. 2019. 'Q and A—The Nexus between Conflict-Related Sexual Violence and Human Trafficking during Peacekeeping Missions: An Insider's View'. *Journal of Trafficking and Human Exploitation* 3 (1): 87–94.

Carby, Hazel V. 1982. 'White Woman Listen! Black Feminism and the Boundaries of Sisterhood'. In *The Empire Strikes Back: Race and Racism in 70s Britain*, edited by Centre for Contemporary Cultural Studies, 212–235. London: Hutchinson.

Carreiras, Helena. 2010. 'Gendered Culture in Peacekeeping Operations'. *International Peacekeeping* 17 (4): 471–485. https://doi.org/10.1080/13533312.2010.516655.

Carson, Lisa. 2016. 'Pre-Deployment "Gender" Training and the Lack Thereof for Australian Peacekeepers'. *Australian Journal of International Affairs* 70 (3): 275–292. https://doi.org/10.1080/10357718.2015.1133561.

Chappell, Louise, and Fiona Mackay. 2021. 'Feminist Critical Friends: Dilemmas of Feminist Engagement with Governance and Gender Reform Agendas'. *European Journal of Politics and Gender* 4 (3): 321–340. https://doi.org/10.1332/251510820x15922354996155.

Cho, Sumi, Kimberlé Williams Crenshaw, and Leslie McCall. 2013. 'Toward a Field of Intersectionality Studies: Theory, Applications, and Praxis'. *Signs: Journal of Women in Culture and Society* 38 (4): 785–810. https://doi.org/10.1086/669608.

Cockburn, Cynthia. 2010. 'Gender Relations as Causal in Militarization and War'. *International Feminist Journal of Politics* 12 (2): 139–157. https://doi.org/10.1080/14616741003665169.

Cohn, Carol. 2006. 'Motives and Methods: Using Multi-Sited Ethnography to Study US National Security Discourses'. In *Feminist Methodologies for International Relations*, edited by Brooke A. Ackerly, Maria Stern and Jacqui True, 91–107. Cambridge: Cambridge University Press.

Collins, Patricia Hill. 1989. 'The Social Construction of Black Feminist Thought'. *Signs: Journal of Women in Culture and Society* 14 (4): 745–773. https://doi.org/10.1086/494543.

Connell, R. W. 2002. 'Masculinities, the Reduction of Violence and the Pursuit of Peace'. In *The Postwar Moment: Militaries, Masculinities and International Peacekeeping, Bosnia and the Netherlands*, edited by Cynthia Cockburn and Dubravka Zarkov, 33–40. London: Lawrence & Wishart.

Cook, Judith A., and Mary Margaret Fonow. 1986. 'Knowledge and Women's Interests: Issues of Epistemology and Methodology in Feminist Sociological Research'. *Sociological Inquiry* 56 (1): 2–29. doi: 10.1111/j.1475-682X.1986.tb00073.x.

Cook, Sam. 2016. 'The "Woman-in-Conflict" at the UN Security Council: A Subject of Practice'. *International Affairs* 92 (2): 353–372. https://doi.org/10.1111/1468-2346.12553.

Cornwall, Andrea. 2016. 'Towards a Pedagogy for the Powerful'. *IDS Bulletin* 47 (5): 75–88. https://doi.org/10.19088/1968-2016.168.

Curran, David. 2013. 'Training for Peacekeeping: Towards Increased Understanding of Conflict Resolution?' *International Peacekeeping* 20 (1): 80–97. https://doi.org/10.1080/13533312.2012.761841.

Curran, David. 2017. *More than Fighting for Peace? Conflict Resolution, UN Peacekeeping, and the Role of Training Military Personnel*. Cham, Switzerland: Springer.

Davids, Tine, and Anouka van Eerdewijk. 2016. 'The Smothering of Feminist Knowledge: Gender Mainstreaming Articulated through Neoliberal Governmentalities'. In *The Politics of Feminist Knowledge Transfer: Gender Training and Gender Expertise*, edited by Maria Bustelo, Lucy Ferguson, and Maxime Forest, 80–96. London: Palgrave Macmillan.

de Beauvoir, Simone. 1997. *The Second Sex*. Translated by H. M. Parshley. London: Vintage. 1949.

de Jong, Sara, and Susanne Kimm. 2017. 'The Co-Optation of Feminisms: A Research Agenda'. *International Feminist Journal of Politics* 19 (2): 185–200. https://doi.org/10.1080/14616742.2017.1299582.

de Lauretis, Teresa. 1989. *Technologies of Gender: Essays on Theory, Film, and Fiction*. Basingstoke: Macmillan.

Deiana, Maria-Adriana, and Kenneth McDonagh. 2018. '"It Is Important, but . . .": Translating the Women Peace and Security (WPS) Agenda into the Planning of EU Peacekeeping Missions'. *Peacebuilding* 6 (1): 34–48. https://doi.org/10.1080/21647259.2017.1303870.

Dhawan, Nikita. 2012. 'Hegemonic Listening and Subversive Silences: Ethical-Political Imperatives'. In *Destruction in the Performative*, edited by Alice Lagaay and Michael Lorber, 47–60. Amsterdam: Rodopi.
DPKO & DFS. 2017. 'Lesson 2.4: Women, Peace and Security'. United Nations. Accessed 19 July 2019. http://dag.un.org/bitstream/handle/11176/400595/FINAL%20Lesson%20 2.4%20160517.pdf?sequence=49&isAllowed=y.
DPKO/DFS. 2010. 'DPKO/DFS Guidelines: Integrating a Gender Perspective into the Work of United Nations Military in Peacekeeping Operations'. Accessed 25 February 2018. https://peacekeeping.un.org/sites/default/files/dpko_dfs_gender_military_perspective.pdf.
Duffey, Tamara. 2000. 'Cultural Issues in Contemporary Peacekeeping'. *International Peacekeeping* 7 (1): 142–168. https://doi.org/10.1080/13533310008413823.
Duffield, Mark. 2001. *Global Governance and the New Wars: The Merging of Development and Security*. London: Zed Books.
Duncanson, Claire. 2009. 'Forces for Good? Narratives of Military Masculinity in Peacekeeping Operations'. *International Feminist Journal of Politics* 11 (1): 63–80.
Duncanson, Claire. 2013. *Forces for Good? Military Masculinities and Peacebuilding in Afghanistan and Iraq*. Basingstoke: Palgrave Macmillan.
Duncanson, Claire. 2018. 'Beyond Liberal vs Liberating: Women's Economic Empowerment in the United Nations' Women, Peace and Security Agenda'. *International Feminist Journal of Politics* 21 (1): 111–130.
Duncanson, Claire, and Rachel Woodward. 2016. 'Regendering the Military: Theorizing Women's Military Participation'. *Security Dialogue* 47 (1): 3–21. https://doi.org/10.1177/0967010615614137.
Dunlop, Rishma. 1999. 'Beyond Dualism: Toward a Dialogic Negotiation of Difference'. *Canadian Journal of Education/Revue canadienne de l'éducation* 24 (1): 57–69. https://doi.org/10.2307/1585771.
Duriesmith, David. 2020. 'Engaging or Changing Men? Understandings of Masculinity and Change in the New "Men, Peace and Security" Agenda'. *Peacebuilding* 8 (4): 418–431. https://doi.org/10.1080/21647259.2019.1687076.
Edelman, Lee. 2004. *No Future: Queer Theory and the Death Drive*. Durham, NC: Duke University Press.
Ellsworth, Elizabeth. 1989. 'Why Doesn't This Feel Empowering? Working Through the Repressive Myths of Critical Pedagogy'. *Harvard Educational Review* 59 (3): 297–325. doi: 10.17763/haer.59.3.058342114k266250.
Elshtain, Jean Bethke. 1982. 'On Beautiful Souls, Just Warriors and Feminist Consciousness'. *Women's Studies International Forum* 5 (3-4): 341–348. https://doi.org/10.1016/0277-5395(82)90043-7
Enderstein, Athena-Maria. 2018. '"First of All, Gender Is Power": Intersectionality as Praxis in Gender Training'. *Studies on Home and Community Science* 11 (2): 44–56. https://doi.org/10.1080/09737189.2017.1420380.
Enloe, Cynthia. 2000. *Maneuvers: The International Politics of Militarizing Women's Lives*. Berkeley, CA: University of California Press.
Enloe, Cynthia. 2014. *Bananas, Beaches and Bases: Making Feminist Sense of International Politics*. 2nd ed. Berkley, CA: University of California Press.
Eriksson Baaz, Maria, and Maria Stern. 2013. *Sexual Violence as a Weapon of War? Perceptions, Prescriptions, Problems in the Congo and Beyond*. London: Zed Books.
Eschle, Catherine, and Bice Maiguashca. 2018. 'Theorising Feminist Organising in and against Neoliberalism: Beyond Co-Optation and Resistance?' *European Journal of Politics and Gender* 1 (1–2): 223–239. https://doi.org/10.1332/251510818x15272520831120.
Farris, Sara R. 2017. *In the Name of Women's Rights: The Rise of Femonationalism*. Durham, NC: Duke University Press.
Fassin, Didier. 2013. *Enforcing Order: An Ethnography of Urban Policing*. English ed. Cambridge: Polity.

'Female Soldiers Are Changing How Armed Forces Work'. 2021. *The Economist*, 24 April.
Ferguson, Lucy. 2015. 'This Is Our Gender Person'. *International Feminist Journal of Politics* 17 (3): 380–397. https://doi.org/10.1080/14616742.2014.918787.
Ferguson, Lucy. 2019a. 'Exploring Privilege through Feminist Gender Training'. *European Journal of Politics and Gender* 2 (1): 113–130. https://doi.org/10.1332/251510819X15471289106059.
Ferguson, Lucy. 2019b. *Gender Training: A Transformative Tool for Gender Equality*. Cham, Switzerland: Palgrave Pivot.
Fetherston, A. Betts. 1998. 'Voices from Warzones: Implications for Training UN Peacekeepers'. In *A Future for Peacekeeping?*, edited by Edward Moxon-Browne, 158–175. Basingstoke: Macmillan Press.
Fetherston, A. Betts, and Carolyn Nordstrom. 1995. 'Overcoming Habitus in Conflict Management: UN Peacekeeping and War Zone Ethnography'. *Peace and Change* 20 (1): 94–119. https://doi.org/10.1111/j.1468-0130.1995.tb00625.x.
Flynn, Elizabeth. 2001. 'Strategic, Counter-Strategic, and Reactive Resistance in the Feminist Classroom'. In *Insurrections: Approaches to Resistance in Composition Studies*, edited by Andrea Greenbaum, 17–34. Albany, NY: State University of New York Press.
Fonow, Mary Margaret, and Judith A. Cook. 1991. 'Back to the Future: A Look at the Second Wave of Feminist Epistemology and Methodology'. In *Beyond Methodology: Feminist Scholarship as Lived Research*, edited by Mary Margaret Fonow and Judith A. Cook, 1–15. Indianapolis, IN: Indiana University Press.
Foucault, Michel. 1991. *Discipline and Punish: The Birth of the Prison*. Translated by Alan Sheridan. London: Penguin. 1971.
Foucault, Michel. 1998. *The History of Sexuality: The Will to Knowledge*. Translated by Robert Hurley. Vol. 1. London: Penguin. 1976.
Freire, Paulo. 1976. *Education, the Practice of Freedom*. London: Writers and Readers Publishing Cooperative.
Freire, Paulo. 2005. *Pedagogy of the Oppressed*. 30th Anniversary Ed. London: Continuum. 1970.
Friedman, Marilyn. 1996. 'The Unholy Alliance of Sex and Gender'. *Metaphilosophy* 27 (1–2): 78–91. https://doi.org/10.1111/j.1467-9973.1996.tb00868.x.
Furia, Stacie Robyn. 2009. 'Memoirs of Captain Fury: An Ethnographic Study of Gender and the Military'. Doctor of Philosophy, Sociology, University of California Santa Barbara.
Ging, Debbie. 2017. 'Alphas, Betas, and Incels: Theorizing the Masculinities of the Manosphere'. *Men and Masculinities* 22 (4): 638–657. https://doi.org/10.1177/1097184X17706401.
Goffman, Erving. 1990. *The Presentation of the Self in Everyday Life*. London: Penguin. 1959.
Goldstein, Joshua S. 2003. *War and Gender: How Gender Shapes the War System and Vice Versa*. Cambridge: Cambridge University Press.
Gore, Jennifer M. 1993. *The Struggle for Pedagogies: Critical and Feminist Discourses as Regimes of Truth*. New York, NY: Routledge.
Gray, Harriet. 2016. 'The Geopolitics of Intimacy and the Intimacies of Geopolitics: Combat Deployment, Post-Traumatic Stress Disorder, and Domestic Abuse in the British Military'. *Feminist Studies* 42 (1): 138–165. https://doi.org/10.15767/feministstudies.42.1.138.
Haaland, Torunn Laugen. 2012. 'Friendly War-Fighters and Invisible Women: Perceptions of Gender and Masculinities in the Norwegian Armed Forces on Missions Abroad'. In *Making Gender, Making War: Violence, Military and Peacekeeping Practices*, edited by Annica Kronsell and Erika Svedberg, 63–74. New York: Routledge.
Haastrup, Toni, and Jamie J. Hagen. 2021. 'Racial Hierarchies of Knowledge Production in the Women, Peace and Security Agenda'. *Critical Studies on Security* 9 (1): 27–30. https://doi.org/10.1080/21624887.2021.1904192.
Halperin, David M. 2012. *How to Be Gay*. Cambridge, MA: Harvard University Press.
Harding, Sandra. 1993. 'Rethinking Standpoint Epistemology: What Is "Strong Objectivity"?' In *Feminist Epistemologies*, edited by Linda Alcoff and Elizabeth Potter, 49–82. London: Routledge.

Hearn, Jeff. 2012. 'Men/Masculinities: War/Militarism—Searching (for) the Obvious Connections?' In *Making Gender, Making War: Violence, Military and Peacekeeping Practices*, edited by Annica Kronsell and Erika Svedberg, 35–47. London: Routledge.
Hemmings, Clare. 2011. *Why Stories Matter: The Political Grammar of Feminist Theory*. Durham, NC: Duke University Press.
Hemmings, Clare. 2012. 'Affective Solidarity: Feminist Reflexivity and Political Transformation'. *Feminist Theory* 13 (2): 147–161. https://doi.org/10.1177/1464700112442643.
Hendricks, Cheryl. 2015. 'Women, Peace and Security in Africa'. *African Security Review* 24 (4): 364–375. https://doi.org/10.1080/10246029.2015.1099759.
Henry, Marsha. 2003. 'Where Are You Really From? Representation, Identity and Power in the Fieldwork Experiences of a South Asian Diasporic'. *Qualitative Research* 3 (2): 229–242. doi: 10.1177/14687941030032005.
Henry, Marsha. 2012. 'Peacexploitation? Interrogating Labor Hierarchies and Global Sisterhood among Indian and Uruguayan Female Peacekeepers'. *Globalizations* 9 (1): 15–33. https://doi.org/10.1080/14747731.2012.627716.
Henry, Marsha. 2013. 'Sexual Exploitation and Abuse in UN Peacekeeping Missions: Problematising Current Responses'. In *Gender, Agency, and Coercion: Thinking Gender in Transnational Times*, edited by Sumi Madhok, Anne Phillips, and Kalpana Wilson, 122–142. London: Palgrave Macmillan Limited.
Henry, Marsha. 2015. 'Parades, Parties and Pests: Contradictions of Everyday Life in Peacekeeping Economies'. *Journal of Intervention and Statebuilding* 9 (3): 372–390. https://doi.org/10.1080/17502977.2015.1070021.
Henry, Marsha. 2021. 'On the Necessity of Critical Race Feminism for Women, Peace and Security'. *Critical Studies on Security* 9 (1): 22–26. https://doi.org/10.1080/21624887.2021.1904191.
Henry, Marsha. 2024. *The End of Peacekeeping: Gender, Race, and the Martial Politics of Intervention*. Philadelphia, PA: University of Pennsylvania Press.
Higate, Paul. 2003. '"Soft Clerks" and "Hard Civvies": Pluralizing Military Masculinities'. In *Military Masculinities: Identity and the State*, edited by Paul R. Higate, 27–42. Westport, CT: Praeger.
Higate, Paul. 2004. *Gender Relations and Peacekeeping in Democratic Republic of Congo and Sierra Leone*. Pretoria: ISS Africa. https://www.files.ethz.ch/isn/118357/91%20FULL.pdf.
Higate, Paul, and Marsha Henry. 2009. *Insecure Spaces: Peacekeeping, Power and Performance in Haiti, Kosovo and Liberia*. London: Zed Books.
Hilhorst, Dorothea, and Nynke Douma. 2018. 'Beyond the Hype? The Response to Sexual Violence in the Democratic Republic of the Congo in 2011 and 2014'. *Disasters* 42 (S1): S79–S98. https://doi.org/doi:10.1111/disa.12270.
Hines, Sally. 2019. 'The Feminist Frontier: On Trans and Feminism'. *Journal of Gender Studies* 28 (2): 145–157. https://doi.org/10.1080/09589236.2017.1411791.
Holmes, Georgina. 2019. 'Situating Agency, Embodied Practices and Norm Implementation in Peacekeeping Training'. *International Peacekeeping* 26 (1): 55–84. https://doi.org/10.1080/13533312.2018.1503934.
Holohan, Anne. 2019. 'Transformative Training in Soft Skills for Peacekeepers: Gaming for Peace'. *International Peacekeeping* 26 (5): 556–578. https://doi.org/10.1080/13533312.2019.1623677.
Holvikivi, Aiko. 2019. 'Gender Experts and Critical Friends: Research in Relations of Proximity'. *European Journal of Politics and Gender* 2 (1): 131–147. https://doi.org/10.1332/251510819X15471289106068.
Holvikivi, Aiko. 2021. 'Training the Troops on Gender: The Making of a Transnational Practice'. *International Peacekeeping* 28 (2): 175–199. https://doi.org/10.1080/13533312.2020.1869540.

Holvikivi, Aiko. 2023. 'Contending with Paradox: Feminist Investments in Gender Training'. *Signs: Journal of Women in Culture and Society* 48 (3): 533–555. https://doi.org/10.1086/723268.

Holvikivi, Aiko, and Kristin Valasek. 2016. 'How to Integrate Gender into Military Curricula'. In *Handbook on Teaching Gender in the Military*, edited by The Partnership for Peace Consortium Security Sector Reform Working Group and Education Development Working Group, 81–98. Geneva: DCAF and PfPC.

hooks, bell. 1994. *Teaching to Transgress: Education as the Practice of Freedom*. Kindle vols. New York: Routledge.

hooks, bell. 2003. *Teaching Community: A Pedagogy of Hope*. New York: Routledge.

hooks, bell. 2009. *Teaching Critical Thinking: Practical Wisdom*. New York: Routledge.

Huddart, David. 2006. *Homi K. Bhabha*. London: Routledge.

Hudson, Heidi. 2016. 'Decolonising Gender and Peacebuilding: Feminist Frontiers and Border Thinking in Africa'. *Peacebuilding* 4 (2): 194–209. https://doi.org/10.1080/21647259.2016.1192242.

Hudson, Valerie M., Bonnie Ballif-Spanvill, Mary Caprioli, and Chad F. Emmett. 2014. *Sex and World Peace*. New York: Columbia University Press.

Hurley, Matthew. 2018a. 'The "Genderman": (Re)negotiating Militarized Masculinities when "Doing Gender" at NATO'. *Critical Military Studies* 4 (1): 72–91. https://doi.org/10.1080/23337486.2016.1264108.

Hurley, Matthew. 2018b. 'Watermelons and Weddings: Making Women, Peace and Security "Relevant" at NATO through (Re)Telling Stories of Success'. *Global Society* 32 (4): 436–456. https://doi.org/10.1080/13600826.2018.1440195.

Hutchings, Kimberly. 2013. 'Choosers or Losers? Feminist Ethical and Political Agency in a Plural and Unequal World'. In *Gender, Agency, and Coercion*, edited by Sumi Madhok, Anne Phillips and Kalpana Wilson, 14–28. Basingstoke: Palgrave MacMillan.

Hutchings, Kimberly. 2018. 'Pacifism Is Dirty: Towards an Ethico-Political Defence'. *Critical Studies on Security* 6 (2): 176–192. https://doi.org/10.1080/21624887.2017.1377998.

Jackson, Lisa F. 2007. *The Greatest Silence: Rape in the Congo*. Women Make Movies.

Jacoby, Tami. 2006. 'From the Trenches: Dilemmas of Feminist Fieldwork'. In *Feminist Methodologies for International Relations*, edited by Brooke A. Ackerly, Maria Stern and Jacqui True, 153–173. Cambridge: Cambridge University Press.

Jaggar, Alison M. 1997. 'Love and Knowledge: Emotion in Feminist Epistemology'. In *Feminist Social Thought: A Reader*, edited by Diana Tietjens Meyers, 384–405. New York: Routledge. Original edition, 1989.

Jauhola, Marjaana. 2010. 'Building Back Better? Negotiating Normative Boundaries of Gender Mainstreaming and Post-Tsunami Reconstruction in Nanggroe Aceh Darussalam, Indonesia'. *Review of International Studies* 36 (1): 29–50. https://doi.org/10.1017/S0260210509990490.

Jauhola, Marjaana. 2013. *Post-Tsunami Reconstruction in Indonesia: Negotiating Normativity through Gender Mainstreaming Initiatives in Aceh*. London: Routledge.

Jennings, Kathleen M. 2019. 'Conditional Protection? Sex, Gender, and Discourse in UN Peacekeeping'. *International Studies Quarterly* 63 (1): 30–42. https://doi.org/10.1093/isq/sqy048.

Johannsen, Agneta M. 2009. 'Training Resources on Security Sector Reform and Gender'. In *Gender and Security Sector Reform Training Resource Package*, edited by Megan Bastick and Kristin Valasek. Geneva: DCAF.

Johnson-Sirleaf, Ellen. 2009. *This Child Will Be Great*. New York: Harper Collins.

Kabeer, Naila. 1991. 'Gender, Development, and Training: Raising Awareness in the Planning Process'. *Development in Practice* 1 (3): 185–195. https://doi.org/10.1080/096145249100076371.

Kandiyoti, Deniz. 1988. 'Bargaining with Patriarchy'. *Gender and Society* 2 (3): 274–290. https://doi.org/10.1177/089124388002003004.

Kaplan, Laura Duhan. 1994. 'Woman as Caretaker: An Archetype That Supports Patriarchal Militarism'. *Hypatia* 9 (2): 123–133. https://doi.org/10.1111/j.1527-2001.1994.tb00436.x.

Kennedy-Pipe, Caroline. 2017. 'Liberal Feminists, Militaries and War'. In *The Palgrave International Handbook of Gender and the Military*, edited by Rachel Woodward and Claire Duncanson, 23–37. London: Palgrave Macmillan.

King, Anthony. 2013. *The Combat Soldier: Infantry Tactics and Cohesion in the Twentieth and Twenty-First Centuries*. Oxford: Oxford University Press.

Kirby, Paul. 2013. 'Refusing to Be a Man? Men's Responsibility for War Rape and the Problem of Social Structures in Feminist and Gender Theory'. *Men and Masculinities* 16 (1): 93–114. https://doi.org/10.1177/1097184X12468100.

Kirby, Paul. 2015. 'Ending Sexual Violence in Conflict: The Preventing Sexual Violence Initiative and Its Critics'. *International Affairs* 91 (3): 457–472. https://doi.org/10.1111/1468-2346.12283.

Korolczuk, Elżbieta, and Agnieszka Graff. 2018. 'Gender as "Ebola from Brussels": The Anticolonial Frame and the Rise of Illiberal Populism'. *Signs: Journal of Women in Culture and Society* 43 (4): 797–821. https://doi.org/10.1086/696691.

Kronsell, Annica. 2012. *Gender, Sex, and the Postnational Defense: Militarism and Peacekeeping*. Oxford: Oxford University Press.

Kunz, Rahel. 2014. 'Gender and Security Sector Reform: Gendering Differently?' *International Peacekeeping* 21 (5): 604–622. https://doi.org/10.1080/13533312.2014.963319.

Kunz, Rahel. 2016. 'Windows of Opportunity, Trojan Horses, and Waves of Women on the Move: De-Colonizing the Circulation of Feminist Knowledges through Metaphors?' In *The Politics of Feminist Knowledge Transfer: Gender Training and Gender Expertise*, edited by Maria Bustelo, Lucy Ferguson, and Maxime Forest, 99–117. London: Palgrave Macmillan.

Kunz, Rahel, Elisabeth Prügl, and Hayley Thompson. 2019. 'Gender Expertise in Global Governance: Contesting the Boundaries of a Field'. *European Journal of Politics and Gender* 2 (1): 23–40. https://doi.org/10.1332/251510819X15471289106112.

Lackenbauer, Heléne, and Richard Langlais. 2013. *Review of the Practical Implications of UNSCR 1325 for the Conduct of NATO-Led Operations and Missions*. Stockholm: Swedish Defence Research Agency. https://www.nato.int/nato_static/assets/pdf/pdf_2013_10/2013 1021_131023-UNSCR1325-review-final.pdf.

Laplonge, Dean. 2015. 'The Absence of Masculinity in Gender Training for UN Peacekeepers'. *Peace Review* 27 (1): 91–99. https://doi.org/10.1080/10402659.2015.1000198.

Lather, Patti. 1991. *Getting Smart: Feminist Research and Pedagogy with/in the Postmodern*. London: Routledge.

Leeds, Christopher A. 2001. 'Culture, Conflict Resolution, Peacekeeper Training and the D Mediator'. *International Peacekeeping* 8 (4): 92–110. https://doi.org/10.1080/1353331010 8413922.

Lewis, Magda. 1992. 'Interrupting Patriarchy: Politics, Resistance and Transformation in the Feminist Classroom'. In *Feminisms and Critical Pedagogy*, edited by Carmen Luke and Jennifer Gore, 167–191. New York and London: Routledge.

Lewis, Tyson Edward. 2010. 'Paulo Freire's Last Laugh: Rethinking Critical Pedagogy's Funny Bone through Jacques Rancière'. *Educational Philosophy and Theory* 42 (5–6): 635–648. https://doi.org/10.1111/j.1469-5812.2010.00690.x.

Lombardo, Emanuela, and Lut Mergaert. 2013. 'Gender Mainstreaming and Resistance to Gender Training: A Framework for Studying Implementation'. *NORA—Nordic Journal of Feminist and Gender Research* 21 (4): 296–311. https://doi.org/10.1080/08038 740.2013.851115

Lombardo, Emanuela, and Lut Mergaert. 2016. 'Resistance in Gender Training and Mainstreaming Processes'. In *The Politics of Feminist Knowledge Transfer: Gender Training and Gender Expertise*, edited by Maria Bustelo, Lucy Ferguson, and Maxime Forest, 43–61. London: Palgrave Macmillan.

Lugones, María. 2007. 'Heterosexualism and the Colonial/Modern Gender System'. *Hypatia* 22 (1): 186–209. https://doi.org/10.1111/j.1527-2001.2007.tb01156.x.

Lugones, María. 2010. 'Toward a Decolonial Feminism'. *Hypatia* 25 (4): 742–759. https://doi.org/10.1111/j.1527-2001.2010.01137.x.

Luke, Carmen, and Jennifer Gore. 1992. 'Introduction'. In *Feminisms and Critical Pedagogy*, edited by Carmen Luke and Jennifer Gore, 1–14. New York and London: Routledge.

Mackay, Angela. 2005. 'Mainstreaming Gender in United Nations Peacekeeping Training: Examples from East Timor, Ethiopia, and Eritrea'. In *Gender, Conflict and Peacekeeping*, edited by Dyan E. Mazurana, Angela Raven-Roberts, and Jane L. Parpart, 265–279. Oxford: Rowman and Littlefield.

Madhok, Sumi. 2020. 'A Critical Reflexive Politics of Location, "Feminist Debt" and Thinking from the Global South'. *European Journal of Women's Studies* 27 (4): 394–412. https://doi.org/10.1177/1350506820952492

Maher, Frances A. 1987. 'Toward a Richer Theory of Feminist Pedagogy: A Comparison of "Liberation" and "Gender" Models for Teaching and Learning'. *Journal of Education* 169 (3): 91–100. http://www.jstor.org/stable/42741791.

Mahmood, Saba. 2005. *Politics of Piety: The Islamic Revival and the Feminist Subject*. Princeton, NJ: Princeton University Press.

Mäki-Rahkola, Anne, and Henri Myrttinen. 2014. 'Reliable Professionals, Sensitive Dads and Tough Fighters'. *International Feminist Journal of Politics* 16 (3): 470–489. https://doi.org/10.1080/14616742.2012.755834.

Martin, Barbara L., and Leslie J. Briggs. 1986. *The Affective and Cognitive Domains: Integration for Instruction and Research*. Englewood Cliffs, NJ: Educational Technology Publications.

Medie, Peace A., and Alice J. Kang. 2018. 'Power, Knowledge and the Politics of Gender in the Global South'. *European Journal of Politics and Gender* 1 (1–2): 37–54. https://doi.org/10.1332/251510818X15272520831157.

Mehta, Akanskha. 2019. 'Teaching Gender, Race, Sexuality: Reflections on Feminist Pedagogy'. *Kohl* 5 (1): 23–30. https://doi.org/10.36583/kohl/5-1-4.

Mertens, Charlotte. 2019. 'Undoing Research on Sexual Violence in the Eastern Democratic Republic of Congo'. *ACME: An International Journal for Critical Geographies* 18 (3): 662–687. https://acme-journal.org/index.php/acme/article/view/1594/.

Mignolo, Walter D., and Wanda Nanibush. 2018. 'Thinking and Engaging with the Decolonial: A Conversation between Walter D. Mignolo and Wanda Nanibush'. *Afterall* 45: 24–29. https://doi.org/10.1086/698391.

Miller, Laura L., and Charles Moskos. 1995. 'Humanitarians or Warriors? Race, Gender, and Combat Status in Operation Restore Hope'. *Armed Forces and Society* 21 (4): 615–637. https://doi.org/10.1177/0095327X9502100406.

Mohanty, Chandra Talpade. 1988. 'Under Western Eyes: Feminist Scholarship and Colonial Discourses'. *Feminist Review* 30 (1): 61–88. https://doi.org/10.2307/1395054.

Moran, Mary. 2012. 'Our Mothers Have Spoken: Synthesizing Old and New Forms of Women's Political Authority in Liberia'. *Journal of International Women's Studies* 13 (4): 51–66.

Motlafi, Nompumelelo. 2018. 'The Coloniality of the Gaze on Sexual Violence: A Stalled Attempt at a South Africa—Rwanda Dialogue?' *International Feminist Journal of Politics* 20 (1): 9–23. https://doi.org/10.1080/14616742.2017.1358908.

Mukhopadhyay, Maitrayee. 2014. 'Mainstreaming Gender or Reconstituting the Mainstream? Gender Knowledge in Development'. *Journal of International Development* 26 (3): 356–367. https://doi.org/10.1002/jid.2946.

Mukhopadhyay, Maitrayee, and Franz Wong. 2007. 'Introduction'. In *Revisiting Gender Training: The Making and Remaking of Gender Knowledge*, edited by Maitrayee Mukhopadhyay and Franz Wong, 11–26. Amsterdam: KIT Royal Tropical Institute & Oxfam GB.

Narayan, Uma. 2000. 'Essence of Culture and a Sense of History: A Feminist Critique of Cultural Essentialism'. In *Decentering the Center: Philosophy for a Multicultural, Postcolonial, and Feminist World*, edited by Uma Narayan and Sandra Harding, 80–100. Bloomington, IN: Indiana University Press.

Noddings, Nel. 1988. 'An Ethic of Caring and Its Implications for Instructional Arrangements'. *American Journal of Education* 96 (2): 215–230. http://www.jstor.org/stable/1085252.

Otto, Dianne. 2014. 'Beyond Stories of Victory and Danger: Resisting Feminism's Amenability to Serving Security Council Politics'. In *Rethinking Peacekeeping, Gender Equality and Collective Security*, edited by Gina Heathcote and Dianne Otto, 157–172. Basingstoke: Palgrave Macmillan.

Otto, Dianne, and Gina Heathcote. 2014. 'Rethinking Peacekeeping, Gender Equality and Collective Security: An Introduction'. In *Rethinking Peacekeeping, Gender Equality and Collective Security*, edited by Gina Heathcote and Dianne Otto, 1–20. Basingstoke: Palgrave Macmillan.

Oyèwùmí, Oyèrónkẹ́. 1997. *The Invention of Women: Making an African Sense of Western Gender Discourses*. Minneapolis, MN: University of Minnesota Press.

Oyèwùmí, Oyèrónkẹ́. 2011. 'Beyond Gendercentric Models: Restoring Motherhood to Yorùbá Discourses of Art and Aesthetics'. In *Gender Epistemologies in Africa: Gendering Traditions, Spaces, Social Institutions and Identities*, edited by Oyèrónkẹ́ Oyèwùmí, 223–238. New York: Palgrave Macmillan.

Oyèwùmí, Oyèrónkẹ́. 2016. *What Gender Is Motherhood? Changing Yorùbá Ideals of Power, Procreation, and Identity in the Age of Modernity*. New York: Palgrave Macmillan.

Paris, Roland. 2002. 'International Peacebuilding and the "Mission Civilisatrice"'. *Review of International Studies* 28 (4): 637–656. https://doi.org/10.1017/S026021050200637X.

Patrick, Otim. 2011. *They Slept with Me*. Refugee Law Project.

Penttinen, Elina. 2012. 'Nordic Women and International Crisis Management: A Politics of Hope?' In *Making Gender, Making War: Violence, Military and Peacekeeping Practices*, edited by Annica Kronsell and Erika Svedberg, 153–164. New York: Routledge.

Pepper, Analee. 2012. *Gender Training for the Security Sector: Lessons Identified and Practical Resources*. Geneva: DCAF. https://www.dcaf.ch/sites/default/files/publications/documents/Gender_Training_for_the_Security_Sector_Lessons_Identified_Practical_Resources_Update-2016.pdf.

Peters, Michael, and Colin Lankshear. 1996. 'Postmodern Counternarratives'. In *Counternarratives: Cultural Studies and Critical Pedagogies in Postmodern Spaces*, edited by Henry A. Giroux, Colin Lankshear, Peter McLaren, and Michael Peters, 1–39. New York: Routledge.

Phipps, Alison. 2020. *Me, Not You: The Trouble with Mainstream Feminism*. Manchester: Manchester University Press.

Plantenga, Dorine. 2004. 'Gender, Identity, and Diversity: Learning from Insights Gained in Transformative Gender Training'. *Gender and Development* 12 (1): 40–46. https://doi.org/10.1080/13552070410001726506

Pratt, Nicola. 2013. 'Reconceptualising Gender, Reinscribing Racial-Sexual Boundaries in International Security: The Case of UN Security Council Resolution 1325 on "Women, Peace and Security"'. *International Studies Quarterly* 57 (4): 772–783. https://doi.org/10.1111/isqu.12032.

Prebel, Julie. 2014. 'Resistance Revisited: Resolving Gender Trouble in the First-Year Writing Classroom'. *Pedagogy* 14 (3): 531–539. https://doi.org/10.1215/15314200-2715832

Prügl, Elisabeth. 2010. 'Gender Expertise and Feminist Knowledge'. Gender Politics in International Governance, Graduate Institute, Geneva, 6–8 October 2010.

Prügl, Elisabeth. 2013. 'Gender Expertise as Feminist Strategy'. In *Feminist Strategies in International Governance*, edited by Gülay Caglar, Elisabeth Prügl, and Susanne Zwingel, 57–73. London: Routledge.

Prügl, Elisabeth. 2016. 'How to Wield Feminist Power'. In *The Politics of Feminist Knowledge Transfer: Gender Training and Gender Expertise*, edited by Maria Bustelo, Lucy Ferguson, and Maxime Forest, 25–42. London: Palgrave Macmillan.

Pruitt, Lesley J. 2016. *The Women in Blue Helmets: Gender, Policing, and the UN's First All-Female Peacekeeping Unit.* Oakland, CA: University of California Press.

Pruitt, Lesley J. 2018. 'A Global South State's Challenge to Gendered Global Cultures of Peacekeeping'. In *Revisiting Gendered States: Feminist Imaginings of the State in International Relations,* edited by Swati Parashar, J. Ann Tickner, and Jacqui True, 123–138. Oxford: Oxford University Press.

Puar, Jasbir K. 2007. *Terrorist Assemblages: Homonationalism in Queer Times.* Durham, NC: Duke University Press.

Puechguirbal, Nadine. 2003. 'Gender Training for Peacekeepers: Lessons from the DRC'. *International Peacekeeping* 10 (4): 113–128. https://doi.org/10.1080/13533310308559352.

Quilty, Aideen. 2017. 'Queer Provocations! Exploring Queerly Informed Disruptive Pedagogies within Feminist Community-Higher-Education Landscapes'. *Irish Educational Studies* 36 (1): 107–123. https://doi.org/10.1080/03323315.2017.1289704.

Rao, Rahul. 2020. *Out of Time: The Queer Politics of Postcoloniality.* Oxford Studies in Gender and International Relations. New York: Oxford University Press.

Razack, Sherene. 2003. 'Those Who "Witness the Evil"'. *Hypatia* 18 (1): 204–211. https://doi.org/10.1111/j.1527-2001.2003.tb00790.x.

Razack, Sherene. 2004. *Dark Threats and White Knights: The Somalia Affair, Peacekeeping, and the New Imperialism.* Toronto: University of Toronto Press.

Razack, Sherene. 2007. 'Stealing the Pain of Others: Reflections on Canadian Humanitarian Responses'. *Review of Education, Pedagogy, and Cultural Studies* 29 (4): 375–394. https://doi.org/10.1080/10714410701454198.

Read, Róisín. 2019. 'Comparing Conflict-Related Sexual Violence: Expertise, Politics and Documentation'. *Civil Wars* 21 (4): 468–488. https://doi.org/10.1080/13698249.2019.1642613.

Reimann, Cordula. 2013. *Trainer Manual: Mainstreaming Gender into Peacebuilding Trainings.* Berlin: Center for International Peace Operations (ZIF) & Deutsche Gesellschaft für Internationale Zusammenarbeit (GIZ).

Rich, Adrienne Cecile. 1995. *On Lies, Secrets, and Silence: Selected Prose 1966–1978.* New York: Norton.

Rich, Adrienne. 2003. 'Notes toward a Politics of Location'. In *Feminist Postcolonial Theory: A Reader,* edited by Reina Lewis and Sara Mills, 29–42. New York: Routledge.

Richmond, Oliver P. 2011. *A Post-Liberal Peace.* London: Routledge.

Rodríguez, Juana María. 2014. *Sexual Futures, Queer Gestures, and Other Latina Longings.* New York: New York University Press.

Roy, Srila. 2022. *Changing the Subject: Feminist and Queer Politics in Neoliberal India.* Durham, NC: Duke University Press.

Ryngaert, Cedric. 2017. 'Peacekeepers Facilitating Human Rights Violations: The Liability of the Dutch State in the Mothers of Srebrenica Cases'. *Netherlands International Law Review* 64 (3): 453–535. https://doi.org/10.1007/s40802-017-0101-6.

Sasson-Levy, Orna, and Sarit Amram-Katz. 2007. 'Gender Integration in Israeli Officer Training: Degendering and Regendering the Military'. *Signs: Journal of Women in Culture and Society* 33 (1): 105–133. https://doi.org/10.1086/518262.

Schniedewind, Nancy. 1987. 'Teaching Feminist Process'. *Women's Studies Quarterly* 15 (3/4): 15–31. http://www.jstor.org/stable/40003433.

Schott, Robin May. 2015. 'The Reflexivity of Tears: Documentaries of Sexual Military Assault'. In *Documenting World Politics: A Critical Companion to IR and Non-Fiction Film,* edited by Rens van Munster and Casper Sylvest, 132–148. London: Routledge.

Scott, Joan Wallach. 1996. *Only Paradoxes to Offer: French Feminists and the Rights of Man.* Cambridge, MA: Harvard University Press.

Sedgwick, Eve Kosofsky. 2003. *Touching Feeling: Affect, Pedagogy, Performativity.* Durham, NC: Duke University Press.

Sexwale, Bunie M. Matlanyane. 1996. 'What Happened to Feminist Politics in "Gender Training"?' In *New Frontiers in Women's Studies: Knowledge, Identity, and Nationalism*, edited by Mary Maynard and June Purvis, 51–62. London: Taylor & Francis.

Shepherd, Laura J. 2006. 'Veiled References: Constructions of Gender in the Bush Administration Discourse on the Attacks on Afghanistan Post-9/11'. *International Feminist Journal of Politics* 8 (1): 19–41. https://doi.org/10.1080/14616740500415425.

Simić, Olivera. 2010. 'Does the Presence of Women Really Matter? Towards Combating Male Sexual Violence in Peacekeeping Operations'. *International Peacekeeping* 17 (2): 188–199. https://doi.org/10.1080/13533311003625084.

Sjoberg, Laura. 2016. *Women as Wartime Rapists: Beyond Sensation and Stereotyping; Perspectives on Political Violence*. New York: New York University Press.

Smele, Sandra, Rehanna Siew-Sarju, Elena Chou, Patricia Breton, and Nicole Bernhardt. 2017. 'Doing Feminist Difference Differently: Intersectional Pedagogical Practices in the Context of the Neoliberal Diversity Regime'. *Teaching in Higher Education* 22 (6): 690–704. https://doi.org/10.1080/13562517.2016.1273214.

Sontag, Susan. 2004. *Regarding the Pain of Others*. London: Penguin.

Spade, Dean, and Aaron Belkin. 2021. 'Queer Militarism?! The Politics of Military Inclusion Advocacy in Authoritarian Times'. *GLQ: A Journal of Lesbian and Gay Studies* 27 (2): 281–307. https://doi.org/10.1215/10642684-8871705.

Spivak, Gayatri Chakravorty. 2010. 'Can the Subaltern Speak?' In *Can the Subaltern Speak? Reflections on the History of an Idea*, edited by Rosalind Morris, 21–78. New York: Columbia University Press. Original edition, 1988.

Spivak, Gayatri Chakravorty, and Elizabeth Grosz. 1990. 'Criticism, Feminism, and the Institution'. In *The Post-Colonial Critic: Interviews, Strategies, Dialogues*, edited by Sarah Harasym, 1–16. London: Routledge.

Spivak, Gayatri Chakravorty, and Sarah Harasym. 1990. 'Practical Politics of the Open End'. In *The Post-Colonial Critic: Interviews, Strategies, Dialogues*, edited by Sarah Harasym, 95–112. London: Routledge.

Spivak, Gayatri Chakravorty, John Hutnyk, Cott McQuire, and Nikos Papastergiadis. 1990. 'Strategy, Identity, Writing'. In *The Post-Colonial Critic: Interviews, Strategies, Dialogues*, edited by Sarah Harasym, 35–49. London: Routledge.

Stoler, Ann Laura. 2010. *Carnal Knowledge and Imperial Power: Race and the Intimate in Colonial Rule*. Berkeley, CA: University of California Press.

Stoler, Ann Laura. 2011. 'Colonial Aphasia: Race and Disabled Histories in France'. *Public Culture* 23 (1): 121–156. https://doi.org/10.1215/08992363-2010-018.

Strathern, Marilyn. 2016. *Before and after Gender: Sexual Mythologies of Everyday Life*. Chicago, IL: Hau Books.

Tallberg, Teemu. 2007. 'Bonds of Burden and Bliss: The Management of Social Relations in a Peacekeeping Organisation'. *Critical Perspectives on International Business* 3 (1): 63–82. https://doi.org/http://dx.doi.org/10.1108/17422040710722560.

Tidy, Joanna. 2016. 'The Gender Politics of "Ground Truth" in the Military Dissent Movement: The Power and Limits of Authenticity Claims Regarding War'. *International Political Sociology* 10 (2): 99–114. https://doi.org/10.1093/ips/olw003.

Titunik, Regina F. 2008. 'The Myth of the Macho Military'. *Polity* 40 (2): 137–163. https://doi.org/10.1057/palgrave.polity.2300090

Trimbur, John. 2001. 'Resistance as a Tragic Trope'. In *Insurrections: Approaches to Resistance in Composition Studies*, edited by Andrea Greenbaum, 3–15. Albany, NY: State University of New York Press.

True, Jacqui. 2014. 'The Political Economy of Gender in UN Peacekeeping'. In *Rethinking Peacekeeping, Gender Equality and Collective Security*, edited by Gina Heathcote and Diane Otto, 243–262. Basingstoke: Palgrave Macmillan.

UN Women. 2013. 'In India, Special Trainings and All-Women Peacekeeper Units Tackle Sexual Violence'. Accessed 5 December 2016. http://www.unwomen.org/en/news/stories/2013/10/in-india-all-women-peacekeeper-units-tackle-sexual-violence.

UN Women. 2015. 'Female Peacekeepers Take the Helm, to End Gender-Based Violence'. Accessed 5 December 2016. http://www.unwomen.org/en/news/stories/2015/5/female-peacekeepers-take-the-helm.

USAFRICOM. 2014. *Preparing to Prevent: Conflict-Related Sexual Violence Mitigation*. Peacekeeping and Stability Operations Institute (PKSOI), U.S. Army College (Pennsylvania). http://pksoi.armywarcollege.edu/default/assets/File/CRSV_Training_Scenarios_Preparing_to_Prevent.pdf.

Väyrynen, Tarja. 2004. 'Gender and UN Peace Operations: The Confines of Modernity'. *International Peacekeeping* 11 (1): 125–142. https://doi.org/10.1080/1353331042000228481.

Virno, Paolo. 2008. *Multitude: Between Innovation and Negotiation*. Translated by Isabella Bertoletti, James Cascaito, and Andrea Casson. Los Angeles, CA: Semiotext(e).

Wadham, Ben. 2017. 'Violence in the Military and Relations among Men: Military Masculinities and "Rape Prone Cultures"'. In *The Palgrave International Handbook of Gender and the Military*, edited by Rachel Woodward and Claire Duncanson, 241–256. London: Palgrave Macmillan.

Welland, Julia. 2013. 'Militarised Violences, Basic Training, and the Myths of Asexuality and Discipline'. *Review of International Studies* 39 (4): 881–902. https://doi.org/10.1017/S0260210512000605.

Westendorf, Jasmine-Kim. 2017. *WPS, CRSV and Sexual Exploitation and Abuse in Peace Operations: Making Sense of the Missing Links*. London: LSE.

Whitworth, Sandra. 2004. *Men, Militarism and UN Peacekeeping: A Gendered Analysis*. London: Lynne Rienner.

Whitworth, Sandra. 2008. 'Militarized Masculinity and Post-Traumatic Stress Disorder'. In *Rethinking the Man Question: Sex, Gender and Violence in International Relations*, edited by Jane L. Parpart and Marysia Zalewski, 109–126. London: Zed Books.

Wiegman, Robyn. 2004. 'On Being in Time with Feminism'. *Modern Language Quarterly* 65 (1): 161–176. https://doi.org/10.1215/00267929-65-1-161.

Wiegman, Robyn. 2014. 'The Times We're In: Queer Feminist Criticism and the Reparative "Turn"'. *Feminist Theory* 15 (1): 4–25. https://doi.org/10.1177/1464700113513081a.

Wiegman, Robyn. 2016. 'No Guarantee: Feminism's Academic Affect and Political Fantasy'. *Atlantis* 37 (2): 83–95. http://journals.msvu.ca/index.php/atlantis/article/view/83-95%20PDF.

Wolf, Diane L. 1996. 'Situating Feminist Dilemmas in Fieldwork'. In *Feminist Dilemmas in Fieldwork*, edited by Diane L. Wolf, 1–55. Boulder, CO: Westview Press.

Wollaston, Sam. 2005. 'Busy Doing Nothing'. *Guardian*, 12 July 2005. Accessed 5 July 2019. https://www.theguardian.com/media/2005/jul/12/tvandradio.comment.

Woodward, Alison E. 2001. 'Gender Mainstreaming in European Policy: Innovation or Deception?' WZB Working Paper. https://www.econstor.eu/bitstream/10419/44052/1/345123883.pdf.

Wright, Katharine A. M. 2016. 'NATO'S Adoption of UNSCR 1325 on Women, Peace and Security: Making the Agenda a Reality'. *International Political Science Review* 37 (3): 350–361. https://doi.org/10.1177/0192512116638763.

Wright, Katharine A. M., Matthew Hurley, and Jesus Ignacio Gil Ruiz. 2019. *NATO, Gender and the Military: Women Organising from Within*. London: Routledge.

Young, Iris Marion. 2003. 'The Logic of Masculinist Protection: Reflections on the Current Security State'. *Signs: Journal of Women in Culture and Society* 29 (1): 1–25. https://doi.org/10.1086/375708.

Zalewski, Marysia. 2000. *Feminism after Postmodernism: Theorising through Practice*. London: Routledge.

Zalewski, Marysia. 2006. 'Distracted Reflections on the Production, Narration and Refusal of Feminist Knowledge in International Relations'. In *Feminist Methodologies for International Relations*, edited by Brooke A. Ackerly, Maria Stern, and Jacqui True, 42–61. Cambridge: Cambridge University Press.

Zalewski, Marysia. 2010. "'I Don't Even Know What Gender Is': A Discussion of the Connections between Gender, Gender Mainstreaming and Feminist Theory'. *Review of International Studies* 36 (1): 3–27. https://doi.org/10.1017/S0260210509990489.

Zanotti, Laura. 2008. 'Imagining Democracy, Building Unsustainable Institutions: The UN Peacekeeping Operation in Haiti'. *Security Dialogue* 39 (5): 539–561. https://doi.org/10.1177/0967010608096151.

# Index

*For the benefit of digital users, indexed terms that span two pages (e.g., 52–53) may, on occasion, appear on only one of those pages.*

affect, 56, 60, 71–72, 83, 91–92, 146, 159. *See also* emotion
Afghanistan, 4–5, 102, 164–65
African Union, 34
Ahmed, Sara
  on 'affect aliens', 83
  on diversity work within institutions, 129, 161–62
  on emotion, 21, 66–67, 76, 78, 142
  on 'feminist killjoys', 103
  on the 'feminist snap', 146
  on the obvious as 'the unthought', 40–41

Belkin, Aaron, 46–47, 71–72, 151–52, 161, 164–65
Berlant, Lauren, 25, 88–89, 118–19, 161–62
Bhabha, Homi
  on coloniality, 46–47, 88, 112, 118–19
  on discontinuous subjects, 129
  on hybrid politics, 163–64
  on mimicry, 147–49
  on 'reading against the grain', 22
Black feminism, 30–31, 122
Boler, Megan
  on emotion, 66, 71–72
  on empathy, 124–25
  on 'pedagogy of discomfort', 110, 135, 139, 159
  on sympathy, 112
  on witnessing, 124–25, 130–31
Bosnia-Herzegovina, 113–14, 143
Britzman, Deborah P.
  on 'difficult knowledge', 56, 139, 159
  on education and psychic life, 93, 125–26
  on education and social engineering, 123
  on education as a 'gamble with meaning', 119, 121–22, 151
Brown, Wendy, 160
Bush, George H. W., 135–36
Butler, Judith
  on binary gender identification, 44
  epistemology and, 21, 31
  resistant feminist politics and, 95
  on sex and gender, xii
  on subversiveness, 150–51

Cammaert, Patrick, 81–82
Carson, Lisa, 39–40, 42
Cohn, Carol, 19
coloniality
  ambivalence and, 88, 118–19
  colonial aphasia and, 42–43, 112–13
  conflict-related sexual violence and, 67–68, 157
  gender training for peacekeepers and, 3, 24, 42–44, 118–19, 157, 158, 163–64
  'light side' *versus* 'dark side' of, 42–44
  motherhood and, 48
  race and, 20, 23, 42–44, 46–47, 112, 114–15, 157
conflict-related sexual violence (CRSV)
  coloniality and, 67–68, 157
  culture-based understandings of, 77–78, 157
  in the Democratic Republic of Congo, 73, 135–36
  emotion and, 68, 70, 71, 73–76, 79–82, 83, 84, 86–90, 118–19, 157–58, 159
  gender training for peacekeepers and, 70–71, 72–77, 78–82, 85–87, 118–19
  HIV/AIDS and, 79–80
  men as victims in, 49–50, 158
  military framing of the problem of, 79–82, 87, 88–89, 118
  police peacekeeping forces and, 85–87, 88–89
  'policy hype' regarding, 67–68
  race and, 43–44, 67–68, 77–78, 157
  reporting structures regarding, 81, 85–86
  training curricula and, 27–28, 33–34, 40–41, 43–44, 61–62, 66–67, 70–77, 78–84, 85–86, 92–93
  victim support services and, 76, 82–83, 85–87
  violence by women and, 49–50, 155

cook, sam, 38–39
Cornwall, Andrea, 6–7, 130–31
critical friendship, 167–69

de Beauvoir, Simone, 30–31
de Lauretis, Teresa, 31–32
Democratic Republic of Congo (DRC), 37, 73, 135–36
Dhawan, Nikita, 39, 145

Ellsworth, Elizabeth, 125–26, 128, 129–30
emotion
 conflict-related sexual violence and, 68, 70, 71, 73–76, 79–82, 83, 84, 86–90, 118–19, 157–58, 159
 excess emotion and, 83–90
 feminist theory and, 71–72
 gender training for peacekeepers and, 66–67, 69, 70, 71, 72–77, 78–82, 83, 84, 87, 118–19
 intersubjectivity and, 66–67, 76, 83
 jokes and, 105
 masculinity and, 68–69, 75, 88, 89
 in militaries, 68–70, 71–72, 75, 84–85, 87–88, 157–58
 peacekeeping and, 66–67, 71–72, 75, 84–85
 pedagogy and, 66–67, 69, 71–72, 75, 83, 87–88, 89–90
 resistance to gender training and, 98–99
 scripts and, 76
 sexual abuse committed by peacekeepers and, 84, 87–88, 159
Enloe, Cynthia, 47–48, 79–80, 149
epistemic authority
 citation of existing power and, 21
 feminist politics and, 32–33
 gendered notions of, 59–60, 62–63, 157
 gender training for peacekeepers and, 21, 59–64
 global power structures and, 7–8, 33–34
 'ground truth' and, 60–62
 homophobia and, 60
 in militaries, 26–27, 59–63, 157
 training curricula and, 32–34, 36, 37–39, 62–63
Eurocentrism, 20, 39, 42–44
European Union, 6, 34

female genital mutilation, 110, 142–43
Feminist Majority (organization), 4–5
feminist pedagogies
 critical consciousness-raising and, 126
 critical friendship and, 167–69
 defining characteristics of, 122–30

 emotion and, 66
 epistemic commitments and, 124–25, 133–34
 ethic of care and, 139–43, 152–53
 feminist politics and, 123–26, 129–30
 feminist theory and, 13–14, 24
 intersubjectivity and, 13–14
 liberal epistemologies and, 66
 politics of difference and, 127–28, 134–35
 power relations and, 123, 124–25, 126–27, 128, 129–30, 134, 142–43, 152–53
 resistance and, 93, 95, 97, 99–100
 subversion and, 121–22, 143–52, 153, 159, 163
 theorizing from experience and, 131–38, 152–53
feminist politics
 distancing from, 106–11, 115–16
 epistemic authority and, 32–33
 'feminist killjoys' and, 103–4
 feminist pedagogies and, 123–26, 129–30
 'feminist snap' and, 146
 gender and, 1–2, 30–31, 42
 gender training for peacekeepers and, xiii, 6–8, 11–12, 13–14, 22–26, 28–29, 118, 159–60, 164
 international development and, 6–7
 martial institutions and, xiv–xv, xviii, 2
 militaries and, 10–11, 23, 164–65
 neoliberal rationalities and, 23
 peacekeeping and, 11–12
 race and, 30–31
 resistance against, 28, 94–96, 99–100, 115, 116–17, 118–19
 resistance within, 95, 100
 trans* subjects and, 23, 30–31
feminist theory
 academia and, 25–26
 emotion and, 71–72
 feminist pedagogy and, 13–14, 24
 gender and, 1, 31, 42, 53–54
 gender training for peacekeepers and, xii–xiii, 22–23, 26–27, 157
 hostility toward, 26
 militaries and, xii, 10–11, 23
 motherhood and, 48–49
 positionality and, 18
Ferguson, Lucy, 13–14, 106, 145
Fetherston, A. Betts, 8
First Gulf War (1991), 135–36
Flynn, Elizabeth, 95–96, 97
Foucault, Michel, 12, 72–73, 74–75, 95, 123, 129–30, 140
Freire, Paulo, 122, 125–26, 130–31

gender advisers
  child protection and, 48
  gender courses for, 16
  hostile audience expectations among, 58
  queerness and, 133
  United Nations and, 30
Geneva Centre for Security Sector
  Governance, 35–36
Global North
  colonial aphasia and, 112–13
  gender mainstreaming efforts and, 11
  gender training curricula and, 26–27, 36, 37–38, 39, 51, 62–63, 157, 168–69
  gender training practitioners and, 7–8, 138, 157, 167
  violence and inequality in, 114–15
Global South
  epistemic authority and, 37–38, 168–69
  gender mainstreaming efforts and, 11
  gender training for peacekeepers and, 36
  global governance structures and, 9–10
  peacekeepers from, 9–10, 36–37, 138
  'Woman-in-conflict' figure and, 38–39
*The Greatest Silence* (Jackson), 73–77, 79–80, 83

Harding, Sandra, 168–69
'He for She' campaign (United Nations), 49–50
hegemonic listening, 39
hegemonic masculinity. *See* masculinity
Hemmings, Clare, 24–25, 42, 69
Henry, Marsha, 9–10, 20
heteronormativity
  gender training for peacekeepers and, 24, 42, 44, 46–47, 118–19, 158, 159, 163–64, 166
  hypermasculinity and, 69–70
  resistance to gender training and, 101–2, 108
  training curricula and, 26–27, 44, 158
HIV/AIDS, 79–80, 119–20
homophobia
  anti-gay laws and, 147–48
  gender training for peacekeepers and, 3, 45–46, 60, 108, 109, 139
  martial institutions and, xi, 2, 116–17
  police and, 45–46
  West Africa and, 45–46
hooks, bell, 93–94, 95, 110, 116–17, 126–27
Hutchings, Kimberly, 164–65
hypermasculinity. *See* masculinity

International Peace Institute, 35–36

Jackson, Lisa F., 73

Jaggar, Alison, 83
Jauhola, Marjaana, 11–12, 133
Johnson-Sirleaf, Ellen, 48–49
jokes
  changes in perspective and, 94–95
  communal bonds reinforced in, 103, 104–5
  emotional discomfort and, 105
  'feminist killjoys' and, 103–4
  misogyny and, 105, 107
  pedagogical strategies involving, 105–6, 116
  performative elements of, 105, 106
  resistance to gender training and, 91, 94, 102–6, 115–16
  separation of norms from realization and, 103
  social hierarchies upheld in, 103

Kabeer, Naila, 13, 37–38
Kaplan, Laura Duhan, 141–42
Klein, Melanie, 121
Kolhatkar, Neel, 107
Kunz, Rahel, 13, 35–36

Liberia, 48–49
Lombardo, Emanuela, 97, 100
Lugones, María, 42–44

Mackay, Angela, 54–55, 56–57, 60–62
Mahmood, Saba, xvii
martial institutions. *See also* militaries; police forces
  co-optation of gender knowledge in, 28, 118, 119, 164–65
  domestic abuse committed by members of, 5–6
  feminist politics and, xiv–xv, xviii, 2
  gender training and, 2, 57–58, 119, 161–62, 164–65
  homophobia and, xi, 2, 116–17
  misogyny and, 2, 116–17
  women's gendered service within, 5–6
masculinity
  emotion and, 68–69, 75, 88, 89
  heteronormativity and, 69–70
  militaries and, 9–10, 19, 68–70, 71–72, 82, 88–89, 135–36, 141–42, 143–44, 154
  misogyny and, 105
  peacekeeping and, 69–70, 82
  police forces and, 69–70, 154
Mergaert, Lut, 97, 100
militaries. *See also* martial institutions
  camaraderie in, 141–42
  class positionality in, 19–20, 21

militaries (*cont.*)
  emotion and, 68–70, 71–72, 75, 84–85, 87–88, 157–58
  epistemic authority and, 26–27, 59–63, 157
  female soldiers in, 11, 16, 23, 48, 100–1
  feminist politics and, 10–11, 23, 164–65
  feminist theory and, xii, 10–11, 23
  gender discrimination in, 53
  gendered positionality in, 18–19, 21
  gender norms in, 5–6, 8–9, 11, 21–22, 100–1
  gender training and, xi–xii, 1–2, 4–6, 16, 19–20, 35, 48, 57–58, 59–63, 118, 147, 154
  humanitarian action and, 84–85
  hypermasculinity and, 9–10, 19, 68–70, 71–72, 82, 88–89, 135–36, 141–42, 143–44, 154
  sexual assault and harassment within, 5
Miller, Laura, 75, 78–79
misogyny
  distancing gender from feminist politics and, 110–11
  gender training for peacekeepers and, 3, 56–57, 166
  jokes and, 105, 107
  martial institutions and, 2, 116–17
  men's rights agendas and, 49–50, 107, 110–11
  'Modern Educayshun' (Kolhatkar), 107, 116–17
Mohanty, Chandra Talpade, 38–39
Moskos, Charles, 75, 78–79

Nordic Centre for Gender in Military Operations, 16–17, 36
North Atlantic Treaty Organization (NATO), 16–17, 34–36, 62

Otto, Dianne, 22–23, 24–25, 161–62
Oyěwùmí, Oyèrónkẹ́, 48

paranoid reading, 119–20
Patton, Cindy, 119–20
Peabody, Elizabeth Palmer, 65
peacekeeping
  child protection and, 48
  emotion and, 66–67, 71–72, 75, 84–85
  female peacekeepers and, 3–4, 11, 37, 47–48, 49–50, 53
  feminist politics and, 11–12
  Global South peacekeepers and, 9–10, 36–37, 138
  hypermasculinity and, 69–70, 82
  local security forces and, 45–46
  neoliberal rationalities and, 10
  Nordic countries and, 69–70
  police forces and, 85–86
  sexual exploitation and abuse by peacekeepers during, 4–5, 19, 43–44, 50–51, 67–68, 76, 79–80, 84, 87–88, 112–13, 158, 159
  sexual harassment by peacekeepers during, 50, 79–80, 84
  United Nations and, 33–34, 47–48
pedagogy. *See also* feminist pedagogies
  emotion and, 66–67, 69, 71–72, 75, 83, 87–88, 89–90
  'ground truth' and, 72–73
  intersubjectivity and, 13–15, 27–28
  jokes and, 105–6, 116
  pedagogy of discomfort, 110, 135–36, 137–38, 139, 159
  pedagogy of gender, 3, 66–67
  pedagogy of the oppressed, 130–31, 138
  pedagogy of the powerful, 130–31, 138
  resistance and, 93
Perry, Ruth Sando, 48–49
police forces
  conflict-related sexual violence and, 85–87, 88–89
  female officers and, 16
  gender discrimination in, 53
  gender training and, xi, 1–2, 16, 45–46, 154
  homophobia and, 45–46
  hypermasculinity and, 69–70, 154
  as peacekeepers, 85–86
  resource shortages and, 85–87
  in West Africa, 45–46
Prügl, Elisabeth, 12, 129–30, 150–51, 159
Puechguirbal, Nadine, 54–55, 59–60, 72–73, 91–92, 108–9

queerness, 45–46, 60, 133

race
  coloniality and, 20, 23, 42–44, 46–47, 112, 114–15, 157
  conflict-related sexual violence and, 43–44, 67–68, 77–78, 157
  femininity and, 42–43
  feminist politics and, 30–31
  gendered power and, 42–43
  gender training for peacekeepers and, 3, 42–44, 46–47, 123–24, 157, 164, 166
  global power structures and, 7–8
  researcher positionality and, 18, 20
Razack, Sherene, 11–12, 77–78, 87–88, 129–30
reparative reading, 120–21, 122–23, 143–44

resistance to gender training
  biological dimorphism and, 100–1
  coloniality and, 101–2
  cultural essentialism and, 111
  denial of the need for gender change and, 97, 100, 101–2
  distancing from feminist politics and, 106–11, 115–16
  emotion and, 98–99
  gender essentialism and, 91, 100–1
  heteronormativity and, 101–2, 108
  jokes and, 91, 94, 102–6, 115–16
  pedagogical responses to, 102, 104–6, 107–9
  performative aspects of, 97–100, 104–5, 106–7, 115
  political ambiguity of resistance and, 94–96
  possibility of negotiation and, 116–17
  projection and, 111–16
  refusal to accept responsibility and, 97, 100
  scripts and, 28, 92–93, 96–99, 101–17
  training curricula's anticipation of, 54–57, 58–59, 91–92, 102
  trivialization of gender equality and, 97, 100, 101, 108
Rich, Adrienne, 148–49

Schniedewind, Nancy, 58, 126–27
Schott, Robin May, 73
Scott, Joan Wallach, 159–60
Sedgwick, Eve Kosofsky, 65, 119–20, 121, 152–53
sexual harassment, 1–2, 5, 50, 51, 80–81, 84
sexual violence. *See* conflict-related sexual violence (CRSV)
Sexwale, Bunie M. Matlanyane, 7–8, 37–38
Spivak, Gayatri Chakravorty
  on deconstruction, 163
  gendered subalterns and, 38–39
  micrological texture of power and, 15–16
  practical politics of the open end and, 24, 28, 151, 153, 163
  on practice and theory, 53–54, 128–29
  on 'white men saving brown women from brown men', 111

Stoler, Ann, 42–43, 112–13
subversion
  anti-gay laws and, 147–48
  feminist pedagogies and, 121–22, 143–52, 153, 159, 163
  gender training for peacekeepers and, 3, 11–12, 13–14, 24, 25, 28–29, 144–49
  mimicry and, 147–49, 150–51
  'small subversions' and, 28, 150–52, 153
  'Trojan horse strategy' and, 144–45, 148–49, 159

Tallberg, Teemu, 71–72
Thapar-Björkert, Suruchi, 20
Tidy, Joanna, 60–61
trans* subjects, 23, 30–31, 46, 108
'Trojan horse strategy', 144–45, 148–49, 159

United Nations
  conflict-related sexual violence and, 4–5
  Core Pre-Deployment Training Manual and, 15–16, 33–34
  Department of Peace Operations and, 33–34, 47–48
  gender training for peacekeepers and, 6, 16–17, 30, 33–36, 39–40, 41, 47–48, 49–50, 54–55
  'He for She' campaign and, 49–50
  peacekeeping operations and, 33–34, 47–48
  Security Council, 30, 33–34, 35, 60
United States Africa Command (USAFRICOM), 70–71

Väyrynen, Tarja, 11–12
Virno, Paolo, 102–3, 104–5, 116–17

wartime rape. *See* conflict-related sexual violence (CRSV)
West Africa, motherhood in, 48–49
Wiegman, Robyn, 25–26, 28–29, 120, 160–62
Women, Peace and Security agenda, 3–4, 33–34, 38–39, 50, 123–24

Yorùbá, 48

www.ingramcontent.com/pod-product-compliance
Lightning Source LLC
Chambersburg PA
CBHW072304090825
30890CB00002B/47